ANARCHISTS OF ANDALUSIA, 1868–1903

Artisan Militiamen in Cádiz, December 1868 (see page 68). From: Luis Mejías y Escassy, Las barricadas de Cádiz (Cadiz, 1869)

Anarchists of Andalusia 1868–1903

Temma Kaplan

Princeton University Press, Princeton, New Jersey

PUBLISHED BY PRINCETON UNIVERSITY PRESS,
PRINCETON, NEW JERSEY
IN THE UNITED KINGDOM: PRINCETON UNIVERSITY PRESS,
GUILDFORD, SURREY

LIBRARY OF CONGRESS CATALOGING IN PUBLICATION DATA
WILL BE FOUND ON THE LAST PRINTED PAGE OF THIS BOOK

PUBLICATION OF THIS BOOK HAS BEEN AIDED BY A GRANT
FROM THE ANDREW W. MELLON FOUNDATION

THIS BOOK HAS BEEN COMPOSED IN LINOTYPE JANSON

PRINTED IN THE UNITED STATES OF AMERICA
BY PRINCETON UNIVERSITY PRESS, PRINCETON, NEW JERSEY

For Jonathan and in memory of the *Old Mole*

Contents

List of Figures

List of Tables

Acknowledgments

Research for this book was carried out primarily at the Institute of Social History, Amsterdam; the newspaper archives or Hemerotecas of Cádiz, Sevilla, Madrid, Valencia, and Barcelona; the Municipal Archive of Jerez de la Frontera; and the Public Records Office, London. I am deeply indebted to Rudolf de Jong and Thea Duijker of the Institute for their guidance and friendship. To thank them for research help would be to underestimate the aid they have provided over the years. The relative disorganization and intrigue associated with work in Spanish local archives, especially in southern Spain, made me doubly grateful for the orientation I received in Barcelona from Josep Fontana, Enric Fuster, and Josep Termes.

Grants from the American Council of Learned Societies and from the Research Committee of the Academic Senate of the University of California, Los Angeles have facilitated my work. The university's humane policy of giving sabbatical quarter-leaves to junior faculty gave me the opportunity to finish the first draft of this study. The *Journal of Interdisciplinary History* and M.I.T. Press have generously allowed me to reintegrate here material I first discussed in "The Social Base of Nineteenth-Century Andalusian Anarchism in Jerez de la Frontera," VI (1975), 47–70. Houghton Mifflin Co. has granted permission to quote extensively from my article, "Women and Spanish Anarchism," from *Becoming Visible: Women in European History* (1977), edited by Claudia Koonz and Renate Bridenthal.

This book has evolved from my habit of seeking rational explanations for extraordinary events such as revolutionary insurrections. When I was an undergraduate, Herbert Marcuse's interest in the Albigensian Crusade of the thirteenth century captured my imagination and aroused my curiosity about religious and cultural components of popular movements. From Frank E. Manuel, I learned how to ferret out people from between the lines of texts. John Womack, Jr. introduced me to Eric Wolf's *Sons of the Shaking Earth* and Fernand Braudel's *The Mediterranean and the Mediterranean World in the Age of Philip II*, which taught me that a sense of geography and work space is essential to grass-roots history. Sitting in Womack's class as his teaching assistant was an object lesson in how to secure general historical patterns by focusing on significant regions. Juan Marichal tutored me in the nuances of Spanish history. David Landes opened my eyes to the field of social history and permitted me to explore the cultural life of the Spanish working class. With him I first read Eric J. Hobsbawm's *Primitive Rebels*, E. P. Thompson's *The Making of the English Working Class*, and Albert Soboul's *The Parisian Sans-Culottes and the French Revolution, 1793–94*, whose influence upon this book will be obvious.

Colleagues and comrades have helped channel my enthusiasm into disciplined activity. Clara E. Lida nurtured my fledgling interest in Spain, persuaded me to make crucial changes in this manuscript, and has encouraged me to pursue my theories even when they diverge from hers. David and Martel Montgomery have absorbed me into their family, and along the way, have given me good advice about labor history. Stephan and Abigale Thernstrom, Michael and Judith Walzer, and Danillo and Margaret Bach refrained from giving advice but gave support. Paul Avrich let me know what I was doing right when everything looked wrong. Barrington Moore, Jr. maintained a lively interest. Gabriel Tortella, Abilio Barbero, José María Moreno Galván, and Roberta Salper made my days in Madrid less lonely. With Ros Baxandall, Nancy Fitch, Linda Gordon, Ruth Kennedy, Juliet Mitchell, Judith Murray, Dale Rosen, Katherine Sklar, Judy Stacey, Meredith Tax, and Susan Tracy, I have found community. William Christian, Jr. came upon the scene just as I was completing the first draft of this study. Hours spent talking to him about Spain, popular worship, and village life forced me to reassess anarchist iconoclasm and my own. He helped me tone down my voice while proclaiming my arguments. Noël Diaz drew the map and graphs. Norma Farquhar prepared the index. My editor, Margaret Case, has been a skillful and gentle midwife.

Through comments upon earlier drafts of this manuscript and related articles, the following people have suggested ways I might improve this study: Paul Avrich, Renato Barahona, Lutz Berkner, Robert Brenner, Milton Cantor, William Christian, Jr., Natalie Zemon Davis, Josep Fontana, Eric J. Hobsbawm, Gabriel Jackson, James Joll, Rudolf de Jong, Clara E. Lida, Peter Loewenberg, Arno J. Mayer, Gerald Meaker, M. J. Meggitt, Franklin Mendels, Jerome Mintz, David Montgomery, T. O. Ranger, Hans Rogger, Stanley Stein, Geoffrey Symcox, Charles Tilly, Joan Connelly Ullman, and John Womack, Jr. As they will notice, I did not always take their advice.

Without the patience and sense of humor of my husband, Jonathan M. Wiener, this book might never have been written. In fact, had we not shared a fascination with the Spanish anarchists, we might never have met. The final debt of gratitude therefore must go to the anarchists themselves.

Abbreviations

NATIONAL ORGANIZATIONS

FRE Federation of the Spanish Region (Federación regional española) of the First International, 1870–1874; clandestine, 1874–1881.

FTRE Workers' Federation of the Spanish Region (Federación de trabajadores de la región española), 1881–1888; collectivist national anarchist confederation.

OARE Anarchist Organization of the Spanish Region (Organización anarquista de la región española), 1888–, political successor to the FTRE. Shortlived and less important than the 1891 agricultural workers' syndicate with the same initials described below. Its members seem to have been a cadre devoted to giving political direction to anarchist organizations.

Pact The Spanish Federation for Resistance to Capitalism (Federación española de resistencia al capitalismo) was also called the Pact of Union and Solidarity (Pacto de unión y solidaridad). Formed in May 1888, just as the FTRE was disintegrating, the Pact was an attempt to coordinate workers' activities in different trades and different areas.

FSORE Federation of Workers Societies of the Spanish Region (Federación de sociedades obreras de la región española), formed in October 1900 as yet another umbrella organization of political trade unions. By 1905 it, too, seems to have disintegrated.

AGRICULTURAL WORKERS SOCIETIES

UTC Union of Field Workers (Unión de trabajadores del campo). Formed as early as 1870 as independent local trade unions of agricultural workers, vinetenders, peasants, coopers, bakers, and carters, the first UTC became a labor section of the FRE in April 1872, and probably remained alive during the clandestine period between 1874 and 1881. It reemerged with the formation of the FTRE in September 1881 as a collectivist labor confederation. Like the early sections, the UTC of the eighties included rural proletarians, peasants, and skilled workers. With the decline of the FTRE in 1888, it disappeared as a national organization, but lived on locally, its 1882 statutes forming the basis for successive labor syndicates in Andalusia.

OARE   Agricultural Workers of the Spanish Region (Organización de agricultores de la región española) was founded in December 1891 as an anarchist national confederation of agricultural workers. It, too, included bakers and other semiskilled workers.

UARE   Union of Agricultural Workers of the Spanish Region (Unión de agricultores de la región española) held a congress in August 1893. It was probably the same organization as the OARE, and adopted the 1882 statutes of the UTC.

SOA   Society of Agricultural Workers (Sociedad de obreros agricultores), founded in November 1901 by José Crespo, a baker active in anarchist affairs as far back as the nineties. This, too, was an anarchist organization that adopted the 1882 UTC statutes.

Bibliographic Abbreviations

Accounts and Papers   Supplement to the Parliamentary Record. House of Commons. Bills, Papers and Reports. State Papers Room, British Museum (London)

Actas   *Actas de los consejos y comisión federal de la región española (1870–1874)*

ACV   Archivo del Consejo Regulador del Vino, Jerez de la Frontera

ADC   Archivo de la Diputación Provincial de Cádiz

AHN   Archivo Histórico Nacional (Madrid)

AMC   Archivo Municipal de Cádiz

AMJF   Archivo Municipal de Jerez de la Frontera

AMS   Archivo Municipal de Sevilla

AS	Archivo de Simancas
BM	British Museum
BMJF	Biblioteca Municipal de Jerez de la Frontera
BN	Biblioteca Nacional (Madrid)
BPA	Biblioteca Pública Arús (Barcelona)
CP	Casa de Pilatos. Archivo de los Duques de Medinaceli y Alcalá
FO	Foreign Office Records, Public Records Office (London)
HB	Hemeroteca de Barcelona
HC	Hemeroteca de Cádiz
HM	Hemeroteca de Madrid
HS	Hemeroteca de Sevilla
HV	Hemeroteca de Valencia
IISG	Internationaal Instituut voor Sociale Geschiedenis (International Institute of Social History, Amsterdam)

ANARCHISTS OF ANDALUSIA, 1868–1903

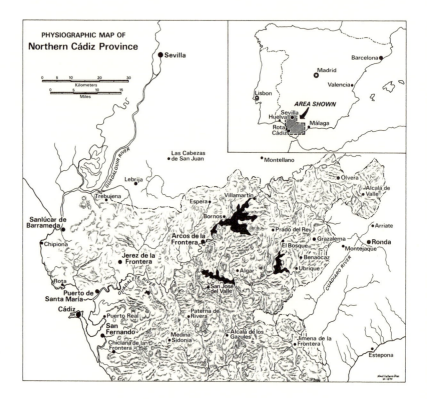

PHYSIOGRAPHIC MAP OF
Northern Cádiz Province

● Sevilla

Kilometers
0 5 10 20 30
Miles
0 5 10 15

Barcelona ●
Madrid ●
Valencia ●
Lisbon ●
AREA SHOWN
Huelva ● Sevilla
Rota ● Málaga
Cádiz

Las Cabezas
● de San Juan
● Montellano

Lebrija ●
● Olvera
Trebujena ●
● Alcalá de
Valle

Espera ● Villamartín
Sanlúcar de
Barrameda ●
Bornos ●
Arriate ●
Chipiona ●
Arcos de la
Frontera ●
Prado del Rey ●
Grazalema ●
● Ronda
El Bosque ●
Montejaque ●
Jerez de la
Frontera ●
Benaocaz ●
Rota ●
Algar ●
Ubrique ●
Puerto de
Santa María ●
GUADALETE RIVER
San José
del Valle ●
Cádiz ●
Puerto Real ●
Paterna de
Rivera ●
San
Fernando ●
Medina
Sidonia ●
Alcalá de los
Gazules ●
Chiclana de la
Frontera ●
Jimena de la
Frontera ●
Estepona ●

GUADALQUIR RIVER

GUADIARO RIVER

The Lay of the Land

This book is about Andalusian anarchism, a grass-roots movement of peasants and workers that grew and flourished between 1868 and 1903 within certain boundaries. Northern Cádiz Province, containing Jerez de la Frontera, the richest sherry district in the world, was the scene of insurrections, strikes, and general strikes throughout the latter part of the nineteenth century. Andalusian anarchism is synonymous with those revolutionary episodes and the gathering of thousands of people into community organizations related to militant trade unions.

This examination of the component forces of the anarchist movement in Northern Cádiz Province seeks to shed light on broader issues of comparative peasant and labor history: how people transform old institutions into collective associations to meet new needs, how old work relationships persist in new social settings, and how the different experiences of male and female peasants, artisans, skilled, and unskilled workers become translated into a particular political ideology.

With such concerns, social history cannot help but be political history as well. Concrete changes in landholding and sherry production altered the political thought of anonymous people. These changes in popular outlook come clear in the movement's strikes and insurrections. Collective action of a particular kind was used to further specific political programs which, since unwritten, are intelligible to the historian only by studying those times in which masses rose up to proclaim them.

Andalusia consists of the provinces of Huelva, Sevilla, Córdoba, Jaén, Granada, Málaga, and Cádiz, roughly south-

3

ern Spain. This study, however, will focus on one area, the district in which lie the vineyards and wheat fields near the city of Cádiz. The section under consideration is defined by mountains, rivers, and anarchist activity rather than by bureaucratic demarcations. It extends west from Ronda to Cádiz and south from Las Cabezas de San Juan to Chiclana de la Frontera (see map, p. 2). Its western frontier is the south Atlantic coast of Spain. Its center lies in the Guadalete River valley, a rich alluvial plain constantly plagued by insufficient rainfall. What is referred to as Northern Cádiz Province includes border towns in the provinces of Málaga and Sevilla, when those towns are in the agrarian and political network oriented toward Cádiz. The southern and eastern portions are in the Betic Mountain range.

Moving west to east, the colors of the land change from the white sands of the coastal beaches and salt marshes, to the parchment white-clay soils near Sanlúcar de Barrameda, Jerez de la Frontera, and Puerto de Santa María, to the ochre valleys rimmed by yellow-brown foothills, into the grey-green mountains of esparto grass scrub and wild oak trees. The area encompasses fertile sherry vineyards and wheat fields in large estates: latifundia. The region also includes the port through which the wine and wheat are shipped and the hill and plains towns that provide the labor to produce them.[1]

It was the poorer people of this rich area who formed a revolutionary community at the end of the nineteenth century to secure the wealth of land and factories. Those interested in sustained revolutionary activity rather than the culture of poverty have always turned to the Spanish anarchists, as Eric J. Hobsbawm did in his pathbreaking book, *Primitive Rebels*. He traced the development of revolutionary politics from banditry and individual crimes against the state through nonhierarchical social movements such as anarchism, to the centralized socialist parties of the twenti-

[1] Vizetelly, *Facts about Sherry*, pp. 88, 93; Sermet, *Espagne du sud*; *Estudio agrobiológico de la provincia de Cádiz.*

eth century. The question he raised about Andalusian anarchism was why, over a period of nearly seventy years, some of the most isolated and seemingly backward peasants in Europe should carry on a sustained, ideologically coherent leftist political movement. He emphasized the exploitation of landless day laborers who lived in towns to explain the continuous militancy of the anarchists. Unlike farm laborers elsewhere, a majority of Andalusian farm workers lived in cities, together with thousands of peasants and workers. This gave them the opportunity to discuss grievances, formulate unified strategies, and act collectively.

In *People of the Sierra*, Julian A. Pitt-Rivers stressed the importance of the enduring pueblo as the basic structure of Andalusian anarchism. He argued that in addition to signifying the township and its government, pueblo "has a third meaning: 'people' in the sense of plebs as opposed to the rich . . . for the rich do not belong to the pueblo but to that wider world which has already been delimited as theirs. In this sense, the pueblo is a potentially revolutionary force. . . ."[2]

Gerald Brenan's *The Spanish Labyrinth*, among its other contributions, focused attention upon the enemy against which Andalusian anarchism was directed. The political boss of southern society was the *cacique* who derived his wealth from latifundist grain production. As Brenan described *caciquismo*, he emphasized certain particular political relationships of the latifundist ruling class to the state and the local peasants: "it was constitutional governments and the popular vote that gave them their real power. Their palmiest days were from 1840 to 1917. . . . The obligations of the cacique to the Government were to see that the right candidates were elected, in exchange for which they were given the protection of the Civil Governors and of the judges and magistrates and of course the active assistance of the police. . . . They appointed the mayors in small towns and villages, [and] controlled the local judges and public

[2] Pitt-Rivers, *People of the Sierra*, p. 18.

5

functionaries."[3] However repressive, *caciquismo* was subject to challenges from republicans and anarchists.

This study, taking off from Hobsbawm, Pitt-Rivers, and Brenan, seeks to discover how ideology and tactics developed over time in a popular movement. Since such a work can focus neither on individuals nor on political parties, it chooses a middle ground, the history of change in certain key cities that became anarchist centers in the late nineteenth century. These cities fall into two categories: hill and inland plain towns, and commercial cities. The two at first seem to bear no resemblance to one another. Yet the hill town Arcos de la Frontera and the commercial center of Sanlúcar de Barrameda were both centers of anarchist activities.

Nothing seems more aloof and isolated than Arcos de la Frontera, standing as it does on a high bluff at a bend in the Guadalete River, just at the edge of the mountains. But despite its geographical isolation on a hilltop, the city was an integral part of the economy of the fertile plain or campiña below, stretching eighteen miles to Jerez de la Frontera. These fields and that city influenced events in Arcos, as did the Guadalete River valley, which formed an anarchist highway along which newspapers, people, and ideas traveled.

People in Arcos turned to the fields for their only important employment, plowing in the autumn and harvesting in the summer. But they lived in town and went out to the fields according to the traditional pattern of Andalusian agro-towns. Only about ten percent of the population was regularly employed as hired hands on large estates or in vineyards. Some were shepherds and goatherds in the mountains. There were very few job opportunities in town except for home industries such as weaving coarse woolen cloth, making candles, performing low-level services such as

[3] Brenan, *The Spanish Labyrinth*, p. 7. There is a vast literature on *caciquismo* originating with Joaquín Costa's pioneering study, *Oligarquía y caciquismo*.

cobbling, or working in the olive and flour mills just out-side town.

In places like Arcos, where in 1902 the average annual expenditure for a family of five was around 675 pesetas, the average annual income for a male day laborer was 500 pesetas. To feed their families, poor housewives kept chickens and sometimes a goat or pig in home stalls. They also tended small gardens on which they planted vegetables for family consumption. Young girls were sent out to be maids in the homes of the rich. Their mothers sometimes peddled eggs or goats' milk in Arcos or neighboring towns. Men went into the mountains to collect esparto grass, used in making *alpargatas*, the cheap, straw shoes worn by the poor. They also made charcoal, cut cork, and poached. What enabled workers to live on such meager incomes was that men and women who worked in labor gangs received their food during the weeks they were in the fields.[4]

At home in late nineteenth-century Arcos, as in other Andalusian cities, poor workers and peasants ate bread mornings and evenings. For dinner in the afternoon, bread was often thrown in with water, onions, garlic, tomatoes, peppers, olive oil, and whatever meat or fish was available, to make a nourishing, thick stew at very little cost to the family. But the stew, like everything else, was seasonal, depending upon the availability of the ingredients. The staple was bread.

Up the Guadalete valley and to the east, into the mountains, similar conditions prevailed. In Grazalema, a prosperous woolen cloth industry, perhaps dating back to the Reconquest, had provided men and women with handicraft work—jobs that were eliminated in the nineteenth century when British machine-made cloth began to flood even these isolated markets. The old fulling mills were turned into

[4] *Instituto de reformas sociales: Resumen de la información acerca de los obreros agrícolas en las provincias de Andalucía y Extremadura*, pp. 44, 48–50, 52.

7

olive and flour mills by the late nineteenth century, providing a few jobs for independent millers. Even peasants (people with access to land, whether through tenancy, sharecropping, or ownership) joined the large majority of the population who descended to the wheat-producing plains, twenty-four to forty-two miles northwest, where grain ripened in June and July, at least a month earlier than their own crops. Women weeded in the grain fields. They also hoed beans and picked olives. A female farm worker from a similar rural context has described her experience weeding and hoeing: "We did what they called the 'light work,' hoeing broad beans, then hoeing the weeds out of the wheat. . . . We weeded down one row loosening the dirt, building it up around each plant, until we came to the end and started up the next row. We were never done and the hoe that weighed five pounds in the morning weighed fifty by nightfall."[5]

Although their primary orientation was toward agriculture, men and women in the hill towns also had social connections with neighboring towns in the mountains through trading networks and contraband. Within a few miles of Grazalema and one another were towns such as Benaocaz, Ubrique, and Montejaque. The poor generally traveled by foot across the steep, narrow, but direct routes over the ridges to the next town. Peddlers smuggled untaxed tobacco and cloth from Gibraltar into the hills. Poor men and women took small consignments to isolated villages. Republican militants took to these same hills in 1869 in attempts to win masses to their cause. Bandits frequented the mountain highways. The terrain made it difficult, though by no means impossible, for the government's excise police or troops to follow smugglers, bandits, and revolutionaries into the mountains.

[5] Cornelisen, *Torregreca: Life, Death, Miracles*, p. 171. This was written by a contemporary Italian field worker, but the hoe must have been as heavy in Spain.

The towns along the coast, Cádiz, Sanlúcar de Barrameda, Puerto de Santa María, Puerto Real, San Fernando, and Jerez (about seven miles inland from Puerto de Santa María), had at least as far back as the eighteenth century been commercial cities that profited from the colonial trade with the Philippines and from wine exports. To service this trade, railroads from Jerez to the ports were proposed as early as 1829. The Jerez to Puerto de Santa María line, the first in Andalusia, was completed in 1854. This was a short trunk, designed simply to move goods, especially wine, to the port. But by the late nineteenth century, railroad and telegraph communication also linked the commercial cities of Cádiz with Sevilla and Madrid, across the Caulina plains to the northeast of Jerez. As trading centers oriented to the Atlantic, these towns were more active than those in the inland plain and hills.[6] But the changes they experienced in the nineteenth century did little to alter their physical appearance. The cities near the port of Cádiz looked then as they are still portrayed in travel posters.

Sanlúcar de Barrameda, at the mouth of the Guadalquivir River, for example, is the town from which Columbus sailed for his third voyage to America. From the beach, where early modern Portuguese merchants built a plateresque portal, the town is divided by a street that leads to the central plaza, where the government offices are located. But the real power lies up the hill. There the castle of the dukes of Niebla and Medina Sidonia, the men who until the early nineteenth century were the town's seigneurs, looks out over whitewashed buildings and red tiled roofs to the Atlantic below. Palm trees dot the landscape, giving Sanlúcar a fluffy, feathery look. Down the hill live the craftsmen, shopkeepers, fishermen, peasants, and agricultural workers. In 1868, about 13,000 people, primarily poor field

[6] García-Baquero González, *Comercio colonial y guerras revolucionarias*; Wais San Martín, *Historia general de los ferrocarriles españoles*, p. 201; *El imparcial* (Madrid), 12–1–1892.

9

hands and vineyard workers, lived in the city or its three inland hamlets. They met farm workers from the hills in the wheat latifundia of neighboring Jerez.

But the most important economic feature for Sanlúcar, as for Jerez and Puerto de Santa María, were the gently rolling, chalky white hills separating them, on which are located the oldest and richest sherry vineyards in the world. Despite the importance of grain production, sherry, not wheat, accounted for the major wealth of the coastal cities. In Sanlúcar, where manzanilla, a dry sherry, is produced, skilled winecellar men mixed the juices to make the distinctive wine; skilled coopers made casks from imported American oak; skilled vinetenders nurtured the grapes and pressed them; carters transported the wine musts in from the vineyards and carried the filled casks from the winecellars. They took them to the harbor, whence they were shipped to England, Russia, France, and the United States.

What begins to account for the relation between Andalusian anarchism and particular regions is wealth, not poverty. The actual and potential wealth of the sherry industry in the coastal cities and Jerez is a good starting point for explanations about Andalusian anarchism. However poor and desolate the hill towns, there were other areas in Spain, such as Almería or parts of Extremadura, where people were as poor and equally outraged by social inequality. In Almería, where almost everyone is poor, the idea of revolutionary social changes might seem utopian, for if everything were equally divided, everyone would be equally poor. But in Sanlúcar, where productivity and wealth were obvious even to the hill people who came down to plow and harvest the neighboring latifundia, a revolutionary ideology based on control of production by workers and peasants might seem very rational.

This work, a highly detailed social and political history with a theoretical purpose, explains particular social and economic relations that created and sustained Andalusian anarchism. Five recent works by Clara Lida, Josep Termes, Manuel Tuñón de Lara, Joan Connelly Ullman, and Joaquín Romero Maura have pieced together the main themes in anarchist political development, permitting this research on Cádiz Province.[7] The following examination, though roughly chronological, is not a consecutive narrative but a series of thematic essays that trace the origins of Andalusian anarchism and its transformation over the nineteenth century.

It shows that Andalusian anarchism was a rational, not a millenarian response to a specific social configuration. By distinguishing among forms of oppression, it demonstrates that even exploited people have political options from among which they choose. This technique is especially necessary when treating a decentralized movement. Much of what was creative in Andalusian anarchism has been overlooked because historians' emphasis on national leadership has left open the issue of popular political consciousness and action. Thus it has been difficult to explain how the movement persisted in certain towns and why insurrections and general strikes came in periodic waves. Investigation of the daily life and times of anarchists in one important late nineteenth-century center, Northern Cádiz Province, indicates that "inarticulate" workers and peasants spoke clearly through their actions and organizations about the kinds of social relationships they desired.

[7] Lida, *Anarquismo y revolución en la España del XIX*; Termes, *Anarquismo y sindicalismo en España: La primera Internacional, 1864–1881*; Tuñón de Lara, *El movimiento obrero en la historia de España*; Joan Connelly Ullman, *La semana trágica*; Romero Maura, *"La rosa de fuego."*

CHAPTER I

Prologue: Sherry and Society in Jerez de la Frontera

The evolution of anarchism in Northern Cádiz Province was inextricably tied to the declining prosperity of independent winegrowing peasants, pruners, and coopers after 1863, and their collective response to their condition. Diminished autonomy in their work induced skilled people to band together, creating new cooperative organizations and modifying old ones. These associations were designed to retain control over what remained of workers' and peasants' power, and to fight against a new system of work relations they opposed. Before discussing how bourgeois and petty bourgeois politics in this area were intimately associated with the fortunes of sherry production and sale, the subject of Chapter II, it is essential to describe the changes in sherry production that brought about new social relationships and new social organizations in Jerez de la Frontera, which was to become an anarchist stronghold.

The commune of Jerez, following the general Mediterranean pattern, consisted of seven villages, the city, and the surrounding fields. It was the largest municipality in the province, with a population of about 52,000 in 1868.[1] Jerez was an agricultural district, covering an area ten by thirteen miles and deriving its wealth from the export of wheat and sherry. The majority of the residents had, from time immemorial, been desperately poor landless day laborers, the

[1] "Jerez de la Frontera," *Diccionario geográfico de España*, XI, 251–265, 253; Madoz, *Diccionario geográfico-estadístico histórico de España*, V, 117. The main archival resource for this chapter is the Archivo municipal in Jerez de la Frontera (AMJF). AMJF: *Archivo memoranda 6* (1879), f.8.

group generally thought to have been the social base of Andalusian anarchism.[2]

Land was more highly concentrated in Cádiz Province than in most other Spanish regions. By the middle of the nineteenth century, 58 percent of its total area was in holdings greater than 625 acres; in some districts all but 4 percent of the land was in large estates.[3] Families of the dukes of Medina Sidonia, Alba, Medinaceli, Montpensier, and the count of Niebla owned large fragments of townships in Cádiz Province. The trend toward increased consolidation of land continued throughout the late nineteenth century, along with the international depression. In Jerez, by the middle of the century, two-thirds of the arable and pastoral land was owned by fewer than two hundred people, who had an average holding of about 250 hectares (approximately 625 acres). Most of the land was in pasture, ranch, and cereals.[4] (See Table 1-1.) The principal wheat-producing lands lay to the north and east of Jerez in the Caulina and

[2] The prevailing view of Andalusian anarchism was first fully articulated by Juan Díaz del Moral in *Historia de las agitaciones campesinas andaluzas* and by Constancio Bernaldo de Quirós, "El espartaquismo agrario andaluz." Gerald Brenan's *The Spanish Labyrinth* and Eric J. Hobsbawm's *Primitive Rebels* add brilliant insights into the social structure and organizational complexity of anarchism, but share the same basic interpretations. In passing, Díaz del Moral mentions that most rural agitation occurred in areas of small holders, and that most anarchist militants were artisans or salaried employees, pp. 185, 226–227, 448. And Brenan specified that cobblers, bakers, and schoolmasters were frequently anarchists, p. 141. For a revisionist view emphasizing class struggle within the anarchist movement, consult Kaplan, "The Social Base of Nineteenth-Century Andalusian Anarchism in Jerez de la Frontera," pp. 47–70.

[3] Madoz, *Diccionario geográfico*, v, 117; Brenan, *The Spanish Labyrinth*, p. 116.

[4] Madoz claims that in 1850, many estates varied between 1,100 and 3,300 acres; *Diccionario geográfico*, ix, 619. In 1930, Pascual Carrión reported that Jerez had 1,390 proprietors; of these, 792 had very small holdings, and 86 percent of the land was owned by 19 proprietors, whose average holding was 2,350 hectares or 5,875 acres. Cited in *Diccionario geográfico de España*, xi, 255.

Table 1–1

Land Distribution in Jerez de la Frontera in 1870

Land Use	Hectares
Cereal production	65,000
Pastures, scrub, mountain	57,500
Vines	7,800
Wasteland and rights of way	5,252
Olive groves	1,500
Irrigated land and horticulture	200

One hectare = 2.5 acres.
Source: AMJF 199:10,506:84.

Tablas plains, along the Gaudalete River. In Caulina, as elsewhere in the province, wheat fields were interrupted by hills on which peasants grew vines. Olive groves were less common in Jerez than elsewhere in Andalusia, but the few there were grew to the north and southeast of the city in the foothills, where they too were interspersed with vineyards.

Vines accounted for only six percent of land use, but provided the greatest income both for the region and the nation. The vineyards around Jerez lay in six districts, to the north, west, and east of the city. Sherry vineyards could also be found near the towns of Sanlúcar de Barrameda, Puerto de Santa María, Chiclana, Chipiona, and Rota in Cádiz Province, in Moguer, Manzanilla, and Niebla in Huelva Province, and in scattered plots in both Córdoba and Sevilla Provinces. Just as champagne grapes can be grown in any wine district but achieve their special taste from the soil of Champagne, France, the *palomino* and *Pedro Ximénez* grapes drew their distinctive taste from the special soils around Jerez. Introduced to Jerez sometime in the sixteenth century, the *Pedro Ximénez* grape grew in the Rhineland and was used for Riesling, but Andalusian soil and special blending created a vastly different wine. The chalky lime *albariza* soils of the hilly slopes could be found only outside the cities of Sanlúcar, Jerez, and Puerto de Santa María. These soils generally produced *palomino* grapes for the finest amontillado and oloroso sherries. Other soils, the red-brown, iron-rich clay known as *barro* and the sandy *arena* soils were plentiful in Cádiz, Huelva, and Sevilla Provinces, lower down on the slopes and in the valleys. *Barro-arena* vineyards could be found northward and toward the east, near Arcos. However, the grapes grown on these soils produced thinner, more sour, though often more plentiful musts than those from the *albariza* vineyards. Demand for all sherries grew until 1863, and so greater areas of inferior land were brought into cultivation.[5]

Labor requirements varied with soil. *Barro-arena* produced more grapes per vine than the *albariza*, and therefore needed more harvesters. In general, all vineyards required constant attention at specific times, as medieval artists had shown in their numerous calendar illustrations of different vineyard tasks performed in the appropriate months. The new vinetending season began shortly after the harvest, which was gathered for two or three weeks in late September and early October. The vines were carefully examined. Since the greatest problem in local agriculture was how to preserve moisture, the major labor task in October was to construct basins three feet square around the roots of vines. Building troughs around 450 vines, generally covering one-quarter of an acre, took one heavy laborer a week's work by 1876. This semiskilled work secured him 54 reales or 13.5 pesetas, a comfortable income for the time.

Between 1863 and 1876, the demand for pruners was altered considerably. In Jerez pruning had always been done in December by the most skilled agricultural workers. Their craft was crucial to proper cultivation of the *palo-*

---

[5] Conard and Lovett, "Problèmes de l'évaluation du coût de la vie en Espagne"; Bernal, "Bourgeoisie rurale et proletariat agricole en Andalousie pendant la crise de 1868"; *El guadalete* (Jerez de la Frontera), 25-XI-1873; Croft-Cooke, *Sherry*, pp. 57–59; Vizetelly, *Facts about Sherry*, p. 45; letter, February 12, 1883, FO 72/1654.

mino grapes, grown predominantly on *albariza* soils. If a branch were cut back too far, it would produce too few grapes. If it were not pruned sufficiently, it would yield bunches of small, sour grapes. Numerous heavy grape clusters might bend or break the stalk. Pruning of *palomino* vines required dexterity, intuition, judgment, and familiarity with the special qualities of specific vines; it also required knowledge of soil conditions. But inferior wines could be produced from relatively sour musts, thus reducing the need for skilled pruning. Since pruners were highly paid vineyard craftsmen, dispensing with their services by substituting other, less-skilled vinetenders considerably reduced labor costs. As more and more vines were introduced into *barro-arena* soil after 1863, demand for the old skills declined. Peasant vinegrowers predominantly on *albariza* soil still required skilled pruners, since the marketability of their much more costly wine juice depended upon its high quality; toward the end of the century, however, demand for their expensive product declined, and so did their need for skilled pruners.

Other semiskilled work followed the calendar. January and February were devoted to choosing and planting new vines, filling in rows, grafting where necessary, and flattening the ridges of the basins constructed in the autumn. Further pruning took place in the spring, when the suckers were removed, soils further built up around the vines, and the weeds pulled. Between April and June, vines were also dusted with sulfur powder to defend the plants against *oidium*, a fungus that attacked the vines, causing the stalks and leaves to shrivel. In wet years, gypsum, to guard against mildew, was also applied. These processes had to be repeated, but required less-skilled labor than pruning. As the vines grew they needed supports to keep the grapes from touching the earth and spoiling. Grape flowers bloomed early in June, at which time, if necessary, they were again lightly pruned. August was a busy month. In addition to digging over the ground around the vines in a desperate effort to preserve what little moisture remained, soil for new plantings also had to be plowed several times. Such digging required a large number of laborers. Again and again in the month before harvest, the soil around the grape vines was hoed with a shorthandled implement designed to remove the weeds without damaging the low-lying grapes. Since the best sherry grapes were produced on the oldest vines, great care was taken to keep them healthy for sixty to a hundred years.[6]

Harvesting grapes required less skill but more hands. Henry Vizetelly, an Englishman who traveled through all the great vineyards of Europe, described the vintage outside Sanlúcar in 1875: "The men are broken up into gangs of ten, each with its separate capataz [foreman], and they certainly seemed to work with a will in a heat that rendered movement of any kind little short of heroic. They were a sturdy-looking, picturesque, raggedy lot, in broad sombreros, shirt-sleeves or linen jackets, and the inevitable scarlet or crimson sash wound tightly round their waists. . . . Some few dexterously plucked the bunches (the size and weight of many of which need to be seen to be credited) with their fingers, but the majority used a small jack-knife— the lower class of Spaniard's habitual companion and weapon of offense and defense—to detach the grapes. When the baskets, or the square wooden boxes known as tinetas, each holding about an arroba of grapes, weighing 25 lbs., were filled, the pickers hoisted them on their heads or shoulders, on which a small round straw knot was fixed for the purpose, and marched off in Indian file to the nearest almijar [courtyard or yard near the central buildings]. Here the bunches were spread out in the sun to dry on circular mats of esparto, thus to remain for from one to three days, while all blighted fruit was thrown aside for conversion into either spirit or vinegar."[7]

[6] Croft-Cooke, *Sherry*, pp. 62–63; Vizetelly, *Facts about Sherry*, pp. 28, 32.

[7] Vizetelly, *Facts about Sherry*, p. 16.

After remaining in the sun, the *Pedro Ximénez* raisins were pressed. Again Vizetelly captures the spirit. "The sun by this time had well-nigh set, and preparations were made for pressing the grapes throughout the night, when with a cooler temperature prevailing, there would be much less chance of precipitating the fermentation of the must. This pressing commenced between seven and eight o'clock, and was accomplished in a detached building under a low tiled roof, but entirely open in front. Passing through the gateway, and stumbling in the dim light afforded by an occasional lamp fixed against the wall, over a rudely-paved courtyard, we found ourselves beside a row of large, stout wooden troughs, some 10 feet square and a couple of feet deep, raised about 3 feet from the ground, and known in the vernacular of the vineyards as lagares. . . . Rising perpendicularly in the centre of each of the four lagares to a height of about seven feet is a tolerably powerful screw, which is only brought into requisition after the grapes have been thoroughly trodden. A couple of swarthy bare-legged pisadores leap into each lagar and commence spreading out the bunches with wooden shovels; and soon the whole eight of them in their short drawers, blue-striped shirts, little caps, red sashes, and hob-nailed shoes, are dancing a more or less lively measure, ankle-deep in newly-crushed grapes. They dance in couples, one on each side of the screw, performing certain rapid pendulum-like movements which are supposed to have the virtue of expressing the juice more satisfactorily from the fruit than can be accomplished by mere mechanical means. Their salutatory evolutions ended, the trodden grapes are heaped on one side and patted about with the shovel, like so much newly-mixed mortar. This causes the expressed juice to flow out in a dingy brown turgid stream through the spout fixed in front of the lagar into a metal strainer, and thence into the vat placed beneath to receive it." The process was completed only when the pressers collected the smashed grapes and, using the screw, pressed out the remainder. For little more than two weeks, treaders and pressers worked fourteen-hour shifts. They generally pressed sixty cartloads of grapes in that time, yielding in good years about sixty butts of must (a butt contains between 108 and 113 gallons).[8] From these pressing sheds in the countryside, the musts were carried in casks by oxcart into the city, where sherry storage, vinting, and blending took place.

Those who worked as pruners, plowsmen, pressers, and treaders were relatively well paid compared to other agricultural workers in the area around Jerez. In the 1870s, a treader might expect to receive 30 reales (a real is 25 céntimos or 0.25 pesetas), and the pressers 27 reales a night, plus their wine. But their life was by no means bacchanalian. Vizetelly noted that although "the Andalusians enjoy the reputation of being light-hearted and gay, . . . in the vineyards their light-heartedness seems to subside into taciturnity, and their gaiety to partake of the lugubrious." Generally about two hundred people might be employed in a large, consolidated vineyard at harvest time. They slept and ate in the same room, the so-called house of the people. While the food varied and was better than that fed to grain harvesters, the facilities were less than luxurious. A nineteenth-century visitor described the vinetenders' usual surroundings: "Ranged at equal distances down the centre of the apartment were a number of low tables, just sufficiently large to support a huge smoking bowl of bread and onion porridge of the circumference of a small sponging bath. Seated around each of these tables, with their eyes intently fixed on the steaming bowl, were seven ravenous men, who, quick as thought, plunged the wooden spoons with which they were armed first into the smoking porridge and next into their distended jaws, taking special care never to make a false movement, and always to pile up their spoons as full as possible, until the once overflowing bowl was utterly

[8] *Ibid.*, pp. 16–19.

void." Then they silently smoked their cigarettes, moved their mats from the wall, and in a temperature that averaged 90° F., they slept.[9]

Control over work and the structure of the sherry industry changed after 1863. Sherry prices for the most expensive musts and wines had increased throughout the first half of the nineteenth century, reaching their peak in 1863 (see Figure 1–1). The opportunity to sell sherry for high prices encouraged merchants to expand into the inferior *barro-arena* soils in Jerez, but also into Huelva, Sevilla, and Córdoba.

At first, cheap sherries could not compete with the more luxurious and expensive wines produced on the older vineyards in the *albariza* districts such as Caulina and Ducha by peasant proprietors and tenants. Exogenous economic factors in the sixties helped expand the market for cheaper, inferior grades of sherry, while reducing demand for the best wines. In 1860, the Cobden Treaty gave French wines preferential treatment in Europe, thus placing all Spanish wines at a commercial disadvantage. The late nineteenth-century depression, especially in Great Britain, reduced demand for costly sherries, which were more expensive than ever. The British bourgeoisie, suffering from cotton shortages due to the American Civil War, cut back on luxury wines. But, within a few years, disaster struck French vineyards. Phylloxera, a disease caused by plant lice, began to spread in 1868, and reached its height between 1875 and 1887, devastating French vines and creating markets for all Spanish musts. As an observer reported in 1883, "the demand for cheap Spanish wines is very great in Spain, and it is on the increase; and Jerez has come in for its share of it. The principal customer is France, where the Spanish wine is skillfully blended with a lighter product of the country and sold afterwards as French wines in England at a lower duty." Overall marketing possibilities persuaded shippers to

[9] *Ibid.*, pp. 18–20, 31.

FIGURE I–I

PRICE OF SHERRY AND AREA OF VINES (1851-1883)

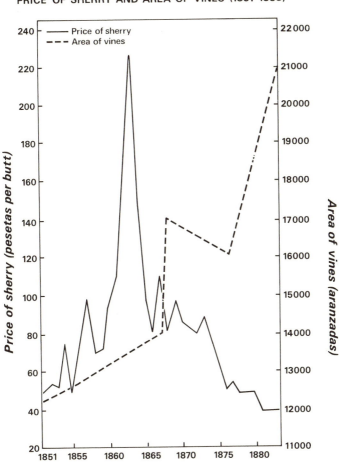

Sources: *Accounts and Papers* (1865) LIII, 658; February 12, 1883 letter, FO 72/1654; *El guadalete*, 7-III-1908; Diego Parada y Barreto, *Noticias sobre la historia y estado actual del cultivo de la vid*, p. 53; AMJF 199:10,506:84; AMJF *Archivo memoranda 6* (1879), f. 8.

Price of sherry is the average selling price per butt in pesetas in Jerez (one butt = 108-113 gallons). Area of vines in aranzadas (one aranzada = .34 hectares or .85 acres).

open up vineyards on the poorer soils in and around Jerez to produce cheap wine. Vinegrowing peasants on the prestigious *albariza* vineyards could find buyers for their musts only so long as they were willing to sell them for the low prices of wine produced on inferior soils. Since most were short of capital, they could not expand acreage and increase volume.[10]

Hence the *albariza* vinegrowing peasant, the aristocracy of his class, suffered severe decline. This was apparent to the British consul in Cádiz, who wrote that "in former years, notably in 1863, 'mostos' ranged at very high rates, and it is from this period that one of the great difficulties of vinegrowers commenced. . . . The fortunes of the vine landowners [peasant proprietors] have in many instances been reduced to the narrowest limits, and persons who were at one time wealthy, are now said to be almost destitute." Unable to pay mortgages and taxes, vinegrowing peasant proprietors began to sell off land, and the average holding per small owner seems to have declined between 1863 and 1883. Yet as late as 1877, there were approximately seven hundred peasant vinegrowers in Jerez alone. They, however, held only one-third of the plots, and had an average lot of one hectare or 2.2 acres. Such people worked alongside their help at harvest time. In greater proportion than the large vineyard owners on *barro-arena* soils, they continued to employ skilled pruners lest their main capital investment, the luxury vines, suffer from improper care. Peasant proprietor and skilled vinedresser shared bad times after 1863.

---

[10] *Ibid.*, p. 46; Warner, *The Winegrowers of France and the Government since 1875*, pp. 1–3; letter of February 12, 1883, in FO 72/1654. The British consul explained that shippers' prices for wine had increased 70 percent in the decade between 1854 and 1864, during which time many shippers bought vineyards. *Accounts and Papers* (1865), LIII, 658. González Gordon, *Jerez-Xerez-Sheris*. The amount of land planted in vines increased from 8,124 aranzadas in 1817 to 21,000 in 1883. Parada y Barreto, *Noticias sobre la historia y estado actual del cultivo de la vid y del comercio vinatero de Jerez de la Frontera*, p. 53.

Had labor costs been the major source of independent peasants' grief, opposition between dressers and vine owners might have taken political form. But peasants seem to have blamed their declining position upon those who prospered, namely the wine shippers, and to a certain degree they were correct that they, as agriculturalists, contributed to the merchants' high profits. For instance, peasant landowners had to pay taxes not only on land but on the musts passing into the city. They also absorbed the cost of gypsum and sulfates dusted on the vines. A local resident reported in 1883 that, largely due to the low price paid for luxury sherries, "there is little encouragement for the owners of vineyards to continue the cultivation of their vines, and it is sad to contemplate that many of the faint hearted and needy landowners have already abandoned their vineyards, preferring to see them a wilderness to laying out money on land without a prospect of future gain. It is calculated that one-third of the entire vineyards of *afueras* or *Albarizas* are left fallow." Both the skilled vinetenders and the peasant proprietors on *albariza* vineyards suffered from declining demand for the product of their labors, a factor noted by Leopoldo Alas [pseud. Clarín] who traced the militance of Jerez' populace to their diminished prosperity after 1863.[11]

NON-VINEGROWING PEASANTS AND AGRICULTURAL WORKERS

Tenants, sharecroppers, and small proprietors who grew grain, chickpeas, or beans were exogenous to the sherry economy, but were active participants in political movements. In 1839, there had been eighty-six *ranchos* or small

[11] Letters of February 12 and June 23, 1883, in FO 72/1654; AMJF 199:10,505:1:1; AMJF *Archivo memoranda 6* (1879), f.8; AMJF: *Protocolos, Año de 1883–1884*; José de Soto Collection, "González-Byass," Palacio del Vino (Jerez) uncatalogued and in disarray; *Accounts and Papers* (1892), LXXXIV, 227–228; Leopoldo Alas, "El Hambre en Andalucía (1883)," in Clara E. Lida (ed.), *Antecedentes y desarrollo del movimiento obrero español*, pp. 441–451.

23

holdings within the commune of Jerez. As costs rose after mid-century, it became profitable for relatively poor independent grain-producing peasants to lease or share plots of land with laborers instead of paying wages. In exchange for land on which taxes and mortgage payments had been paid, the sharecropper plowed the land five or six times to break up clods, while keeping the furrow only a few inches deep in order to prevent evaporation and erosion of topsoil. During the dry summers, the clay baked in the sun, making each year's plowing as difficult as the last. The iron plows that had contributed to the agricultural revolution in northern Europe could not be used in the thin soils of southern Spain. There plowmen continued to use the Roman atrium, or light plow, which the sharecropper could make himself. Oxen to pull the plow were generally provided by the landowner. The sharecropper, however, had to provide seeds and pay two-fifths of the crop to his landlord. Except for vinegrowing peasants, small cultivators kept livestock and, depending upon their numbers, employed a goatherd or a shepherd.[12]

But twenty-nine percent of Jerez' land was devoted to cereal production, most of which was held in latifundia cultivated by landless workers. Although viniculture was more labor intensive, in that the vines required regular attention, the greater extension of grain production meant that the total number actually employed in this sector was larger. Almost everyone in the Guadalete valley and the hills above it, except for the vinetenders and small vineyard owners, was involved in grain production sometime during the year. Even peasants who employed labor on their own plots supplemented their incomes by working on the latifundia in the valley at harvest.[13] Most of those who plowed, planted, and harvested the wheat, barley, and oats grown around Jerez were landless day laborers. In 1871 about 1,300 local workers were regularly employed on the large estates. The harvests required about 10,000 workers, of whom 5,000

[12] Portillo, *Noches jerezanas*, II, 164; *El imparcial*, 12-VI-1883.
[13] AMJF 199:10,506:80–81; AMJF 199:10,505:2:1; *Actas* I, LXIII.

generally came from Jerez and the remainder from Portugal, Huelva, and the hill towns of the Sierra.[14]

If exploitation and oppression alone had been enough to turn people into revolutionaries, agricultural day laborers in Cádiz Province would have been the vanguard. Their economic and social situation was miserable. When they were employed, they generally cultivated wheat and barley in huge labor gangs, sometimes as contract laborers. Others found jobs picking olives, chickpeas, beans, and grapes. Between November and May in any given year there was almost no work except for the skilled laborers who tended vines. Increasing bread prices and shortages in the last half of the nineteenth century fell hardest upon field workers. During harvests, the gangs that lived in barracks in the fields on the plains were fed *gazpacho* or garlic soup. There were constant disputes between the foremen and the laborers about the quality of food, especially the bread, which workers claimed was largely sawdust. Furthermore, heads of households had to feed their families, who were not in the gangs; by 1871, a kilo of bread cost a laborer nearly a whole harvest day's wages (see Figure 1-2). Indeed, beans, chickpeas, meat, and salted cod were so expensive that day laborers could rarely, if ever, afford them.[15]

In Andalusia one-third to one-half the arable land was often left fallow because owners followed a three-field system in which one portion was planted, one plowed and aerated, while one returned to scrub. Some owners, who

[14] AMJF 199:10,505:1:1. The 1871 survey reports that there were 12,445 workers in Jerez, of whom 5,527 were craftsmen of one kind or another.

[15] Sánchez-Albornoz, *Las crisis de subsistencia de España en el siglo XIX*; *España hace un siglo*, pp. 119–134. For the turn of the century, see R. J. Harrison, "The Spanish Famine of 1904–1906"; *El guadalete*, 24–X–1868, 25–XI–1873. Women often worked in labor gangs for nothing but food; Bayo, *Trabajos duros de la mujer*, p. 115. Between 1876 and 1886, women in agriculture generally earned one-half a male laborer's salary, or about one-half a peseta a day, the price of a loaf of bread. AMJF 199:10,505:1:8.

FIGURE 1–2

4 reales = 1 peseta

GENERAL TRENDS IN BREAD PRICES AND FIELD WORKERS' WAGES IN JEREZ (1850-19C

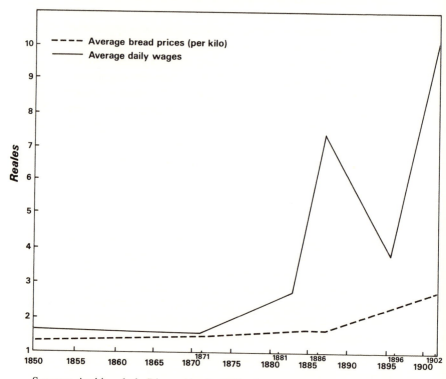

Sources: Archivo de la Diputación de Cádiz: letter, November 7, 1850, *Interrogatorio*, 1850; Archivo municipal de Jerez de la Frontera: 199:10,505:1–2; "Monografias del salario," *Revista social* (Madrid), 1–IX–1881, 8–IX–1881; *AMJF* 199:10,506:73–81; "Aritmética revolucionaria," *El socialismo* (Cadiz), 28–II–1886; "Revista semanal: Cádiz," *El corsario* (La Coruña), 26–III–1896; Instituto de reformas sociales: *Resumen de información acerca de los obreros agrícolas en las provincias de Andalucía y Extremadura* (Madrid, 1905), pp. 44, 48.

used the land as a safe investment after a major financial crash in 1866, had no intention of cultivating it. As a result, work at any wage was in demand most of the year. Yet at harvest time there were tremendous labor shortages. Reapers who were relatively skilled could often bargain over piece rates.[16] While almost anyone could harvest barley, chickpeas, or beans, occupations in which women and children were increasingly employed towards the end of the nineteenth century, the massive demand for labor increased faster than supply, especially between June and September, when all the major products were harvested. Despite population growth, most of Spain was underpopulated in the nineteenth century. In 1839 and 1864 observers complained that a shortage of labor in Andalusia was always evident during harvest season and prevented the opening up of new arable land. For this reason, Portuguese contract laborers, employed at piece rates, were encouraged to work during the harvests in Jerez.[17] From the laborers' point of view, however, "underpopulation" at such times was a blessing that enabled them to demand wage increases.

Especially between November and May, unemployment was generally so great, and poverty was so visible, that municipal governments all over Andalusia organized public works projects in the hopes of reducing the possibility of social disorder. Work constructing roads or renovating monasteries to be used as public buildings and wineries earned the poor less than the prevailing rates in private business, and the mayors and their crews were believed to be "eating up" much of the money assigned to the relief opera-

[16] *El guadalete*, 25-XI-1873; letters of February 12, 1883 and June 6, 1883 in FO 72/1654.

[17] Portillo, *Noches jerezanas*, II, 166; *Accounts and Papers* (1865), LIII, 662–663. Spain was not overpopulated, but underindustrialized. Jordi Nadal argues that the rate of Spanish demographic growth, which was .63 percent a year between 1797 and 1860, actually fell to .49 percent a year between 1860 and 1910—one of the lowest in Europe. "The Failure of the Industrial Revolution in Spain, 1830–1914," p. 535. Between 1851 and 1889, Jerez experienced population decline because of cholera and out-migration. AMJF *Archivo memoranda 6* (1879), f.22; AMJF "Padrón de 1889: Distrito municipal de Jerez de la frontera: número de habitantes de Octubre de 1877," *Archivo memoranda 10* (1889), pp. 75–77. Also see Cutileiro, *A Portuguese Rural Society*.

tions. Aside from public works, there were few sources of economic aid to the needy except cutting wood or gathering esparto grass in the mountains. Local authorities raised private subscriptions to prevent "threatening and imposing" street begging. Sometimes the poor were divided into allotments and awarded to unwilling landowners simply to keep the unemployed occupied and off the streets. With jobs scarce, private charity organizations in Jerez sold soup to the poor.[18]

In times of high unemployment or in periods of government repression, individual acts of violence were widespread. Food was stolen, and occasionally vines were cut, and wheat fields or olive groves burnt. Bandits and robbers made it impossible for the rich to live on their country estates.[19] Given the desperation of the poor and their frequently expressed loathing for the rich, it is no wonder that the landless laborers have been viewed as the social group that directed anarchism in Andalusia. But in periods of famine or high unemployment, the people lacked the means by which to attack their employers in a way that would win them economic gains. In such periods, their misery and desperation may have led them to theft or incendiarism, but desperation was not conducive to disciplined, sustained organizational activity. Most people were unemployed much of the year; when they did have jobs, the constantly fluctuating membership of the agricultural work gangs and the large number of migrants and outsiders made it extremely difficult for them to form stable organizations. Nevertheless, as the ratio between bread prices and field workers' wages improved between 1871 and 1902, they did build

[18] *Accounts and Papers* (1897), XCIII, 403; AMJF 199:10,506:103, 110. The practice of stealing relief money was common throughout Andalusia. See Fraser, *Tajos: The Story of a Village on the Costa del Sol* and Guichot y Parody, *Historia general de Andalucía*, VIII, 155.

[19] For an account of a kidnapping for ransom, see Turbino, *La historia de un cautiverio*.

such unions, many of which persisted over the course of the late nineteenth-century. At least during the first phase of Spanish anarchism, between 1869 and 1883, the agricultural proletariat benefited from its connection with craftsmen, skilled workers, and peasants (defined as tenants, sharecroppers, and small landowners), and their notions of workers' control that developed out of the circumstances and ideology of the small producer. Of this group, the coopers and blenders were the most important.

Skilled Workers and Craftsmen in Jerez

Contrary to what is often argued about Andalusia, in Jerez scarcely a majority of the permanent adult male population considered agriculture to be their primary occupation. In this regard, a report made to Jerez's local government in 1871 is informative (see Table 1–2). Many of those

Table 1–2

Occupational Distribution of
Jerez' Urban Population in 1871

Masons	1293
Servants	751
Coopers	480
Carpenters	447
Bodega Workers	436
Shoemakers	414
Bakers	359
Wagon and Coach Makers	150
Muleteers	127
Stone Cutters	119
Barbers and Surgeons	92
Locksmiths	90
Painters	80
Blacksmiths	50
Potters	50
Total	4938

Source: AMJF 199:10,505:1:1.

listed as urban workers were often employed in agriculture, at least as harvesters in the grain fields. Of the rest, almost everyone was in some direct or indirect way connected with wine production. Wagon makers constructed the means of transporting casks of musts in from the fields. Muleteers carried grapes. Carpenters, masons, and painters helped construct or reconstruct the *bodegas*, or winecellars, in which the sherry was actually manufactured. And blacksmiths, coopers, and winecellar workers contributed their skills to the transformation of grape juices into prestigious sherry wine.

Some grapes were pressed in the *bodegas* or cellars rather than in the fields. A familiar sight on the roads was "troops of mules laden with panniers of dust-covered grapes, and occasionally carrying a couple of blue-shirted, crimson-sashed, hulking muleteros as well." The mules, known to prefer grapes to all other food, were kept muzzled with esparto grass. When the grapes were pressed in the fields, the juices were poured into casks and allowed to bubble away in first fermentation. Then they were carried by ox-cart into town. At the gates of the city, an excise tax or *consumo*, the financial burden of the vineyard owner, was collected. Once at the *bodega*, the vineyard owner was paid for his grapes or juices, and the process of making sherry began. Henry Vizetelly, one of the earliest and most observant travelers, reported that "the mosto on being conveyed from the vineyard to the bodega is transferred . . . into fresh casks, which, after being filled to within about a tenth of their full capacity, are ranged in rows one above the other, the lowest butts being placed on stone supports." The juices were permitted to go on fermenting until February or March. Then a small amount of brandy, said to be less than 2 percent, was added to the musts to fortify them. The best vintages were preserved intact for five to ten years. Then they, like other sherries that were kept intact only four to six years, were manufactured according to the solera system, whereby older wines were blended with newer ones. Barrels were stacked, sometimes as many as ten high, with the oldest wines at the bottom. "As the older wines are drawn off to supply orders, the deficiency created in the butts was made good by the addition of wine of the same character but a year younger, the place of which was supplied in a like manner by still younger wine, and this process was continued all down the scale."[20]

The blending operations were carried out by skilled *arrumbadores*, or cellarmen. The best sherries are made with the best vintages, but sherry is a blended wine, and those tutored in the ways of making the olorosos and amontillados held a secret crucial to the local and national economy. An old firm, Manuel Misa and Company, had in 1875 as many as eight hundred barrels of old wines, blended in 1815, 1820, 1824, 1831, and 1843; these were only used as starters for other sherries. Only the winecellar men knew how to begin to reproduce them. After siphoning off wine from different barrels, they ascertained the quality of each variety, allowing for changes from one year to the next even in juices grown on the same vines and plots as the year before; then they created a recipe for that year. Making such choices was a skill handed down from father to son. Even the owners of sherry companies did not know what proportions went into the special blends that bore their company's names.[21]

Supervising the blending operations, the *arrumbadores* would order barrels removed from their places in the pile. Less skilled winecellar workers inserted funnels into the holes and drew specified proportions from one barrel and poured it into the next. At each pouring, they would draw small quantities off from the barrel and test them for color and taste in comparison with the foreman's sample. Adjustments for taste and texture were again made. Large quanti-

[20] Vizetelly, *Facts about Sherry*, pp. 15, 21, 23–24, 45, 47, 51, 73.
[21] *Ibid.*, pp. 52, 76.

ties of the concoction were poured into barrels, branded, loaded onto wagons or trolleys, and, after 1854, carried by railroad to port.

Coopers were even more highly skilled than pruners and blenders. As far back as the middle ages, caskmakers had strictly controlled production of butts through apprenticeship programs and guild control on quality. They produced their own barrels, and sold them to blending plants. With increased output of cheap sherry, demand for barrels grew, but the old process of making them was too costly in proportion to the price of the new wines. As the blending firms entered into grape production by opening up vineyards in *barro-arena* soils and buying old *albariza* vineyards from bankrupt or credit-poor peasants, they also added their own cooperages. What had previously been the single most important handicraft in Jerez had, by the late nineteenth century, become somewhat mechanized. Up until mid-century, coopers had controlled their own production process. After that time, the majority were forced to become employees in the cooperages attached to winecellars. Independent coopers, like the vinegrowing peasants on *albariza* soils, found that demand for their product declined while demand for shoddier goods increased.

Cooperage employees, while earning relatively high wages, experienced the process of proletarianization in two ways. First and most important was the introduction of piece rates. The labor practice in almost all jobs in Jerez until about 1870 had been to pay daily wages plus food. This had permitted the worker to set his own pace. While blenders, masons, carpenters, and bakers were still paid by the day in 1871, field hands, shoemakers, stone cutters, and cooperage employees had been forced to accept piece rates.[22] The second factor in the proletarianization of coopers was the reduction in skill required, due to greater division of labor and to the mechanization of production.

[22] Croft-Cooke, *Sherry*, pp. 106–107.

Compared with steel production, for example, caskmaking retained many features of a handcraft, the main innovation being the introduction of steam power. But by the 1870s in the cooperage of the González-Byass Company, the most modern in Jerez, the production of barrels had been broken up into distinct jobs, robbing the cooper of the right and the skill to make a cask from start to finish. One group of workers in the sawmill now cut the aged American oak staves into precise lengths. Other workers manned the incline along which truckloads of planks were sent upstairs to the cooperage. The staves were then trimmed and planed with traditional tools by skilled workers. The men straddled slanted benches that held the staves down, freeing both hands for the trimming and planing. They joined the staves, plugged holes and crevices, and put the barrels together. The staves were gathered at the top and splayed at the bottom, held in place by iron hoops. Over a blazing fire, the wood was molded. The charred insides were scraped, bottoms and tops inserted, edges bevelled, and bung holes drilled. The final steaming was then done by steam-driven machinery that revolved the casks. Since this last process had traditionally been the one in which the artisan cooper perfected his work, mechanization of this process symbolized the cooper's loss of control over the quality of his product. Further innovations came with introduction of bottling plants in the late nineteenth century.[23]

Changes in Work and Economy

The economic changes that occurred in Jerez between the late eighteenth century and 1863 objectively improved the social situation in Jerez, which, like the rest of Andalusia, had long suffered from the problems of under-industrialization and underutilization of land. But after 1863,

[23] González Gordon, *Jerez*, pp. 446–447; Vizetelly, *Facts about Sherry*, pp. 54, 64–65, 72.

33

declining demand for the excellent old sherries hurt the vine-growing peasants and cut into the profits of winecellar owners, who stockpiled costly quantities of the old luxury sherries. The expansion of vinelands into *barro-arena* districts meant that new lands were opened up, providing jobs for wage laborers. But the flood of manufactured goods, imported in exchange for sherry, helped bring about the decline of the independent handicraftsmen, such as handloom weavers, *navaja* or jackknife makers, and tinsmiths, whose products could not compete with foreign machine-made goods. Many former *albariza* vineyard owners were forced to sell their land and become tenants or wage laborers on what had been their own vineyards when demand for their grapes, and consequently their earnings, declined after 1863. Such peasants may actually have improved their economic situation, because they would no longer have had to pay the high costs of labor, new vines, gypsum, and sulfur; nor did they have to absorb the entire loss in years of drought. But they lost the power to judge, to decide, and to control production.[24]

The turmoil caused after the sharp drop in demand for luxury sherry after 1863 caused all sectors of Jerez society to organize. Petty producers and skilled workers in Jerez responded to the worsening economic and social situation after 1863 by drawing on old organizational forms and creating new ones—by forming cooperative societies, protective associations and unions to defend their interests and to preserve their old patterns of work. Craftsmen in Jerez, including coopers, tinsmiths, hat manufacturers, and belt makers had been organized into strong guilds until the early nineteenth century, when laissez-faire capitalist legislation had abolished the guilds along with aristocratic, clerical, and municipal corporations. The guilds had been exclusionary, but they were the only traditional institutions through which craftsmen could defend their rights and set their own

[24] Portillo, *Noches jerezanas*, II, 152; *Accounts and Papers* (1884), LXXX, 577–578.

standards. Without them and the journeymen's associations, small producers and employees were forced to fight against economic change as isolated individuals. Some of Jerez' craftsmen probably held onto their associations, despite legal impediments, disguising them as cultural organizations. Many beneficial societies, producers' cooperatives, and even rudiments of trade unions may have grown out of such organizations, but since they were clandestine, there is no way to know for sure.[25]

By 1870, there were in Jerez, approximately fifty different societies to which artisans, small proprietors, and workers belonged. For instance, the thirty-one member "Star" society was a consumer and producer cooperative that had a factory and warehouses for food and wine. It more than tripled its capital within three months of operation. Jerez' masons, carpenters, blenders, and skilled vineyard workers had had no traditional institutions of which authorities were aware until the 1860s, when they, too, began to organize. Perhaps one of the most impressive groups was the "Abnegation" society, founded in 1864. By 1870, it rented two vineyards with a total of 8,000 vines, and had a small winecellar and 15,000 pesetas capital. In 1868, the ninety-member "Primitive" construction society collectively built and continued to operate a blending plant and winecellar. In less than two years they had accumulated capital of 7,500 pesetas.[26]

[25] AMJF 199:10,505:1:24; González Gordon, *Jerez*, pp. 142–143. Garrido, *Historia del reinado del último Borbón de España*; Nettlau, "Impresiones sobre el desarrollo del socialismo en España." Josep Termes and Clara Lida stress anarchism's debt to utopian socialism and cooperative movements, and Iris Zavala discusses anarchism's connection to republican secret societies. See her *Masones, comuneros y carbonarios* and *Ideología y política en la novela española del siglo XIX*.

[26] Garrido, *Historia de las clases trabajadoras*, III, 245; IV, 131–132, 134. David Montgomery's "Trade Union Practice and the Origins of Syndicalist Theory in the United States" (unpublished, mimeographed copy available from author) supports many of my views

Some of the associations attempted to unite diverse groups. The "Development" society was formed in January 1869, to serve as a credit union; another organization, "Fraternity," was founded in 1870, and yet another, "Hope," began in November 1872. Dues for "Development"—an 8-peseta entrance fee and 1.24-peseta monthly subscription—certainly excluded all but the more prosperous members of the petty bourgeoisie. "Fraternity" had one hundred members who agreed to create a secular primary school that would teach crafts.[27]

Guilds and journeymen's associations had previously organized skilled workers in order to monopolize production and certify competence; in Jerez after midcentury, cooperatives and employees' associations, which included peasant proprietors, artisans, vinedressers, coopers, and semiskilled workers, performed a different function. The cooperative societies and trade unions provided their members with workers' control through collective ownership of property, and the credit unions accumulated capital for workers' enterprises. But these associations also had a social dimension, insofar as they provided cooperative ways by which people of different classes could fight against the growing power of the sherry firms. Thus the existence of a powerful group of skilled vinetenders, caskmakers, blenders, and peasants who were relatively well organized assured that the process of centralization of work activities, which normally leveled all workers to semiskilled roles, might meet organized opposition in Jerez.

---

about the relationship between craftsmen's societies and notions of workers' control.

[27] Garrido, *Historia de las clases trabajadoras*, p. 135; AMJF 199: 10,505:1:17; AMJF 8:12,627.

CHAPTER II

Capitalist Development and Bourgeois Politics in Northern Cádiz Province

Changes in the work process and the politics that developed from them were products of larger social transformations attributable to the growth of capitalism. More than merely an economic system centered on the sherry industry, capitalism represented the most fundamental reordering of relationships since the Reconquest. No facet of life was left untouched. No individual remained aloof.

Spain, like Prussia and many other nations, became a capitalist country in the nineteenth century in a futile attempt to preserve the remnants of the Old Regime. This reactionary goal led the governors of the Spanish state to set in motion a series of innovations that, in the early half of the nineteenth century, welded together the progressive bourgeoisie with more prosperous workers and peasants in Northern Cádiz Province, an alliance that came undone in 1868.

Under pressure from its creditors, the Spanish state accelerated the pace of capitalist agricultural development between 1814 and 1820, and again between 1836 and 1855, first by forcing most farmers to the marketplace, and then by creating vast amounts of private property through the disentailment of seigneurial corporate estates. Liberalized land policies stimulated commercial enterprises, such as sherry wine production, since the availability of land permitted sherry producers to expand operations by opening new vineyards. Investment opportunities attracted foreigners who provided capital for small mercantile firms in Cádiz. Grape-growing tenants and sharecroppers, coopers, carters, and

37

tradespeople in Northen Cádiz Province prospered with the sherry boom, but suffered from the system of taxation.

The Spanish state, always on the verge of bankruptcy in the early nineteenth century, attempted to raise the maximum amount of revenue they could, without hurting the agricultural bourgeois latifundists of Castile and Andalusia, who dominated the government. They embarked upon a tax program that protected one capitalist enterprise, wheat production, while penalizing Cádiz' commercial and petty bourgeoisie by imposing heavy luxury taxes on wine, and by permitting the continuation of the *consumo*, or internal tariff, upon goods passing into cities. Protection and internal tariffs were inconsistent with the kind of laissez-faire capitalism the Cádiz merchants wished to promote.

Had the Spanish state pursued a progressive capitalist tax policy, encouraging the sale of grain and wine, both the agricultural and mercantile bourgeoisie of Northern Cádiz Province would probably have supported the state. Instead, national protection of grain, combined with the government's failure to negotiate favorable foreign import taxes on sherry, and continued double excise taxes on wine (taxing both the musts passing from countryside to winecellar and the imported bottled wine, which was bottled in Great Britain until the late nineteenth century), reduced mercantile and petty bourgeois profits. One special piece of treachery was the Spanish government's refusal to negotiate most-favored-nation treaties, which would have helped sherry producers prevent foreign governments, especially France and Great Britain, from classifying sherry with brandy and liquors of the highest proofs instead of with wine, which paid significantly lower duties. In order to protect the wheat growers, the government sacrificed the wine producers. Such a policy turned the commercial and petty bourgeoisie in Cádiz Province against the agricultural bourgeoisie, and against the state. This antagonism assumed political expression in the Democratic party.

Agricultural capitalism was firmly established in Andalusia by 1840, if that term indicates that land itself was a commodity that could be bought and sold; that laborers increasingly lost access to land; and that production for a cash economy shaped social and political relationships. This development was not a consequence of a self-conscious political program, but the result of short-term fiscal decisions that had been carried out after the Napoleonic period. These trends, delineated by Josep Fontana for the period between 1814 and 1820, held, with certain variations, until 1868. Under Ferdinand VII, the Spanish government tried to reform the state without disrupting privileged groups, a task that proved to be impossible. To meet extraordinary national debts incurred during the Spanish-American wars of independence, the servicing of which accounted for over 30 percent of the national budget as late as 1860, Spain was forced to reorganize its financial base.[1] To extract more revenues from the predominantly rural sectors, the government attempted to reduce the clerical hold on land and abolish seigneurial claims to the agricultural surplus. Ferdinand VII therefore attempted to impose what amounted to an agricultural revolution from above through the use of a direct tax system. It was hoped that such a policy would

[1] Not everyone will agree with this definition of capitalism. At a conference that discussed the Spanish bourgeoisie, A. M. Bernal argued that what defined the Andalusian agricultural bourgeoisie was their system of exploiting the land they held. In debate, Manuel Tuñón de Lara, taking issue with the notion that there was a rural bourgeoisie in Andalusia, reminded the audience that the bourgeoisie is defined by its relation to the means of production, its system of market relations, its investment of capital, and its interest in productivity. My views about what defines the bourgeoisie, the prime movers of capitalism, are consistent with his, but I believe that such a bourgeoisie was active in northern Cádiz Province. *La Question de la "bourgeoisie" dans le monde hispanique au XIXe siècle*, pp. 77, 84–85; Fontana, *La quiebra de la monarquía absoluta*; Hennessy, *The Federal Republic in Spain: Pi y Margall and the Federal Republican Movement 1868–74*, p. 107.

force self-sufficient peasants to produce crops in excess of what they and their landlords could consume or sell to local markets. To raise money for taxes, the peasants would have to specialize in market crops, and give up attempts to produce the variety of subsistence goods necessary for themselves and their families. Once at market, selling their specialized crops for money, they would buy the goods they no longer produced, thus creating an internal national market for items produced elsewhere in Spain. Through direct taxes, the state tried to increase overall productivity, raise demand, and skim off dividends from expanded production and trade. With this system, Ferdinand went a long way toward creating a capitalist economy.

While wheat producers favored excise taxes as a means of providing state revenue, Andalusian commercial interests claimed that expanded free trade was the only way to do so. As far back as the Napoleonic period, Cádiz' liberal bourgeoisie, consisting primarily of sherry merchants, had favored the elimination of tariffs (or the negotiation of most-favored-nation treaties) and the reduction of excises.[2] The king clearly threw in his lot with the conservatives on the tax question. But his destruction of feudal property relations, the result of direct taxes combined with disentailment, alienated clergy, many aristocrats, and landowning peasants. Although Ferdinand and his advisers stopped short of direct attacks on the church, which were postponed until 1837, the state's financial needs, particularly its desire for regular taxes from the peasants, brought it into conflict with the clergy, who supported themselves through tithes paid in kind. Peasant proprietors, tenants, and sharecroppers were

[2] Important discussions of the politics of tariff and trade can be found in Sánchez-Albornoz, "La legislación prohibicionista en materia de importación de granos, 1820–1868," in *Las crisis*, pp. 13–45; and in Fontana, "Formación del mercado nacional y toma de conciencia de la burguesía," in *Cambio económico y actitudes políticas en la España del siglo XIX*, pp. 13–53. An important theoretical discussion of taxation and political reactions to it can be found in Ardant, *Théorie sociologique de l'impôt*, p. 21.

caught between the church's demand for tithes and the state's new demands for taxes. To the extent that the government's policy succeeded, it exacerbated the misery of the peasants. But the state alienated crucial classes without achieving the income that would have permitted it to pay its debt and provide regular salaries to the army. When Ferdinand was attacked in 1820 by armed forces opposed to the Spanish-American wars, he had no mass base to which he might turn for support. He was returned to the throne in 1823, not because he had regained popularity, but because the Holy Alliance preferred him to more radical elements. His death in 1833 set off another series of uprisings, as much in opposition to the form of economic liberalism he represented as for dynastic political reasons.

Between 1820 and 1868 the Spanish state was committed to protecting wheat prices in order to assure high profits for Andalusian and Castilian grain-producing capitalists. This policy, while assuring important revenues for the government, had deleterious effects on the rest of the population. One of the most articulate and consistent sources of opposition came from the Northern Cádiz wine merchants and peasants. Since genuine sherry was produced only in the Jerez district and towns bordering on Cádiz Harbor, local merchants had nothing to fear from foreign competition, but they had everything to lose from unfavorable terms of trade on the international wine market. One result of Spain's policy of excluding foreign grain through high tariffs was foreign retaliation against Spanish wines, including sherry.

The Northern Cádiz merchants and vinegrowing peasants wanted absolutely free trade or government support in arranging mutual trade agreements with sherry-purchasing nations, usually the former. The *consumo*, Spain's version of the French *octroi*, was a tax on all goods coming into a city's limits, even from its own hinterland. The excise fell upon food and drink, as well as on other products. Cádiz merchants had demanded the abolition of the *consumo* and the substitution of a land tax for a long time. Their reason for opposing the *consumo* was that it tended to raise the costs of all items of consumption, thus reducing local demand for cheaper sherries. Vineyard owners, whether peasants, shippers, or winecellar men, had to pay taxes on musts passing into town to be blended and stored, while retailers and customers paid the luxury tax on bottled wine, liquor, olive oil, and meat.[3]

Although the commercial bourgeoisie in Cádiz succeeded in winning free trade and the abolition of the *consumo* only for limited periods in the nineteenth century, they did profit from the creation of a land market after 1837. Between 1836 and 1837, Juan Álvarez de Mendizábal's government, strapped for funds to supply its side in the 1833–1840 civil war, broke the entail primarily on church land that constrained about seventy percent of the Spanish land mass and at least fifty percent of all the land below the Guadalquivir River. A subsequent disentailment carried out by Pascual Madoz between 1854 and 1856 nearly completed the job by disentailing municipal lands. While the principal aim of Mendizábal's reform was to raise necessary war revenues, not to end seigneurial landholdings, the disentailment and abolition of the tithe effected a major land and tax reform. The same legislation that abolished seigneurial juridical rights also brought to market common land in pastures, meadows, and wastes attached to townships like Jerez, Sanlúcar, and Puerto de Santa María. By 1850 an observer in Jerez reported that "the large farmers have benefitted from the suppression of the tithe to the church in recent years. Their situation has also improved as a result of other legal guarantees. In general, they have gotten richer."[4]

[3] Sánchez-Albornoz, *Las crisis*, p. 16; letter, November 7, 1850, signed by Pedro Gordon and Francisco de Lauta, president and secretary respectively of the Royal Economic Society of Jerez de la Frontera. ADC: *Interrogatorio, 1850*, uncatalogued. Pedro Gordon was a leading sherry producer.

[4] Canga Argüelles, *Diccionario de hacienda con aplicación a España*, vol. v: *Baldíos; Diccionario razonado de legislación y jurisprudencia* (1874), xi, 9, cited in Ramos-Oliveira, *Historia de España*, ii, 193;

Many social groups were hurt by this capitalist legislation, notably small landowning peasants who had formerly had certain rights to township lands. Until the 1855 disentailment in Jerez, the 80 full-time grain producing peasants had "rights to extensive pastures on which they [could] graze their goats, pigs, and oxen. They shared these rights with other local peasants who [rented] their land." This common land was sold to private parties after 1855. Other tenants and sharecroppers who had provided the labor on aristocratic or clerical land were often driven off by new landowners who preferred to hire day laborers. One piece of ecclesiastical land that had supported 6,000 families before disentailment supported only 240 afterward.

The church, especially the religious orders, was hardest hit by special legislation promulgated between 1837 and 1855, which made all church property, including real estate, national property. Written by reformers, many of whom were anticlerical, the laws were designed to fill state coffers while wiping out a powerful enemy by depriving it of its economic base. Clerical orders not engaged in teaching or hospital work were dissolved. Mendizábal himself and many of his ministers were from Cádiz, where the landed power of the orders was especially great. For instance, in Jerez de la Frontera in 1824 there were only eight orders with a total membership of 51, including novices, but these tiny religious orders controlled considerable wealth. Between 1797 and 1824, the total number of regular clergy in Spain had declined by ninety percent, but their land remained intact. Orders such as Jerez' Discalced Mercedarians, with

Bernal, "Formación y desarrollo de la burguesía agraria sevillana: Caso concreto de Morón de la Frontera," in *La Question de la "bourgeoisie,"* p. 48. A general review of the literature on the disentailment process in Spain can be found in Ponsot, "Révolution dans les campagnes espagnoles au xixᵉ siècle," in Anes Álvarez, "La agricultura española desde comienzos del siglo xix hasta 1868," p. 245; and in Herr, "El significado de la desamortización en España." ADC: *Interrogatorio, 1850.*

only one member in 1824, continued to hold land. It was argued in 1834 that, given the wealth brought in by rentals and tithes, each monk or nun in Jerez was guaranteed an average annual income of more than 5,000 pesetas, while the average laborer earned 120.[5] The twelve Carthusians who inhabited La Cartuja, to the southeast of Jerez, and owned some of the major vineyards in the township, almost certainly had incomes well above the local average.

The disentailments seem to have changed some of this. The Carthusian vineyards were nationalized and sold—primarily, it appears, to local wine merchants. The Carmelites, of whom there were six in 1824, owned the del Valle vineyards until 1855. Friars and urban monks not engaged in charitable activities were relatively hard hit by the disentailments in Jerez. The Santo Domingo monastery in town became a grain storage warehouse and winecellar, as did the Veracruz and Descalzo monasteries. A more common pattern was for an old monastery to become a public building. What had once been the monastery of Our Lady of Bethlehem became the jail. The Church of St. Christopher was, by 1868, used as Democratic party headquarters.

Franciscan convents of the Mothers of God and the Poor Claires, which in 1850 had 27 and 16 nuns, respectively, continued doing charitable works. The nuns of the Immaculate Conception and the Nazarenes merged and ran a philanthropic home for the aged female poor. Philanthropic activities, performed primarily by female religious in Jerez, ensured that women's orders would persist where most of the male orders went under. After 1837 those clergy who survived were financially dependent on the charity of former aristocrats whom the disentailments had trans-

---

[5] ADC: *Interrogatorio, 1850*; Lazo, *La desamortización eclesiástica en Sevilla (1835-45)*, cited in Anes, "La agricultura española," pp. 248–249, 251; Ponsot, "Révolution dans les campagnes," p. 117; *Xerez de la Frontera*. Representación dirigida al rei en 1824 (cited hereafter as *Representación*), pp. 19–20; Portillo, *Noches jerezanas*, p. 213.

formed into agricultural capitalists, and on the commercial bourgeoisie.

The law of 1837 permitted people who could make large down payments to hold sixteen-year mortages at 5 percent interest. Those who wanted to pay in government bonds could get eight-year mortages at 10 percent. Since government bonds were depreciating below face value, due to the state's inability to service its national debt, the second condition was more favorable, for bondholders could use their worthless certificates to buy land, the value of which was increasing. One indication of the growth of land value is that rents in western Andalusia doubled between 1814 and 1840. The law of 1837 was, therefore, a bonanza to the monied classes. Although some legislators conceived the law as a way to provide land to peasants, few but the wealthiest freeholders and tenants could afford to buy land.

Modern latifundism, based on private property rather than on seigneurial relations, can be traced to the development of agrarian capitalism that culminated in the disentailment legislation. Land was transformed into a commodity. Sales were most rapid where the commercial bourgeoisie was best developed, near the port cities. Long deprived of land by entail, the Cádiz merchants purchased land that they often rented out to tenants and sharecroppers, many of whom had cultivated it before 1837 as peasant proprietors or as tenants of the church or the aristocracy.[6] Aristocrats, formerly prohibited by entail from selling land, could put their property on the market and pocket the profits; they could also buy new land to consolidate holdings. Both aristocrats and merchants bought land; but political and economic differences continued to divide the agricultural bourgeoisie, dependent solely on agricultural production

[6] Madoz, *Diccionario geográfico*, ix, 618–619; *Representación*, p. 19; *El guadalete*, 22-x-1868; Anes, "La agricultura española," pp. 249–251, 255; Bernal, "Formación y desarrollo," p. 51; Ponsot, "Révolution dans les campagnes," pp. 118–120.

45

and land speculation, from the commercial bourgeoisie in Cádiz Province, whose primary interest lay in the sherry trade.

SHERRY AND THE COMMERCIAL BOURGEOISIE

The two new segments of the capitalist elites consolidated their power. Between 1837 and 1855, a second series of disentailments took place, this time dissolving all corporations, including guilds, and abolishing the municipal public domain. Prior to 1837, there were approximately five hundred small mercantile houses and blending firms in Jerez de la Frontera. Their owners could not buy much land, since those who had owned it held it as entailed property, but they could make a profit merely acting as wine merchants. At the end of the eighteenth century a minor Swiss noble, Pedro Domecq, came to aid his mother's cousin, Juan Carlos de Haurie, a wine merchant in Jerez. The old man died; brothers and cousins followed from Switzerland. After the disentailment of 1837, the family bought property (including the towered mansion, now the company trademark) from the Marcharnudo vineyards, which had been awarded by Alfonso X to one of his retainers after the thirteenth-century reconquest of Jerez. The Domecqs built one of the foremost sherry houses in the world. The late eighteenth-century British consul in Cádiz, Sir James Duff, who helped local merchants raise money to resist Napoleon, was a wine shipper in Puerto de Santa María and founder of the Duff-Gordon Company, more famous for its gin than its sherry. Manuel María González Ángel, the son-in-law of a leading Cádiz merchant, created his own winecellar, the Sacristy, which had previously belonged to a disentailed church. He bought out other, older cellars, purchased vineyards, and raised money from the English importer, Robert Blake Byass, who by 1855 was a partner in the firm.

After 1837, British mercantile families began to invest in Spanish shipping firms and wine cellars, often providing the capital for the purchase of vineyards when they came on the market. George William Suter moved to Jerez at mid-century, formed Cramp Suter and Co. as a sherry shipping firm, and remained in town taking care of business and acting as the British vice consul and business adviser for the district. Like these men, many other Englishmen built local companies, intermarried with Spanish sherry producers (who, until after the seventies, were socially distinct from the grain latifundists), and formed the Anglo-Andalusian bourgeoisie that was to become so important in the region's subsequent history. Names like Patricio (Patrick) Garvey emerged, along with González and Domecq, as synonyms for sherry.[7]

As sherry markets expanded in the forties, sherry warehouse owners needed to be sure that the wines they shipped were the same from lot to lot, a task for which owners of large stocks were better suited than those with small cellars. Shippers and owners of large *bodegas* therefore tried to consolidate sherry production from vine to wine. The first step in this process was for shippers and blenders to buy old *albariza* vineyards or to establish new ones on *barro-arena* soil. The latter again required capital. According to an 1852 newspaper report, each new vineyard required at least 150,000 to 200,000 pesetas at the outset. Most new land was divided into plots of 15 *aranzadas*, approximately 13 acres. These plots, scattered as far away as Huelva, Sevilla, and Córdoba, were far larger than the old *albariza* vineyards. In and around Cádiz Province, the big shippers often consolidated seven or more old peasant holdings on both *albariza* and *barro-arena* soils.

After the initial land purchase, the costs in new vineyards mounted. In addition to buying vines, erecting sheds for

[7] Anes, "La agricultura española," pp. 253–254; Bernal, "Bourgeoisie rurale," p. 333; Delgado y Orellana, *La casa de Domecq d'Usquain*, pp. 31–32, 34; Portillo, *Noches jerezanas*, I, p. 154; *El guadalete*, 22-II-1908; 11-II-1868; *"Old Sherry": The Story of the First Hundred Years of González Byass & Co., Ltd., 1835-1935*.

wine presses, and building a house for the foreman, who lived on the property with his family, the would-be vineyard owner had to invest money to have his land fenced and guarded from July to September, when the grapes ripened. Having constructed all this, the cash value of his fifteen-*aranzada* plot in 1852 would have been 17,500 pesetas, and its value would not increase for at least four years, until the vines started producing. But must prices increased between 1848 and 1863, making such long-term investments profitable. Prices reached an all-time high in 1863. Because potential profits mounted accordingly, sherry merchants who were also grape producers were generally willing to take great risks. In Jerez in 1817, only 8,124 *aranzadas* had been in vines; by 1851, there were 12,369. Between 1851 and 1867 the amount increased an additional 13 percent, and in the next three years it rose another 23 percent.[8]

With their new fortunes, Cádiz sherry merchants and blending firm owners began to invest in banks, railroads, and mines. By 1890, the González-Byass family company owned outright about fifty buildings, vineyards, railroad lines, and seven steam engines. They regularly employed 250 workers and still more laborers at harvest. They ran two model schools for employees' children. The company's founder, Manuel María González Ángel, sponsored the first railroads in Andalusia, including the 1854 Jerez line, which carried sherry to port. By 1837, members of the sherry families had become prominent in local political and economic affairs. For example, Manuel Domech [*sic*], Patricio Garvey, Cayetano Rivero, Ventura Misas, Julián Ibarbura, and Francisco Pérez de la Riva, all important sherry cellar owners and merchants, sat on the Jerez Chamber of Commerce.[9]

[8] AMJF:112; 116; *El guadalete*, 15-11-1908, 22-11-1908; *Archivo memoranda 6* (1879), f.22.

[9] Del Castillo, *Gran diccionario geográfico, estadístico e histórico*

Between 1837 and 1868 the commercial groups of Cádiz Province, consisting primarily of wine shippers and vineyard and cellar owners, increasingly came to form a self-conscious class of bourgeois liberals. They fought against imposition of state excises. Most important, they articulated popular opposition to the *consumo* not only because it raised the price of musts and bottled wine passing into the city, thus hurting vineyard owners and retailers, but also because it increased the cost of food and drink for the largely urban population. Dependent as they were on foreign markets, the Cádiz mercantile community gravitated toward a decentralized administration that would liberate them from an inept and unsympathetic Madrid. As early as 1821, Cádiz merchants had attempted to create a republican city state.[10]

Like other European liberals, the Cádiz commercial bourgeoisie promoted democratic participation in government by all property holders. They were at the forefront of the nineteenth-century movement to gain participation in the management of the state, for the Cádiz commercial bourgeoisie did not have political influence commensurate with their economic importance. "The State is the instrument for conforming civil society to the economic structure, but it is necessary for the State 'to be willing' to do this; i.e. for the representatives of the change that has taken place in the economic structure to be in control of the State," as Antonio Gramsci has argued.[11] The agricultural bourgeoisie was represented in the government, but the commercial bourgeoisie was left out. In Cádiz, at least, the latter took up the flag

---

de España y sus provincias, ii, 377; *Propuestas para la Junta de Comercio de Jerez de la Frontera para 1837*, ADC: uncatalogued.

[10] Cádiz had always had trouble with Madrid, but the struggle took on new dimensions with the development of capitalist agriculture, which exacerbated old antagonisms. For discussions of how Cádiz circumvented Madrid's rules about transshipping, see Stein and Stein, *The Colonial Heritage of Latin America*. Zavala, *Masones, comuneros y carbonarios*, p. 109.

[11] Gramsci, *Selections from the Prison Notebooks*, p. 208.

of opposition, joined by small producers who opposed the state because of its devastating grain policy.

It is impossible to divorce the subsistence problem from the development of capitalism, on one hand, and from the articulation of democratic and anarchist politics, on the other. One result of capitalist cereal production was increased productivity, which might have brought reduction in the unit cost of grain and lower bread prices. Instead they were kept artificially high by state protection. Between 1833 and 1871, although Spanish wheat acreage doubled and grain production also doubled, the price increased about 20 percent. Cities such as Jerez and Cádiz, particularly those in or near ports, suffered from high bread prices because grain was easily shipped out to European markets, where it fetched high prices. Until the Andalusian railroads were built after 1854, poor river transportation and lack of roads made it difficult to move grain grown inland. While the government could have attempted to subsidize cereals in order to keep the prices down, they chose to place a floor on grain prices in order to assure high profits for grain producers. Moreover, Spanish grain producers were under no obligation to provide national markets if they could get better selling prices elsewhere. On the other hand, after 1820 western Andalusia was prohibited from importing foreign grain except in dire emergencies. Spain suffered subsistence crises in 1803, 1804, 1808, and most notably in 1857 and 1866. Regional famine, such as occurred in Cádiz, Málaga, and Huelva in 1835, had to reach extraordinary heights before civil governors were permitted to import foreign grain to feed the population. A contemporary critic of this policy wrote, "The system of protection is in fact carried to such an extent in this country that the classes protected are in a state of commercial prostration, and apparently enjoy the fruits of their petty monopolies at the expense of, and detriment to, the well-being of the great masses of the population. . . . The prohibitory provisions in the Tariff against the importation of foreign grain still in force, and established for the protection of the Castilian [and Andalusian] corn-growers, seemed likely a short time since [1866] to produce serious consequences in the southern provinces. On account of the high price of bread, representations were made from various quarters to the Government, with a view to obtaining the free admission of foreign corn, or at least some measure to relieve the condition of the poor; but to such an extent have the landed proprietors surrounded themselves with protective defences, that the Government have no power to grant the relief sought for until the price of corn averages a certain fixed price in the three frontier provinces of the kingdom."[12] Such a policy assured high grain prices throughout the first part of the nineteenth century.

Textile manufacturers in Catalonia and incipient iron, steel, and machine producers of the Basque country also favored protection, which they hoped would enable them to compete with the cheaper northern European goods that otherwise flooded the Spanish market in the nineteenth century. So Cádiz' mercantile community, along with individual economic liberals scattered in other port cities, were left alone to fight for free trade. Free trade was a political issue supported in Andalusia by *El guadalete* of Jerez de la Frontera and *La discusión* of Sevilla. The issue also helped create more stable political organizations. As early as 1857, during a period of famine due, in part, to four extraordinary years of exporting grain to Europe when the Crimean war prevented Russian wheat from reaching its usual markets, economic liberals Laureano Figuerola, Gabriel Colmeiro, and Gabriel Rodríguez formed the Association for the Re-

---

[12] Statistics are given in Garrido, *Historia de las clases trabajadores*, III, 254; Tortella Casares, *Los orígenes del capitalismo en España*, pp. 163–201; *The Economist*, 19–1–1856, cited in Sánchez-Albornoz, *Las crisis*, pp. 16–21, 58; Sánchez-Albornoz, "Determining Economic Regions from Time Series Data"; "Report by Mr. West, Her Majesty's Secretary of Legation, on the Commerce, Finance, &c, of Spain. Madrid, July 1, 1867," *Accounts and Papers*, LX (1868–1869), 228.

form of Tariffs and Customs Duties. A successor to the 1846 Cádiz Association for Free Trade, modeled upon the English Anti-Corn Law League, the 1857 association was especially significant because among its members were some of Spain's most important liberals and, subsequently, Republicans: Laureano Figuerola and Juan Echegaray were successively ministers of interior and development in the governments of 1868 to 1874; Emilio Castelar and Práxedes Mateo Sagasta were presidents of the Republic and of the Restoration Monarchy; Antonio Cánovas del Castillo, who with Sagasta alternated as prime minister of the late nineteenth-century monarchy was also a free trader in 1859 (although by 1874 he had reversed himself). Leaders of all subsequent Republican factions, José María Orense and Joaquín María Sanroma, were also members.[13]

Despite the formation of the Association for Tariff and Trade Reform, in itself merely a lobbying group, few alterations in trade policy were effected. Many of the Cádiz economic liberals, men such as Ramón de Cala, Fernando Garrido, and José Paúl y Angulo, were therefore increasingly drawn to more formal political organizations, such as the Democratic party, to achieve their goals. The merger of commercial bourgeois, petty bourgeois, and proletarian interests was epitomized in the leadership of Cala, Garrido, and Paúl. The roots went deep in local history. Joaquín Abreu, a Cádiz landowner exiled in France, met Charles Fourier and became converted to his principles of social organization and his ideals. He attracted younger men, such as Manuel Sagrario de Veloy, who in 1841 attempted to establish a phalanstery or model community at Tempul, about 24 miles from Jerez. Other young men, including Garrido, Cala, and Guillén, were attracted to Fourierist ideas, especially ideas about the need for social reorganization rather than mere political change.

Cala moved from Fourierism to the Democratic party, to

[13] Sánchez-Albornoz, Las crisis, pp. 31–33; Artola, La burguesía revolucionaria (1808–1869), p. 269.

the Federal Republicans after 1868. He helped organize the Abnegation sherry cooperative in 1864. As Mayor of Jerez during the revolutionary regime of November 1868, he organized work, in effect creating national workshops, to provide employment for the starving by paying them to dismantle monasteries and build roads. He also followed the traditional local practice of demanding that migrant labor depart within 48 hours. A somber, quiet, and after the death of his wife, a melancholy figure, Cala participated in Jerez' politics, sat in the Constituent Cortes as Jerez' representative, and later edited the important Federalist newspaper *La igualdad*. Once anarchism was established, he became a leading defender of its right to exist as an opposition organization.

Fernando Garrido united the tradition of cooperative economics, which had been strong in Cádiz at least as far back as the sixties, and the new Democratic-Republican movements. His activities as a painter, novelist, journalist, polemicist, and labor historian still left him a great deal of time for political activity. Stocky, jolly, and robust, greying by 1868, he was a born and practiced conspirator whose honesty and sincerity won him friends even among his political opponents. Garrido was well known among Jerez' craftsmen, to whom he introduced visiting anarchists such as Anselmo Lorenzo and foreign dignitaries such as the ethnographer Elie Reclus. Something of an amateur sociologist, Garrido studied the associationist tradition in Spain and knew Cádiz' cooperative societies, collective vineyards, wine-cellars, and construction crews.

José Paúl y Angulo, the heir to a family of large landowners and wine producers from Jerez de la Frontera, seems to have been one of the most important links between Democratic politics and incipient anarchism in Cádiz. A hothead and an adventurer, perhaps romantically moved by what he perceived to be the spontaneity of the masses, he was at the center of insurrectionary politics in the years following the 1868 Revolution. As early as the forties, he supported tax reform in Cádiz Province. He joined the Democrats around 1866.[14]

Cádiz' mercantile community scarcely constituted a majority in the region, let alone in the nation, but they discovered allies among the more articulate, educated, and politically conscious petty bourgeoisie. The bakers, carpenters, shopkeepers, coopers, wine blenders, the relatively prosperous tenants, sharecroppers, small vineyard proprietors, vinetenders, local journalists, notaries, and physicians—scarcely 5 percent of the population of Cádiz Province—were crucial to the development of bourgeois liberal political practices.

As Karl Marx wrote about the German small producers in 1850, "Far from desiring to revolutionize all society for the revolutionary proletarians, the democratic petty bourgeoisie strive for a change in social conditions by means of which existing society will be made as tolerable and comfortable as possible for them." Commonly, the petty bourgeoisie called for "the diminution of state expenditure by a curtailment of the bureaucracy and shifting the chief taxes on to the big landowners, . . . the abolition of the pressure of big capital on small, through public credit institutions and laws against usury, . . . the establishment of bourgeois property relations in the countryside by the complete abolition of feudalism." To win these goals, Marx claimed that the petty bourgeoisie needed "a democratic state structure, either constitutional or republican, that will give them and their allies a majority; also a democratic communal structure that will give them direct control over communal property and over a series of functions now performed by

[14] Eiras Roel, *El partido demócrata español (1849–1868)*; Garrido, *Historia de las clases*, III, 134–135; IV, 125; "Ramón de Cala," *Tierra y libertad*, 19-VII-1902; Reclus, "Impresiones de un viaje por España en días de revolución (1868–1869)," p. 97; Muchado, *La hacienda de España*, p. 257; de Góngora, *El periodismo jerezano; apuntes para su historia*; Paúl y Angulo, *Verdades revolucionarias*; Hennessy, *Federal Republic*, pp. 273 ff.; Bozal Fernández, *Juntas revolucionarias, manifiestos y proclamas de 1868*, pp. 130–131.

the bureaucrats."[15] Elements of this program that Marx noted in Germany are to be found in Spain in the formation of the Democratic party, which expressed simultaneously the needs of Cádiz' progressive commercial and petty bourgeoisie.

The army was one of the state institutions that united the commercial bourgeoisie and the small producers against the latifundists or agricultural capitalists. By 1871, twenty-four percent of all draftees were substitutes. To gain exemption from conscription for a six-year term, a recruit or his family could pay the government a bounty—about 1,000 pesetas in 1872—but the price was too high for most small producers to pay, and was about five times the annual income of most proletarians. The latifundists, who controlled power at the local level, provided limited political and economic benefits to key employees among the landless laborers, thus turning them into allies among the poor. One such benefit was to pay the bounty for draft exemption for key workers, in return for obedience from the masses. The commercial bourgeoisie could afford to pay the bounty for themselves, but they realized that the system provided a hold for the latifundists over their workers, who formed the majority of the population in Cádiz Province. So they joined the petty bourgeoisie in opposition to the draft, and their wishes were taken as an important plank of the Democratic party, which favored the abolition of the draft and the creation of a volunteer army.[16]

Another local issue that united the petty bourgeoisie and the commercial bourgeoisie was the issue of excise taxes and *consumo*. Taxes on sherry, often reaching between 15 and 25 percent of its value, provided important state revenues. There were also excise taxes on legal documents, meat, salt,

[15] Karl Marx, "Address to the Central Committee of the Communist League," cited in Miliband, "Marx and the State," p. 288.

[16] Sales de Bohigas, "Some Opinions on Exemption from Military Service in Nineteenth-Century Europe," p. 286; Hennessy, *Federal Republic*, p. 179.

and tobacco. Of the last two, one was a necessity, the other one of the few luxuries enjoyed by the Spanish poor. Opposition to this form of taxation was widespread. So was antagonism to the *consumo*, which provided municipalities with the revenues to pay local bureaucrats and the police force. Whereas grain producers who shipped their cereals out of the region direct to the ports were exempt from the *consumo*, vineyard owners and others whose primary product moved from one area to another to be processed had to pay the tax. Small producers who sold their grapes or grain to local markets also had to pay, as did shopkeepers bringing in wares, and even those returning from the countryside with sausages given to them by relatives. This tax alone united merchants, small producers, and the proletariat. Administered by local officials, often viewed as representative of latifundist *caciques*, the *consumo* was an active symbol of the political class control exercised by wheat producers. Since the same bureaucrats who administered that tax also collected state taxes, in Cádiz at least, hatred for the state, agricultural capitalism, and latifundist power was merged.[17]

To counter all three institutions, dissidents formed political and economic associations, of which the Democratic party was the most important in uniting commercial capitalists and small producers. As early as 1840, shortly after the resignation of the Regent María Cristina, democratic and republican ideas began to take shape in newspapers and pamphlets. Some went so far as to demand that the new national government be a federal republic, the state consisting of a confederation of independent cantons. The 1840 program, like its successors, called for creation of an elected committee instead of a monarch to run the government. The *leitmotif* of reduced national spending, abolition of excises and their replacement with land taxes, volunteer army, religious freedom, and free secular elementary school education

[17] Artola, *La burguesía revolucionaria*, p. 268.

was well established among bourgeois liberals before midcentury. When the Democratic party itself was formed in 1849, it drew followers on the basis of these proposals and on the platform of ending wheat protection. Republicanism grew concomitantly. In the spring of 1841, on the anniversary of the 1812 Cádiz Constitution, local militias in Andalusia, made up of petty bourgeois property holders and bourgeois liberals, called for a republican Spain; this action was not organized by a party, but it certainly was not spontaneous, either.

Whatever their own social class origins, political leaders such as Nicolás María Rivero and José María Orense began at midcentury to express the principles most near and dear to the hearts of small producers and merchants. The growing political presence of such people can be seen in December 1841, when free traders and tax reformers won municipal elections in Sevilla, Huelva, and Cádiz. Many of the same men and most of the same issues reemerged in 1854 to 1856, and again between 1868 and 1874. The issues stayed alive because the problems created by the slow and uneven growth of Spanish capitalism, dominated by agrarian rather than commercial interests, remained the same and were perceived in Cádiz Province as part of a continuous process of incompetence, malevolence, and discrimination.[18]

The 1854 June Revolution began as a typical military uprising, but by July it had generated a popular movement in Madrid, establishing a pattern that emerged again in 1868 and in subsequent republican *putsches*. When the provisional government was forced to call a referendum on November 30, 1854, on the form the new government should take, twenty-one deputies, among them Rivero, deputy for Sevilla, and Manuel Bertemati, scion of a leading Jerez sherry family, called for a republic. Both men

[18] Eiras Roel, *El partido demócrata*, pp. 93–95, 97, 105, 136, 151, 215. For a general history of the evolution of Spanish republicanism, refer to Albornoz, *El partido republicano*.

articulated their positions in *La discusión,* between 1854 and 1866 Spain's leading demo-republican newspaper. As representatives of a class conscious of itself and eager to promote legislation—and, if necessary, revolution for itself—such men and the Democratic party were more significant for late nineteenth-century Spanish politics than the party's pathetic and sometimes infantile policies would at first indicate.

Formed in 1849, dedicated to the now familiar principles of a volunteer army, free trade, single tax, universal education, and separation of church and state, the Democratic party specifically committed itself late in life, just before descending underground in 1857, to a republican form of government. While it was clandestine, the party adopted a *carbonari* structure of cell organization common to many nineteenth- and twentieth-century secret groups. Their basic unit was the *choza* of ten people, only one of whom knew anyone else in the organization. This one knew nine other designated leaders of other cells. From these a central committee, the Phalanstery, was chosen. Over 80,000 people, primarily in Catalonia and Andalusia, were said to be organized in this way.[19] Like the anarchists after them, the Democratic party was extremely versatile, forming associations, clubs, and other public groups through which the Democrats could act semiofficially.

Clandestinity breeds insurrectionary politics. In the summer of 1857, Sixto Cámera and Fernando Garrido were involved in attempts to create a republic through mass insurrections. Cámera was killed, twenty-five others died near Benoajan in the mountains east of Jerez, and twenty-four young artisans were taken prisoner and executed. Another massive insurrection with Democratic overtones was led by the notary Rafael Pérez del Álamo in 1861 in Loja, Granada.

Precipitous rebellions, such as the abortive military coup following the 1866 financial crash, indicated the instability

[19] Eiras Roel, *El partido demócrata,* pp. 136, 199, 214–215, 226–227, 237–238; Garrido, *Historia del reinado del último Borbón,* III, 358–359.

of the Spanish national government and its inability to appease the army, Democrats, other Republicans, or even those who favored a more responsive monarchy. In the Pact of Ostend of August 1866, Democrats allied with more conservative members of the upper bourgeoisie, who for the previous eight years had united with reformist generals into a group called the Liberal Union. Its left wing, the Progressive party, led by Sagasta, had long pushed for free trade and increased taxes on agriculture. Thus Democrats, representing largely petty bourgeois interests, Progressives, led by Sagasta, and liberal military men all agreed to accept the leadership of General Francisco Serrano in overthrowing the Monarchy of Isabella II. In a separate conspiracy, exiled Democrats Francisco Pi y Margall and Emilio Castelar, subsequently leaders of the Republican party, also began to plot the establishment of a new government.

The Democrats, though divided, were the spearhead of the revolutionary bourgeoisie in Cádiz. Like the French progressive bourgeoisie of 1848, whom they so resembled, they reached out to the popular masses, particularly to the substantial small producers. Like their French counterparts, they too discovered that popular supporters with different social priorities, once unleashed, were hard to restrain. Had it not been for the work of Cádiz Province Democrats such as Paúl, Guillén, and Cala, however, the 1868 Revolution might have taken a less popular course. Paúl persuaded Prim to tie his star to the Democrats, despite his fear of their radicalism. Once the revolt had broken out, the triumvirate of Paúl, Cala, and Guillén orchestrated events in Cádiz Province to promote the Democratic demands for free press, universal male suffrage, jury system, free association, secularization, free trade, abolition of excises, the creation of income taxes, and abolition of the draft.[20]

---

[20] Eiras Roel, *El partido demócrata*, pp. 250, 328–336, 353; Bernaldo de Quirós, "El espartaquismo," pp. 8–14; Pérez del Álamo, *Apuntes sobre dos revoluciones andaluzas*; Hennessy, *Federal Republic*, p. 58; Bernal, "Bourgeoisie rurale," p. 342. In December 1868, Elie Reclus

For a brief moment, in the revolutionary municipal committees dominated by the commercial bourgeoisie and supported by artisans, the plans of the Democratic party came to fruition. So long as these groups, formerly outside the power structure, fixed their gaze on latifundism, monarchism, and the incompetent Spanish state as the enemy, they could ally. But their ultimate goals were quite different. Few of the Democrats in Cádiz Province wanted to go beyond reforms in civil liberties and in the tax system. The masses, led by the small producers, assumed that social change, including work for the unemployed and redistribution of land, were a necessary part of any revolution. Once the underlying classes began to move independently to achieve their own power rather than accept the democratic privileges meted out to them by the bourgeoisie, the unstable alliance began to disintegrate.

---

noted the similarity between the French bourgeoisie of 1848 to 1851 and Jerez' republicans. "Impresiones de un viaje," p. 235. The outstanding analysis of the class relations of the period in France can be found in Marx, *The 18th Brumaire of Louis Bonaparte.*

CHAPTER III

Bourgeois Revolution and Andalusian Anarchism: The First Phase, 1868 to 1872

The political history of Spanish anarchism has been adequately documented, largely within the past decade. But the connections between the Republicans and early anarchists have not been explained, nor has the way in which anarchists fused their ideology with local working class and peasant culture been analyzed, nor has the process by which anarchism threw down such deep roots in Northern Cádiz Province been described. Attempts by wine producers to wrest control of their trade from an unsympathetic state provided impetus to the local Republicans, and linked them to workers and peasants engaged in the wine trade. The structural basis for early anarchism in Andalusia, however, was the petty bourgeois and working-class labor unions and communal cultural institutions that grew out of more formal working-class associations.[1] Without the women's

---

[1] Throughout this book, the word "union" is used to describe political labor organizations, the ultimate goal of which was to control society rather than to win economic reform of working conditions. In Spain the terms *sindicato* and *sindicalismo* were not employed until the end of the nineteenth century, but the Spanish anarchists did successively speak and write about their *secciones de oficio*, *uniones*, and toward the end of the 1880s, their *sociedades obreras de resistencia al capitalismo*. In the late nineteenth century, they called their movement *societarismo obrero*, roughly workers' collectivism or labor mutualism. "Communalism," though not a term the anarchists themselves used, is employed to express their notion of community solidarity. Likewise, the term "political" is exogenous to anarchist vocabulary, but will be used to indicate organization of power relations. The Andalusian anarchists took political to mean bourgeois electoral politics, which they rejected. They generally employed the word "administration" to describe their kind of councils

sections, libraries, consumers and producers cooperatives, and secular schools, anarchism might have been destroyed shortly after it was created even though it met the ideological, social, and economic needs of certain groups under stress. The movement survived because it became imbedded in popular culture.

The gradual division between bourgeois Democrats and anarchists developed between 1868 and 1873, largely over the social content of revolution. Once the Revolution of 1868 succeeded in overthrowing Queen Isabella, Democrats regrouped as Republicans. They all preferred the formation of a Spanish republic to the creation of a constitutional monarchy with a new king. The Republicans, while working in the same movement, were divided into those who simply wanted a republican form of government with power centralized in a legislature and a president, and the Federalist Republicans, who wanted the state to be a confederation of autonomous city states or cantons. Most of the leading Democrats around Cádiz Province were drawn to the Federalists, the extreme left wing of the party. Republicans also split between those who favored parliamentary methods and the Intransigents, who believed in mass insurrectionary politics. The Intransigents were strong in Jerez.

The revolution began September 18, 1868, in Cádiz when Admiral J. B. Topete and his fleet mutinied. The underfed and dissatisfied troops of Queen Isabella II fought only one major battle in defense of the regime, the Battle of Alcolea at a bridge outside Sevilla, and lost. Within a few days, the generals seized power in Madrid. While the armed forces joined the Democrats in attacking Isabella, they did not join them in calling for a Republic. General Prim merely wanted to substitute a new, efficient monarch for the old one. The provisional government he established in Madrid

---

and trade union organizations, but the function of such associations was political, despite their opposition to the word.

was still dominated in practice, if not in person, by monarchist latifundists, among them the duke of Montpensier, brother-in-law to the deposed queen and a large landowner in Cádiz Province. But events followed their own rules.

In Cádiz Province, the revolution proceeded like clockwork. Within hours of Admiral Topete's revolt, long-time democrats such as Paúl, Cala, Guillén, Eduardo Benot, and Francisco Lizaur, formed the first provincial government. Revolutionary committees were established throughout Cádiz Province and the rest of Andalusia, and within four days of the September 18th Revolution, the provinces of Cádiz, Huelva, and Sevilla were secure for the revolution.[2] Most of the revolutionary committees confirmed the Democratic party platform of 1849, calling for civil guarantees, such as rights of assembly, association, religious dissent; and political liberties, such as universal male suffrage. They also demanded social and economic reforms, such as the creation of free universal elementary education, an end to the draft, abolition of excise taxes, and the formation of a constitutional convention.

The junta in Jerez went beyond these to demand the overthrow of the six-month-old municipal police force, and to a create a committee to feed the people. They abolished the *consumo*, salt, and tobacco taxes. And within a month they instituted mixed juries of employers and employees to resolve labor disputes. In the attempt to achieve social peace between workers and employers, the junta proclaimed that they understood "the differences which can develop between vineyard owners, supervisors, and workers about wages and conditions; therefore it has been decided that the only way to resolve differences is to create a jury on which

[2] Guichot, *Historia general de Andalucía*, VIII, 118–148; Eiras Roel, *El partido demócrata*, pp. 365, 377–378; Bozal Fernández, *Juntas revolucionarias*, pp. 92–93; "Suplemento," *El porvenir* (Seville), 20–IX–1868. The best general survey of the events of 1868 can be found among the articles in Lida and Zavala, eds., *La revolución de 1868: Historia, pensamiento, literatura*.

all classes are represented by trusted delegates." Each group was to choose three representatives to this arbitration board. The government claimed that their decisions would have the force of law and would be defended by the junta.[3] In Jerez, at least, it appears as if a bourgeois revolution dedicated to providing minimal civil liberties, reforming economic relations, without threatening private property, was beginning to take place.[4]

Sherry magnates were prominent among the revolutionary leadership. Examining the occupations of members of Jerez' revolutionary municipal council indicates why the September Revolution, if bourgeois revolution it was, succeeded so rapidly, and why Jerez' revolutionary junta called at once for the establishment of a decentralized republic in Spain. Of the seventeen men who made up the junta, four had for several years prior to the revolution been leaders of Democratic party politics in Cádiz Province. They were Cala, Guillén, Paúl, and Bertemati. The latter had voted for the establishment of a republic at the 1854 Constituent Convention. At least nine of the seventeen were engaged in sherry production and sale, Carlos Haurie and Manuel Sánchez Misa being two of the most important sherry magnates in town (see Table 3–1). It was in the collective social

[3] *El guadalete*, 2–IX–1868, 21–IX–1868, 22–X–1868.

[4] At the Bordeaux conference session on the emergence of the bourgeoisie of Andalusia, Manuel Tuñón de Lara challenged the speakers to defend their notion of rural bourgeoisie, arguing that if there was a bourgeoisie in Andalusia, they opposed a bourgeois revolution. See *La Question de la "bourgeoisie,"* p. 85. One explanation is that the bourgeoisie was divided against itself in Andalusia. The latifundists supported a moderate monarchy because, with few exceptions, the Spanish monarchy had protected their interests. The mercantile bourgeoisie in Cádiz and Jerez realized, however, that their economic and social interests were best served by a decentralized republic, which would permit them maximum autonomy and would allow them to deal with their peasants and working class according to certain paternalist but democratic principles, such as those embodied in the idea of mixed juries of workers, foremen, and employees for labor arbitration.

Table 3–1

Jerez' Revolutionary Junta: September 1868

Name	Previous party affiliation	Occupation
José Bertemati	Democrat	sherry producer
Manuel Bertemati	Democrat	sherry producer
Ramón de Cala	Democrat	journalist
Juan Carredo	unknown	unknown
Francisco García Ruiz	unknown	unknown
Rafael Guillén	Democrat	journalist
Carlos Haurie	unknown	sherry producer
Pedro López Ruiz	unknown	unknown
Manuel Mayot	unknown	unknown
Manuel Paradas	unknown	unknown
José Paúl y Angulo	Democrat	sherry producer
Antonio Pérez de la Riva	unknown	sherry producer
Manuel Piñero	unknown	unknown
Manuel Ponce y Soler	unknown	sherry producer
Francisco Revuelta Montel	unknown	sherry producer
José Sánchez Misa	Democrat	sherry producer
Manuel Sánchez Misa	Democrat	sherry producer

Sources: *El guadalete*, 11–I–1868; 21–IX–1868; *Propuestas para la Junta de Comercio de Jerez de la Frontera para 1837*. ADC: uncatalogued.

and economic interest of wine producers to gain control of their trade from an unsympathetic state. Elsewhere in Cádiz Province—in Chipiona, Chiclana, and Medina Sidonia, for example—the members of the revolutionary junta were also Democrats. In Chipiona most of the Democrats derived their wealth from olive mills and winecellars.[5]

Scarcely two weeks after the September Revolution, many Democrats, preparing to press their own demands for a decentralized federal republic, organized the Federal Republican party. Familiar faces reappeared. The national leaders included Pi y Margall, Orense, Castelar (another Andalusian), and Figueras. Garrido, Cala, Guillén, and Paúl were

[5] *El guadalete*, 11–I–1868, 21–IX–1868, 24–IX–1868; J. Maurice, "Le thème des 'nuevos ricos' en Andalousie de la Restauratión à la IIe République," *La Question de la "bourgeoisie,"* pp. 71, 75.

the party's Andalusian cadre. In early October 1868, they mounted a popular campaign to elect federalist delegates to the constitutional convention. Important newspapers including *El club democrático* renamed itself *El club republicano democrático federal*, lest there be any doubts about its shift from Democratic party to more developed Federal Republican principles, and *El club y la revolución* promoted the cause in Jerez.[6]

Federalist triumphs on their home ground in Cádiz Province were challenged in October and December 1868, as the provisional government in Madrid, dominated by monarchists, began to erode some of the autonomy seemingly won by the municipalities in September. On October 21, 1868, the government announced that "the officials chosen at the moment of revolutionary fervor ought to be replaced by other individuals who, instead of being elected by all the citizens of the city, would be elected by *barriada* (borough) thereby reducing the power of popular leaders." This attempt was resisted in Jerez, among other places. The government probably acted because it became evident that social forces were on the move in the south. Two weeks before the dissolution order, a crowd estimated at between eight and nine hundred armed people attacked the Sisters of Charity convent in Jerez, demanding the release of police officers believed to be taking asylum in the convent.[7] Fear of the always hungry masses, and suspicion that some of the Federalists were too sympathetic to the poor and too anticlerical, must have influenced the provisional government to attempt to centralize its powers.

The second major attack on revolutionary local politics came when the November 12, 1868, manifesto of the national revolutionary coalition pledged to "create the Mon-

[6] Eiras Roel, *El partido demócrata*, p. 390; de Góngora, *El periodismo jerezano*.

[7] Reclus, "Impresiones de un viaje," pp. 417–420; *El guadalete*, 25–X–1868; Bozal Fernández, *Juntas revolucionarias*, p. 34; *El porvenir*, 10–X–1868.

archy" and scheduled elections for January 15, 1869. During hungry December, the beginning of the starvation months in bad years, the provisional government provoked uprisings in Puerto de Santa María and Cádiz by Republicans who refused to allow their popular militias to be disarmed. The uprising began when local councils in Puerto de Santa María and Cádiz, without funds from the provisional government, were unable to feed the hungry. The money ran out in Puerto on December 4, 1868, and the working class, which had been armed during the September Revolution, took to the barricades and demanded food. Troops from Jerez and Cádiz were called in to disarm the population, and four militiamen were seriously wounded in the struggle. In Madrid, the provisional government, having decided on its own to establish a new monarchy rather than hold a popular plebiscite about the form of the new government, used the Santa María insurrection as an excuse to disarm all the local militias and reimpose the draft.[8] Monarchist strength lay in the wheat-producing regions. But in the ports, especially in Cádiz, the Federalist Republicans could not be subdued without disarming the militias. Eighty delegates in the Provisional Cortes, the majority from Barcelona, Valencia, and Andalusia, opposed the government's decision, but the government proceeded with its plan.[9]

Cádiz revolted on December 5th. For reasons that are unclear, the provisional governor of Cádiz, Gregorio Alcalá Zamora, had left town in early December, and his lieutenant governor, also a monarchist appointed by the provisional government, turned over power to the military. They called upon the National Guard in Cádiz to aid the governor in putting down the Santa María uprising. When they refused,

---

[8] Hennessy, *Federal Republic*, pp. 48–49; Mejías y Escassy, *Las barricadas de Cádiz*, pp. 12, 17; *La república federal* (Cadiz), 10-XII-1868; *La federación andaluza* (Cadiz), 21-VI-1873; Guichot, *Historia general de Andalucía*, VIII, 150, 156–157; Reclus, "Impresiones de un viaje," pp. 289, 291–292; *El guadalete*, 6-XII-1868, 7-XII-1868.

[9] Eiras Roel, *El partido demócrata*, p. 395.

they were ordered to lay down their own arms. They answered, "Certainly. If you want our arms, come and get them." News that the guard had mutinied spread through the city of Cádiz. The militia men, "the large majority of whom were artisans," had seized guns and ammunition from the military garrisons during the September Revolution, two months earlier. They swarmed into the streets and began constructing a labyrinth of barricades made up of beds, chairs, furniture, and boxes, to defend them against an army advance. The army called upon the population to disarm.

Throughout town, the workshops, stores, and factories emptied as the militia marshaled its forces. The army artillery prepared to move. Militiamen confronted them, apparently trying to win them over to the people's side. They were arrested and taken to army headquarters in the customs office. The remaining militiamen distributed weapons to the peasants and laborers who gathered in town. Armed with shotguns and revolvers, they occupied City Hall and other government buildings for three and one half days, beginning at 3:30 P.M. on December 5th. Women and children at windows threw rocks and small objects at the troops. Upon the rumor that government forces from Jerez would land at Caleta Beach, the militiamen moved a captured cannon through the streets in preparation for a massive defense at the beachhead. The rebels, mostly aged sixteen to twenty-two, were poorly equipped to fight alone against the Navy, which bombarded the city. Ironically, the Navy was represented by the same force that had mutinied against the queen in September, initiating the 1868 Revolution. Many sailors now refused to shoot at the citizens in Cádiz, yet they were easily repressed.[10]

An armistice was declared on December 10th, following a pitched battle and siege that left thousands starving. After the week-long siege, about a thousand people were incarcerated as rebels. Since the Republican party leadership had

[10] Mejias, *Las barricadas de Cádiz*, pp. 12–13, 21–130; Reclus, "Impresiones de un viaje," pp. 353–355.

been away, attending a party meeting, when the revolt took place, they entered the city only after the battle, and argued that the army bore complete responsibility for the violence. The Republican delegates from Cádiz to the Cortes pleaded for amnesty, but their request was denied. When the elections were held on January 15, 1869, for the Constituent Cortes, virtually under the rifles of a conquering army, the officials elected to the Cortes and the municipal government in Cádiz were all Republicans.[11]

Republican willingness to confront the state through military insurrection against the armed forces should not be assumed to imply more radical social aspirations. In early December 1868, shortly before the Santa María and Cádiz revolts, a political disagreement among Jerez Republicans underlined the limits of bourgeois politics in Andalusia. A local Republican leader, referred to only as "Caro," had roused the ire of other party leaders at a weekly meeting by describing social inequities and urging a war of the poor against the rich. The consensus among the Jerez Republicans was, apparently, that no one should raise social questions until the primary goal, the creation of a national federal republic, had been achieved. Caro was expelled from the party for his statements. One irate Jerez Republican, described by Elie Reclus as a millionaire with huge wine cellars, shouted furiously, "I have one thousand pesetas in my purse for anyone who will get rid of the insolent rogue." When Reclus tried to interrupt him, saying, "It is precisely in this way, Señor, that one provokes social war; it is this kind of behavior that provokes June Days [in Paris, 1848] like those of December [in Spain, 1868], the consequence of which is a period of despotism which lasts twenty years or more," the ranting bourgeois refused to listen and shouted disconcertedly, "I myself, I myself will kill this *canaille* if it is necessary."[12]

In spite of some Republicans' opposition to popular social

---

[11] Mejías, *Las barricadas de Cádiz*, pp. 167–198.
[12] Reclus, "Impresiones de un viaje," p. 235.

revolution, other Andalusian Republicans never ceased con-
spiring to overthrow the state through insurrection. Among
the most important proponents of armed revolt were Paúl
and Guillén of Jerez, who worked through Republican
clubs to get the people to rise up against the new centralist
monarchy, symbolized by the conscription, which had been
reimposed. Since the financial crash of 1866, Pi y Margall
and his followers had attacked the existence of a national
standing army, viewing it as an institution through which
the centralized state robbed people of their autonomy and
liberty. The Democrats had blamed the 1866 depression in
part on military expenditures. At that time nineteen percent
of all government spending went to pay the Army and
Navy, while national debt payments took up another thirty-
two percent.[13] Democrats had hoped to cut expenditures by
reducing the army to a small corps of volunteers, a policy
that won support among the peasants, craftsmen, tradesmen,
and proletariat upon whom the brunt of service generally
fell. In place of the conscript army, Federal Republicans in
1868 proposed a property-owners' militia based on the
model they established throughout Cádiz Province during
the first months of the 1868 revolution.

Two of the most important links between Republicanism
and anarchism in Cádiz Province were José Paúl y Angulo
and Fermín Salvochea. Following Admiral Topete's mutiny,
Paúl was one of the Federal Republican organizers in Cádiz.
To represent Jerez at the 1868 Constituent Cortes, he had
moved to Madrid, where he edited *El amigo del pueblo* in
1869 and *El combate* in 1870, but he frequently returned
to his home in Jerez. Accused of assassinating General Prim
at the end of December 1870, he fled to South America,
where he lived nearly a decade, after which he settled in
Paris and pursued radical republican politics with the financial support of his Jerez landowning in-laws. Workers in
Jerez, worried in 1869 that, as a result of his work as a

[13] Eiras Roel, *El partido demócrata*, p. 402; Hennessy, *Federal Republic*, pp. 54, 106.

journalist and revolutionary, Paúl was neglecting his Jerez land, decided to till some vineyards Paúl owned in the district. One hundred men did the work for which Paúl would reap the profits, and when Paúl's mother tried to tip them, they apparently refused even a cigarette. They were reported to have said that as communists [i.e., anarchists] they wanted to work freely for those rich men who worked for the community.[14]

Fermín Salvochea came to national Republican prominence as the 26-year-old leader of the December 1868 Cádiz Insurrection. A respectable young gentleman from a wealthy mercantile family, between ages 15 and 20 he had studied business in London and Liverpool; but his learning was not limited to the world of negotiations. As he later explained, "living in England I read Thomas Paine for the first time. His writings converted me into an internationalist and even today I remain under his influence. 'My country is the world, all men are my brothers, and my religion consists in doing good deeds.' These words produced an unforgettable impression on me. Each word was profound, and they have been engraved indelibly upon my mind. Later I met Robert Owen who taught me the sublime ideal of communism and Bredlow [i.e., Charles Bradlaugh] who introduced me to the atheist view."

Salvochea returned to Spain in 1862, a radical and a utopian socialist. It is not clear whether he affiliated with the Democratic party or whether he even considered himself a Republican before the September Revolution. In September 1868, however, he seems to have been elected to the Cádiz Revolutionary Committee and chosen as commander of the second battalion of the Volunteers for Liberty. When the government forces demanded that the people disarm in December 1868, Salvochea was among the militiamen who organized armed defense. As a result of the city's defeat, he was then taken prisoner and domiciled in nearby Santa Cata-

---

[14] I am grateful to Clara Lida for the French police archival material on Paúl. Garrido, *Historia de las clases*, III, 245.

lina Castle until, along with other political prisoners, he was given amnesty two months later.[15]

EARLY ANARCHISM

Founded in London in September 1864, the International Workingmen's Association, or First International, attempted to merge labor movements with socialist political associations. The attempt at consolidation was constantly thwarted. Most of the local and national organizations were legally suspect and subject to persecution. Moreover, it proved impossible to break the conspiratorial habits of men like Michael Bakunin, the father of modern anarchism. He and his political followers had principled objections to mass politics without the guiding hand of a political and intellectual elite.

Bakunin was obsessed with conspiracy. Were the issues of secrecy and conspiracy not so fundamental to early anarchism, they might seem comical. Bakunin's string of secret associations must have frustrated and infuriated all who favored more open political organization. Struggles between Bakunin and Karl Marx over the form and means of control of an international socialist workers' and peasants' movement left their imprint on the Federation of the Spanish Region (Federación regional española, FRE), the Spanish branch of the First International. Invited by Karl Marx to join the First International shortly after its founding in 1864 (though he did not join until later), Bakunin, tutored in the schools of Masonry and Carbonarism, had organized instead one of his many secret societies, the International Brothers' Alliance (Alianza de los hermanos internacionales), with its seat in Italy.[16] Two years later, in 1866, he founded the

---

[15] Rocker, *Fermín Salvochea: Precursores de la libertad*, p. 13. For quite a different interpretation of Salvochea's development, see Vallina, *Crónica de un revolucionario*.

[16] Arthur Lehning is the foremost biographer of Bakunin. See espe-

International Fraternity (Fraternidad internacional), composed of republican insurrectionists. Later he attempted to infiltrate pacifist organizations such as the League of Peace and Liberty (Liga de la paz y de la libertad) in hopes of promoting his social ideas among politically advanced groups.

Insofar as Spanish anarchism was concerned, his most important political vehicle was the International Alliance of Socialist Democracy (Alianza internacional de la democracia socialista), organized in September 1868. A month later, true to habit, Bakunin established a secret branch of this Alliance, henceforth called the Secret Alliance. The public Alliance applied to the First International for membership. Their application was accepted only on the condition that the Alliance agree to the International's statutes and pledge to dissolve its secret cell. In early 1869, Bakunin agreed to these conditions and announced the abolition of the Secret Alliance. To replace the public Alliance, he helped organize the Geneva Section of the First International. Thereafter Bakunin used the Geneva Section as his private secretariat, and the Secret Alliance took on a new identity.

As early as 1866, when the International had held the First Congress, a Spaniard had been elected to its General Council. Attempts had been made to disseminate its program in Barcelona. Catalan workers had sent a message to the Second Congress in 1867. Sarro Magallán (Antonio Marsal Anglora) represented Catalan workers at the Third Congress in early September 1868, but there is no evidence that workers or peasants in Cádiz Province had any contact with the International until late 1868, when the Frenchmen

cially his *Michel Bakounine et les conflits dans l'Internationale, 1872*. See also Lida, *Anarquismo y revolución*, pp. 128–129. The outstanding consideration of this series of organizations and an analysis of their significance can be found in Lida's introduction to Max Nettlau's *Miguel Bakunin: La Internacional y la alianza en España (1868–1873)*, p. 14.

Elie Reclus, Aristide Rey, and Alfred Nacquet went to Spain. Of the group, at least Aristide Rey was an active member of the Secret Alliance. Bakunin also sent Giuseppe Fanelli to Spain, seemingly on a separate mission.

When Fanelli left Switzerland he had already joined the Alliance, the statutes of which he introduced to Spain. During his absence he was unaware of Bakunin's maneuvers to win acceptance of the Alliance by the First International. The Spaniards were taught the principles of the Alliance, rather than those of the International. The crux of the difference lay in how society would be governed once socialism had been achieved, but this debate had profound implications for how the First International would function. The Alliance emphasized that "the universal union of free associations" would replace national states, but nothing was said about the role of secret societies in the new regime. The International envisioned a rather strong directing role for the General Council, which acted as an executive board empowered to execute the wishes of its membership. Claims and counterclaims may go on, but it seems clear that both the Alliance and the International's leaders talked about local control and initiative, but arrogated power to themselves as an elite. In the case of the International, the directorate was the General Council. In the case of the Alliance, it was the clandestine inner core, or Secret Alliance.

The same was true of the FRE, which owed its formation to Fanelli. In early December 1868, he addressed Republicans and workers in Madrid, where he also met Fernando Garrido. Men such as the engraver Tomás González Morago, the typographer Anselmo Lorenzo, and the shoemaker Francisco Mora, Fanelli's associates in Madrid in January 1869, formed the nucleus of the Madrid Federation, or local section of the First International. Fanelli went from Madrid to Barcelona, where he met republicans and intellectuals who five months later organized the Barcelona section of the International. Among those he proselitized in Barcelona were young Andalusian professionals temporarily in Catalonia. They included the four most important Andalusian-born Spanish anarchists: José García Viñas, a medical student from Málaga; Antonio González García Meneses, a medical student from Cádiz; Trinidad Soriano, an engineering student from Sevilla; and an Andalusian student called Ferrán.[17] Of these, only Soriano returned to live in Andalusia in the seventies, so only he might possibly have had contact with the workers and peasants' associations that formed the core of southern anarchism.

Upon his return to Switzerland, Fanelli learned that Bakunin had pledged to destroy the Alliance to which Fanelli had recruited members in Spain. This embarrassed Bakunin, and he again dissolved the Alliance; but the die was cast. Not only was the program of the Alliance recognized as the program of all those publicly affiliated with the Spanish branch of the International, but sometime between the summer of 1869 and the spring of 1870, a secret alliance, to which García Viñas, Antonio González Meneses, and Trinidad Soriano belonged, was established in Spain. In fact, organization of the alliance preceded the formation of the FRE at its First National Congress in Barcelona in June 1870. At that time, 90 delegates, representing 40,000 workers organized into unions and associations, heard Rafael Farga Pellicer of the Barcelona section proclaim the goals of the FRE: "We want the end to the domination of capital, the state, and the church. Upon their ruins we will construct anarchy and the free federation of free associations of workers." The statutes adopted as the rules of the FRE were those of the Alliance rather than those of the International.[18]

[17] The actual statutes of the Alliance as listed in 1872 can be found in Nettlau, *Miguel Bakunin*, pp. 96–98. See also Lida, *Anarquismo y revolución*, pp. 133–134, 139, 143 and Termes, *Anarquismo y sindicalismo*, p. 135.

[18] The Spanish alliance was not merely a branch of the Secret Alliance based in Jura, but an indigenous secret alliance (henceforth given in lower case) dedicated to similar principles, but not directed from Switzerland. Lida in Nettlau, *Miguel Bakunin*, p. 21; Termes,

Andalusian Anarchism

At least as early as May 1870, there were anarchist cells in the cities of Jerez and Cádiz. In June 1870, Jerez' anarchist delegates attended the First National Congress of the FRE. At that time they listed among their supporters skilled vineyard workers, wine cellarmen, masons, and bakers. By that summer, the Cádiz branch had eight sections, including a women's association and unions of masons, carpenters, bakers, and vineyard workers.[19] But in October 1870, the Cádiz chapter reported to the FRE's Federal Council, the group ostensibly responsible for coordination and communication among all the anarchist branches, that membership had not increased as it should have because local government officials had used a bakers' strike as an excuse for persecuting all organized workers. Another bakers' strike in neighboring Jerez had provided the mayor there with an opportunity to outlaw the First International and all those syndicates with which it was affiliated. To meet the political threat, in February 1871 workers and peasants in Jerez reconstituted themselves the Casino Universal de Obreros, or workers' center. The following autumn, the same organization submitted a constitution to the FRE, changing themselves back again into the local federation of anarchists. This process, simple and dangerous as it may seem, allowed Andalusian workers to maintain connection with the larger movement at the same time that they protected themselves at home. The chameleon-like nonstructure of anarchist institutions, as it merged with local working-class culture, enabled the anarchists to function.

Anarquismo y sindicalismo, p. 135; Maestre Alfonso, *Hechos y documentos del anarco-sindicalismo español*, p. 31.

[19] For the history of the First International and its successors in Spain, see Joll, *The Anarchists*, and Woodcock, *Anarchism*. Details about the origin of anarchism in Cádiz and Jerez can be found in Nettlau, *La Première Internationale en Espagne (1868–1888)*, 1, 79, 120; *Actas* 1, 12; Bruguera, *Histoire contemporaine d'Espagne*, p. 266.

The same process took place in Sanlúcar de Barrameda, where the actual workers' federation got off to a slow start. Cells were established as early as 1871, but local correspondents complained that the branch was having problems keeping a stable membership. By autumn 1872, however, Sanlúcar had 200 vinetenders enrolled in a labor syndicate, 106 agricultural laborers engaged in another one, and an unspecified number of shoemakers in still another. It appears that the agricultural sections took responsibility for organizing other workers. At the same time, the local had established a consumer's cooperative with 80 members, a collective barbershop, and a cooperative bakery, where they claimed to produce better bread more cheaply than in commercial bakeries. Anselmo Lorenzo, a leading anarchist, was sent in 1872 to visit Jerez, San Fernando, and Cádiz to promote the national anarchist federation. By then Jerez already had more than twenty-five anarchist sections, including a union of vinetenders, a society of masons directed by Pedro Vázquez, and an omnibus section (*secciones varias*), or union of miscellaneous occupations, to which journalists, physicians, notaries, and housewives might belong.[20]

Smaller towns in Cádiz Province also affiliated with the FRE, but the local ruling class' ability to blacklist workers increased in inverse proportion to the size of the locality. The big growth in anarchist strength in smaller cities in Cádiz Province seems to have come in the autumn of 1872. At that time, towns such as Medina Sidonia reported twenty members, Paterna de Rivera announced a propaganda campaign, and San Fernando reported iron workers' and shipwrights' sections and a miscellaneous syndicate. Puerto de Santa María also reported an omnibus syndicate. Hundreds of handwritten broadsides and newspapers, many of which appeared only once, were carried from place to place.

[20] *Actas* I, 35, 44, 80, 127, 256–257, 289, 336–337, 368; *Cartas comunicaciones y circulares del III consejo federal de la región española* (hereafter cited as *Cartas*), I, 148; Lorenzo, *El proletariado militante*, I, 254.

Often, the decrees of the FRE's annual congresses were printed and distributed, probably carried by peddlers and carters, although it would be impossible to prove this. Word of mouth was also important, since so many of the workers in Cádiz Province were migrants at least part of the year. For instance, Diego Rodríguez Vargas of Medina Sidonia read or heard about the International and was brave enough to write to the Federal Council of the FRE for literature. Along with some neighbors he must have proselytized, he organized a local.

The workers in each local were also encouraged to affiliate with regional or national trade syndicates such as the Union of Field Workers (Unión de trabajadores del campo, UTC), the only regional body to achieve any importance in late nineteenth-century Andalusia. Francisco Tomás, a member of the Federal Council, wrote in late 1872 to machinists, dockworkers, and stevedores throughout anarchist Spain, urging them to consolidate their local syndicates into an iron-workers' union that would transcend municipal lines. But despite the activity, and despite attempts to consolidate syndicalist sentiment through regional unions, there was—with the exception of the Union of Field Workers, constituted in April 1872—virtually no regionally coordinated body in Andalusia.[21] Despite its name, the Union of Field Workers organized bakers, coopers, and carters as well as peasants and landless day laborers.

Whether skilled or unskilled, anarchist workers were interested in "the great politics of labor, of organized sections or syndicates, and [in] the economic federation of all workers," a commitment that caused Federal Republicans to call them "undemocratic," since they attempted to go on strike and tried to convince scabs to join them. Bourgeois republicans often intimated that workers' interest in forming unions distracted them from the pressing need to create a republic. However, as the economic situation worsened between 1868

[21] *Actas* I, 253, 280, 288–289; *Cartas* I, 94, 270, 272, 371–372, 388; II, 93, 213; Lorenzo, *El proletariado militante*, II, 65.

and 1873, both skilled and unskilled workers, squeezed in the vise of agrarian depression, may have been less concerned with governmental form than with their own economic position. But if anarchism had been nothing more than a system of trade unions without a program for broader social change, local workers would probably have remained allies of bourgeois Republicans even longer than they did.

Unions of producers formed the fundamental structure of Spanish anarchism. These associations bore little resemblance to English or American craft unions because they were general industrial unions that organized all workers in a given trade, regardless of skill. More important, the Spanish unions seem to have been political cells dedicated to destroying capitalism and the bourgeoisie, rather than trade unions designed to secure reforms within the capitalist economic system. Syndicates were the means by which producers would control future anarchist society, and the instruments through which they would fight contemporary authorities. In towns with strong Republican histories such as Jerez and Cádiz, however, many workers may have continued to seek paternalist support from such Federalists as Garrido. Government repression of the anarchists in 1872 may also have slowed the pace of organizing.

In the Andalusian context, therefore, the Federal Republicans, who defended workers' rights to associate and attempted to ameliorate the execrable economic situation of the poor between 1868 and 1872, appeared as saviours. They not only attempted to create and maintain arbitration boards or mixed juries, but they established market committees to deal with individual workers' grievances. For example, in October 1868, a Jerez vineyard worker, Juan Lazo, complained that his foreman and the baker, José Benítez, had conspired to shortchange the workers for whom bread was part of their salaries. Lazo claimed that the loaves he and his fellow workers received were two and one half ounces short. His grievance was resolved by Manuel Sánchez Misa, a sherry producer and Federalist Republican, who was chairman of the marketing subcommission of the revolutionary junta's commission on local administration. So long as class struggle between workers and supervisors could be resolved by bourgeois political institutions supervised by Federalist Republicans, the anarchists would be hard pressed to win supporters.[22]

To counteract the pull of bourgeois politics, the anarchists sought to create labor unions that would unite small producers with employees, peasants with proletarians, and skilled with unskilled workers. The FRE's directing body consciously sought a populist alliance between laborers, sharecroppers, tenants, and small peasants by calling for reduced rents, increased shares, and workers' control of selling prices. Anarchism's general principles appealed to craftsmen, skilled workers, and peasants in three ways: the anarchists viewed the small productive unit, organized in labor syndicates, as the core of future social arrangements; they guaranteed each individual the benefits from what he or she created, thus eliminating the boss and middleman; and they identified the key sources of oppression as the state and the bourgeoisie rather than the class of employers. Anarchist strategy thus opposed reformist strikes against employers in favor of a revolutionary general or social strike against the local and national government. Anarchists were warned that they would lose economic strikes. Their real goal was to wait and make the ultimate and only revolution, the Social Revolution.[23]

The goal of such an anarchist revolution was to establish a society in which all workers would be organized into collectives or political labor unions. These sections would

[22] *Cartas* I, 347; "Los huelguistas," *La federación andaluza*, 15-VI-1873; *Le Révolté* (Geneva), 24-VI-1882; "Crónica local: Primera comisión de administración local: Subcomisión del mercado," *El guadalete*, 24-X-1868.

[23] *Cartas* I, 117, 397; "La huelga general," *El condenado* (Madrid), 11-VIII-1873 to 2-IX-1873; "La huelga general," *La alarma* (Seville), 27-IV-1890.

be federated nationally and internationally around the trade. Different unions would unite into a local council that would make pacts to facilitate credit, exchange, education, and public health within the municipality. The local council would make treaties with other local federations for credit, exchange, communication, transportation, and public services.[24] These, in turn, would make further contracts with other provinces and nations. Intermediate governments or states would be superfluous, since the section and the local councils could perform necessary administrative tasks.

The workers' union would be at the center of economic and political life in each municipality. These unions and the individuals in them would own the means of production; thus everyone would contribute to production and consume the fruits of his or her own labor without exploitation and without wages. The question of ownership was always blurred in the early phase of Spanish anarchism. For example, under the program promoted by Michael Bakunin's Spanish followers, there was to be collective ownership of tools, shops, land, and means of communication and transportation, but not of the goods produced. Property would theoretically belong to the union, whose members would work cooperatively, each receiving a dividend proportional to his or her labor. This distributive system theoretically would encourage everyone to work at maximum

[24] This structure was first adopted by the First National Congress of the FRE. It was proposed to the convention by a medical student from Cádiz, Antonio González García Meneses, who claimed to represent associations of cabinetmakers, masons, carpenters, and shoemakers in Cádiz, although he himself was a member of the Barcelona section. Nettlau, "Impresiones sobre el desarrollo del socialismo en España," p. 229; Maestre Alfonso, *Hechos y documentos*, p. 31. See also "A.I.T.-F.R.E. Circular 28; La comisión federal a los consejos de las uniones de oficio y comisiones periciales de la federación de oficio," *El condenado*, 11–IX–1873; "A los trabajadores del campo," *El trabajo* (Malaga), 17–XI–1882; "F.T.R.E. Manifiesto, 8 de julio, 1887," *Le Révolté*, 23–VII–1887; Ricardo Mella, "La cooperación libre y los sistemas de comunidad."

capacity and would give the workers' association what the petty producer lacked—economies of scale, credit, and cheap labor. Small producers and skilled workers, for whom the notion of justice and freedom entailed exclusive control of one's own labor and the value it created, may have found that anarchism spoke to their situation.

The FRE was from the beginning based upon unions of all workers engaged in producing the same product; they were to be organized by town, district, region, and nation. Where these unions by trade (uniones de oficios símiles) existed, among Cádiz' agricultural and vineyard workers, coopers, bakers, and cobblers, for example, they resulted in district and regional ties among Andalusian anarchists.[25] Originally, there were to be two structures of labor organization within the anarchist national federation—the local council in each town, and national unions for each branch of production. In Jerez, as in the rest of Andalusia, when a particular occupation was strongly represented, there were large local sections of that trade; the rest of the unions clustered around the local council, which was roughly equivalent in organizational form to a city trades assembly in the United States.

All the official anarchist national organizations tried to impede strikes for higher wages or reduced hours, a policy particularly attractive to vinegrowing peasants seeking to cut labor costs as luxury wine prices fluctuated downward

[25] In a work first written in 1910, José Prat, a leading twentieth-century anarcho-syndicalist, argued that although the term "syndicalism" ("sindicalismo") was new at the turn of the century, the concept was old. The system of organizing people into politically militant sections generally around their trade had in the nineteenth century been called workers' collectivism (societarismo obrero) until the new term "syndicalism" was introduced from France. See Prat, *La burguesía y el proletariado. La federación* (Madrid), 18–XII–1870; *Le Révolté*, 23–VII–1887; Nettlau, "Impresiones," pp. 229–230; Díaz del Moral, *Historia de las agitaciones*, p. 430; Lorenzo, *El proletariado militante* II, 75–79; Romero Maura, "The Spanish Case," in Apter and Joll, eds., *Anarchism Today*, pp. 66–67.

after 1863. The FRE strike policy promoted the worst kind of bureaucratic impediments to action, even though, in principle, anarchists were antagonistic to bureaucracy. According to the FRE, bad treatment by employers or the possibility of using labor shortages to win higher wages were not in themselves sufficient grounds for an official strike. The anarchist organization permitted strikes only when an employer was trying to *increase* exploitation by cutting wages or by increasing hours. As Francisco Tomás, speaking for the Federal Council of the FRE said, "We accept struggle whenever we are provoked, and, if today we choose not to provoke strikes, remaining in a defensive position, at the same time we will not permit sections to accept reduced wages, nor increased hours without increased wages, nor blacklisting because of membership in the International."

Workers who wished their strikes to be sanctioned by the FRE had to submit a list of their goals to the local commission that had jurisdiction over their vocational group. The request then went to the regional commission governing that trade. Even if the commission approved the petition, it had still to go to the committee of the entire local and then to the Federal Council. Since the whole process, including five different stages, might take as many as eight weeks, the only reason any group might go through the intricate process would be to enlist the political and financial support of organized workers outside the district. The whole process was designed to discourage reformist strikes and to promote social revolution.

This system obviously encouraged the most powerful local unions to ignore the anarchist councils and go out on strike when they believed they had some leverage over their employers. Wildcat strikes took place because it was impossible to persuade even anarchist workers to hold out for the revolution when their unions gave them immediate power over their bosses. Workers could take advantage of seasonal labor shortages to demand better working conditions, higher wages, or even a measure of control. One British sherry exporter complained in his newsletter that "the disturbed state of Spain . . . has influenced the shipments from there, and, in consequence of the coopers and labourers having demanded shorter hours of work, great difficulty is experienced in obtaining casks, and higher prices are asked by shippers to meet the increased expense."[26]

Jerez' coopers, who had had the longest associational tradition of any group in town, had been prominent in pre-anarchist cooperative societies and constituted kind of an elite among the skilled workers. In 1870 self-employed and salaried coopers and vinetenders were among the first to organize as labor unions affiliated with the First International. Throughout the nineteenth century, the coopers remained tied to official anarchist organizations, and were at the same time the most militant in demands designed to defend their skills.[27]

Anarchist Communalism

Although the unions provided the structural basis of Andalusian anarchism, the movement really established itself in Cádiz through its cultural and intellectual activities, which welded petty bourgeois and proletarian elements against the big bourgeoisie of all political affiliations. This process was slow, but succeeded in uniting all the "little people," whatever their class or sex, against the rich.

Anarchism threw down deep roots partly because it was able to assimilate and transform traditional working class and petty bourgeois culture. Andalusian anarchism's cul-

[26] Lorenzo, El proletariado militante 11, 78–80; Nettlau, La Première Internationale 1, 368; Cartas 11, 22; Nettlau, "Impresiones," p. 229. Letter, April 7, 1873 in the José de Soto Collection of the Archivo del Consejo regulador del Vino, Jerez de la Frontera, uncatalogued.

[27] "Asociación Internacional: Reglamento de la Sección de Vinicultores de Jerez de la Frontera," cited in de Góngora, Materiales para la historia de la M.N. y M.L. ciudad de Jerez de la Frontera, p. 130. Nettlau reported that there were big coopers' strikes between 1874 and 1881. "Impresiones," p. 327.

tural branches, their women's sections, secular schools, libraries, and cafes were coordinated by local anarchist councils, often consisting of all who might consider themselves anarchists. They determined social policy, founded cooperatives, raised money to support strikers, and created a collective sense of identity. Since social and psychological change was a major anarchist goal, and since such matters could only be discussed and implemented by all local anarchists acting in concert, the local council swiftly became synonymous with anarchism in towns such as Arcos, Jerez, and Sanlúcar. The council and anyone else who cared, often including people from the neighborhood, generally met in a cafe, the Paris Bar in Jerez, for example.[28] Because the anarchists collected membership dues only irregularly, anyone who happened by could claim to be a member and could express his or her views. This meant that there was a convergence between local anarchism and prevailing working-class and peasant culture in Andalusia.

Cádiz' anarchists won support around such issues as anti-clericalism, mass secular education, and women's emancipation. Although local anarchists often referred to Christ as the first anarchist, to themselves as Christians, and to their leaders as apostles, they identified the established church with the prevailing latifundist bourgeoisie and opposed it, if for no other reason than that their enemies seemed to support it. The ruling class used Catholicism to buttress its own position. For instance, in 1871, when a gang of people calling themselves Republicans burnt a vineyard belonging to a monarchist Cortes delegate, José Pemartin, the winecellar itself was saved. Local newspapers attributed the "miracle" to the statue of Jesus that stood in the bodega chapel. Iconoclasm led crowds to destroy pictures of popes and images of saints as well as convents, monasteries, and homes of priests whenever the opportunity arose. Rulers and ruled shared the idea that the church favored the monarchist lati-

---

[28] Lorenzo, *El proletariado militante* i, 254.

fundists, upon whom the religious depended for support after the disentailments.

Anarchist hatred for the institutional church had more fundamental roots, however, than simple anticlericalism. The anarchists hated the authoritarianism inherent in the concepts of God and saints, although they continued to employ a religious idiom to express communitarian sentiments. As a fundamentally antihierarchic movement, dedicated to the belief in human will to the social good, they simply rejected one thousand years of Christian culture that inculcated fatalism and dependency upon higher powers. But Andalusian women found in the church a place where they could gather to reassert female community through gossip and commiseration. Just as Cádiz men would never have tolerated a demand for the abolition of their cafes, but took them over, transforming them into anarchist centers, working-class women did not tolerate Republican or anarchist demands for the destruction of their church. Daily Mass formed the core of poor women's society, just as the local bar or cafe was the center of poor men's social life.

Women were won to the anarchist movement because of its cultural activities rather than its union structure. Female anarchists also created some of their own means of bringing other working-class, peasant, and petty bourgeois women to anarchism. A movement especially important in Northern Cádiz Province, the system of infant initiation into anarchism as a substitute for baptism, seems to have emerged from the women's sections. In 1873, for instance, the Sanlúcar de Barrameda women's branch initiated a boy called "Gateway to Human Progress" and a girl named "Anarchist Europe."[29] These occasions generally provided the opportunity for women gathered together to sing anarchist

---

[29] *El debate* (Madrid), cited in *La legalidad* (Cadiz), 3–VI–1872; *El condenado*, 27–III–1873. Portions of the following section have appeared in Temma Kaplan, "Women and Spanish Anarchism," in Claudia Koonz and Renate Bridenthal, eds., *Becoming Visible: Women in European History.*

songs, discuss how their lives and those of their children would be changed after the revolution, and assert female goals.

Without the September Revolution, however, it is unlikely that the issue of women's equality would have come so dramatically to the fore. Quite early in the revolutionary period, Cádiz' Federal Republicans formed a Women's Republican Association, among the goals of which were to grant women equal property rights. But the Republicans stressed the need for women to continue their roles as guardians of the family.

The anarchists distinguished their position on women from that held by the Federal Republicans through a theoretical attack on the bourgeois family as distinct from the working-class family. Anarchists claimed that women and children were tyrannized by paternalism as institutionalized in the family. Internationalist José Mesa, later a leading Spanish Marxist, stressed this point when he argued at the FRE 1871 Valencia Congress that "the family should be based on love, liberty, and equality." Both the family and the church were believed by anarchists to teach the poor to acquiesce to tyranny. Having learned submissiveness literally at their mothers' knees, poor people then became docile before all authorities, including the ruling-class latifundists and the state. The anarchists maintained that if the authoritarian family provided the model for the authoritarian state, then democratic family life ought to be encouraged to prepare people for anarchism. Anarchists seem to have been among the earliest social theorists whose mass movement grasped the relationship between family psychology, revolutionary personality, and political freedom.

Historians have generally emphasized the ignorance and resulting fanaticism of Cádiz' masses, but, in fact, literacy in Cádiz Province, about 30 to 45 percent, was as high as in Catalonia and central Spain (see Table 3-2). It was higher than any place else in Andalusia or Valencia, where in 1877 average literacy was only between 15 and 30 percent.

Table 3-2

1868 Literacy Rates in Cádiz Province

Judicial district	Population	Percent literate
Algeciras	30,079	30%
Arcos	32,618	20%
Cádiz	71,521	52%
Chiclana	23,477	20%
Grazalema	17,352	18%
Jerez	52,158	29%
Medina Sidonia	24,689	24%
Olvera	25,313	11%
Puerto de Santa María	28,970	29%
San Fernando	35,339	33%
Sanlúcar de Barrameda	25,479	40%
San Roque	24,310	17%

Source: *El guadalete*, 2–11–1868.

Among anarchists the rate was higher still. In 1872, for instance, 56 percent of Jerez' anarchists could read, in a population where only 29 percent were literate; and in neighboring San Fernando, 88 percent of the anarchists could read, when only 33 percent of the general population had that skill. While general literacy rates were lower in inland towns such as Arcos, Grazalema, or San Roque, averaging 20 percent as compared to the coastal cities' 30 percent, anarchists in the hill towns were relatively well educated in comparison with the general population.[30] Thus throughout Cádiz, anarchists could depend upon the written word to spread news about their activities and goals. And, as educated people, Andalusian anarchists put faith in education as an organizing tool. The need for mass education

[30] *El pacto federal: Diario republicano* (Cadiz), began VII–1868, no. 2 undated, no. 23; Lorenzo, *El proletariado militante* II, 196; Artola, *La burguesía revolucionaria*, p. 281; Maurice, "A propos d'une réédition récente: Remarques sur l'anarchisme andalou," p. 320, chides Díaz del Moral for overlooking anarchists' literacy. *Actas* I, 280–281.

was also recognized by Federal Republicans, but again the anarchists went a step further. Whereas the Federalists would have been content to create a reasonably literate electorate, Andalusian anarchists envisaged a new human nature.

To the extent that primary education was available to the Andalusian poor at midcentury, it was generally in the hands of clergy, at least insofar as the church tried to prepare poor children for communion and confirmation. Religious instruction was often the only formal education anarchist youth received. For girls, this meant that, if they attended school at all, they generally learned sewing, decorum, and religious ritual from nuns who tied them to the church by a mixture of benevolence and fear.

Anarchists opposed this subordination of rationality to fear. As libertarians, they hoped to develop means by which they could destroy superstition, the magical thinking and religiosity that they believed prevented human beings from recognizing their individual native intelligence and potential creativity. They believed that personal freedom lay in a system of social relations in which everyone, regardless of sex or occupation, was autonomous and equal. Education played a key role in this personal reform program. At the FRE's Second National Convention in Zaragoza in the spring of 1872, the organization supported a program introduced by the Sevillian member of the alliance, Trinidad Soriano. Called Integral Education, the program called for each local to institute schools, libraries, and laboratories. Based upon Charles Fourier's idea for an école-atelier in which physical as well as mental skills would be developed, Integral Education attempted to destroy the conflict between intellectual and manual labor. Fourier's idea had become the basis for the educational theories of such different socialists as Proudhon, Marx, and Bakunin. And the latter had added instruction in the sciences to the mix. The sequence of the proposed curriculum in Spain was quite simple. All learning would proceed from study of natural history and scientific method, to psychology and logic, and then to evolutionary theory. Students would explore all these disciplines through simple laboratory study. This sequence roughly organized human knowledge into secular categories of nature, mind, and change.

Such a theory attempted to replace a supernatural Catholic universe, interpreted by church dogma, with a positivist cosmology that posited the continuity between nature and egalitarian society. Human beings, women included, were creatures of nature. Human consciousness was subject to the scientific laws of nature rather than to God and the church. Integral Education thus substituted evolution for the will of God, since, as anarchists were fond of saying, revolution would merely speed up evolution. History, anarchists argued, was on their side; but the pace of evolution could be influenced by anarchist politics, since the development of anarchism could be retarded by ignorance. Anarchist educational programs not only attempted to refute religious beliefs and superstition, but they were also designed to challenge church-state authority, since it was widely assumed that adherence to religious precepts assured social order and the status quo. Even more important, anarchists tied the issue of secular education to anarchist political consciousness. Scientific education, they said, could tutor the will by liberating people from fear of the supernatural. The educational regimen was designed to strengthen the will of peasants and workers to withstand exhortations by the clergy, and to overcome fear based on superstition.

After 1872, if not before, anarchist locals throughout Northern Cádiz Province tried to organize coeducational schools, buy books, and establish museums and laboratories wherever possible. The Sanlúcar de Barrameda local established a grammar school in October 1872. The FRE Commission praised their action as a "great stride on the road to emancipation." Most anarchist locals could provide only meager resources, however. The new education was more often in the hands of men like Juan Ruiz, a dedicated teacher who went to the hamlet of Alcornocalejo, near San José del

Valle, where he joined the local anarchist chapter and taught school in people's homes. Taking on fifteen students at a time, he collected about two pesetas a month from each. While students did wage labor to pay his fees, he also worked part-time as a watchman to earn additional money.[31]

The anarchists in Northern Cádiz Province thus succeeded in identifying their movement with militant trade unionism and with working-class culture. Because anarchists emerged as the most literate and perhaps the most articulate among the local peasants and workers, and because anarchist rituals and institutions modified older collective forms, after 1872 anarchism became synonymous with the popular movement to transform society.

[31] Kaplan, "Women and Spanish Anarchism"; Clara E. Lida, "Educación anarquista en la España del ochocientos"; *Cartas* I, 305; *El guadalete*, 8–III–1883.

CHAPTER IV

Insurrectionary Politics, 1869 to 1873

Bakuninist leaders and Intransigent Republicans in Cádiz Province shared a commitment to insurrectionary politics directed by a political elite. Against this tendency, local anarchists in Andalusia attempted to create a popular movement, organized around sections and militant trade unions, the goal of which was to win local control for the masses of working people. There was, in effect, a two-way split between Intransigents and local groups. All this was complicated and masked by the united struggle of both against the Spanish state between 1868 and 1873.

At first, in late 1868, the militance of Republican forces in the south won them popular support, but their fears of social revolution and its potential to destroy even the most radical republicanism were aroused by the 1869 Jerez draft riot. The people, on the other hand, seem to have become discouraged about left Republican insurrectionism, according to which an elite, organized into political cells, would rouse the masses and lead them to spontaneous victory, and the secession of the region from the state. Despite temporary alliances between Intransigents and anarchists, notably in the Cantonalist Insurrection of 1873, Andalusian anarchists increasingly turned against Republican politicians. At the same time, in the Sanlúcar de Barrameda Canton of 1873, local anarchists improvised a revolutionary structure, one that national anarchist leaders had only begun to consider. Through their sections and unions, they seized the town and transformed it into an anarchist commune.

In the spring of 1869, as the constitutional convention in Madrid prepared the statutes that would govern a new monarchy, left Republicans such as Paúl and Guillén plotted through political clubs to convince the populace that armed revolt was necessary.[1] They wanted to avoid an easily repressed preemptive uprising, but this is just what occurred in March 1869.

General Juan Prim, then head of state, had ordered a levy of 25,000 men to put down the Cuban Revolution. The draft lottery in Jerez was scheduled to begin at 7:30 A.M. on the morning of March 16, 1869.[2] The drawing attracted hostile crowds that gathered at central points in Jerez. As the draftees were chosen, one young man, dressed in baggy black pants, white shirt, and cummerbund, disrupted the proceedings. Others joined him. When the police charged the youth and his comrades and began carrying him off to the neighboring jail, the crowds attacked them. The Plaza de Arenal, just down the street from the jail, was suddenly filled with flying stones, empty wine bottles, and masonry. Police reinforcements at the jail repulsed the crowd, which withdrew to the petty bourgeois and working-class districts, where they erected barricades.

Reacting by a show of force, the Madrid government called up the troops from Málaga, Córdoba, Cádiz, and Sevilla. By late afternoon, three companies reached the working-class sections on the outskirts of Jerez. Along with the Guardia Civil and the excise police, they marched down Calle Larga, the main street, toward the Cruz de la Victoria barricades. There an hour-long pitched battle took place. Snipers could be heard long into the night, and there were many casualties, but the barricades were rebuilt during the night. Three thousand men under the command of General Pozo were sent to pull them down at 5 A.M., which led to two more hours of fighting until the townspeople were defeated.

When the bodies were counted, a hundred government troops and at least two hundred local citizens had been

[1] Eiras Roel, *El partido demócrata*, p. 402.
[2] *La Andalucía* (Seville), 19-III-1869; AMJF *Archivo memoranda 2* (1869), pp. 244-246.

wounded or killed. Over six hundred people, among them substantial citizens, including some Federal Republicans, were sent to a penal colony at Ceuta.[3] Despite the bloodbath in Jerez, which individual Intransigents like José Paúl tried to prevent, the Intransigents went ahead with their plans for a coup that autumn—in large measure because in June 1869 the Cortes, by a vote of 214 to 56, proclaimed its preference for a monarchy rather than a republic. Pedro Bohorques, Rafael Guillén, Fermín Salvochea, and Paúl took to the mountains east of Jerez that fall with about five hundred men, primarily from Paterna de Rivera, Medina Sidonia, and Ubrique, in an attempt to rouse the hill people against the centralized state. The coup aborted, and Salvochea narrowly escaped with Paúl to Gibraltar; government forces killed their two comrades. Salvochea spent the next two years in Paris and London among other radicals, returning only in 1871, when amnesty was declared.[4] After the coup, the government suspended constitutional guarantees for two months. Under martial law, neither Federal Republicans nor anarchists enjoyed their civil rights. Nevertheless, the anarchists continued to build their syndicates and establish schools and laboratories, just as the Federalists continued to plot for the overthrow of the monarchy and the creation of a decentralized bourgeois republic to replace it. But the

[3] AMJF *Actas capitulares* (1869), pp. 272–273; *El progreso* (Jerez), 18–III–1870, commemorates the previous year's events. It is included in "Expediente para socorrer a la clase jornalera a virtud de la miseria que se experiencia por las continuas lluvias, 1870," in AMJF 224: 11,250; see also *El progreso*, cited in *La Andalucía*, 20–III–1869, 21–III–1869; and AMJF *Archivo memoranda 2* (1869), pp. 244–246. All newspapers for March 1869 are missing from the Jerez archives.

[4] Rocker, *Fermín Salvochea*, pp. 19, 21–23; Vallina, *Crónica de un revolucionario*, pp. 17, 24; Clara Lida cites a note in *La federación* (Barcelona), 5–XI–1871 that Salvochea had joined the anarchist local in Sevilla, but she and I have both been unable to confirm this evidence. Lida, *Anarquismo y revolución*, p. 161. *La opinión nacional* (Cadiz), 19–VIII–1869; Guichot, *Historia general de Andalucía*, pp. 194–199.

coup of 1869 and its aftermath marked a major change in workers' and peasants' relationship with bourgeois politicians in Andalusia.

Between 1871 and 1872, the relationships among Spanish anarchists were, in turn, altered by both internal and international developments. Following the repression of the Paris Commune in the spring of 1871, many refugees, among them the son-in-law of Karl Marx, Cuban-born Paul Lafargue, fled to Spain. That summer in Madrid he joined the editorial board of *La emancipación*, the First International's foremost Spanish journal. Lafargue helped its editor and founder José Mesa to promote Marxist rather than Bakuninist principles. Through it, they launched the Marxist attack upon the Bakuninist alliance in Spain, and upon conspiratorial leftist politics.

In the wake of the Commune, in late May 1871, the Spanish Cortes had debated whether the International Workingmen's Association should be outlawed. Although no official decree was passed until the following January, on June 3, 1871, Práxedes Mateo Sagasta sent a circular to the provincial governors, attacking the First International. The Federal Council, the governing board of the FRE, fled to Lisbon where, in July 1871, they founded the Portuguese section of the International.[5] The local councils in Andalusia and elsewhere went underground. In September, the FRE began what was to be a long tradition of secret meetings with a clandestine convention in Valencia.

On November 16, the Cortes ratified Prim's selection of

[5] For details on the Paris Commune and its effect on Spanish politics, see Álvarez Junco, *La comuna en España* and Vergés Mundó, *La I Internacional en las cortes de 1871.* Those interested in the Portuguese anarchism should consult Vianna, *A evolução anarchista* [sic] *em Portugal* and Fonseca, *A origem da 1º Internacional em Lisboa.* Detailed examination of the relation between national politics and the development of Spanish anarchism in late 1871 can be found in Morato, *Historia de la sección española de la Internacional (1868–1874),* pp. 87–112.

Amadeo of Savoy as the new king of Spain. Federal Republicans opposed the new monarch, whom Paúl and his Madrid supporters called Macarroni I, but the anarchists remained preoccupied with their own problems. When Prim was shot on December 27 and died three days later, Paúl was blamed, not the anarchists.

Still interdicted, the FRE held its Second National Convention secretly in Zaragoza in April 1872. The Bakuninists were attacked by *La emancipación*, which published a list of those who belonged to the alliance; just before the meeting, the secret society claimed to have dissolved itself, but did not really do so. Thinking they had, Bakunin was annoyed and wrote to Paulo (Tomás González Morago, a member of the FRE's Federal Council) in May 1872 that the role of the International should not be confused with the task performed by the alliance. Whereas the International was designed to gather masses of workers, the alliance existed to shape the movement, giving it a revolutionary direction. Bakunin claimed that while the International continued to perform necessary work, "it alone was incapable of organizing the popular force . . . and for this, a secret organization was necessary." He claimed that the mutual trust and insight necessary to guide the masses could only be secured through a secret organization.[6] Though he selected his words carefully, Bakunin undoubtedly tried to portray the alliance as a vanguard party.

Bakunin and his followers were struggling to maintain not only the Spanish alliance, but more centrally, the frequently dissolved Secret Alliance of Switzerland, mother of all the other alliances. This struggle was the precipitating cause of the division into two warring factions of the Spanish workers movement. It also led to the collapse of the First International itself. The Bakuninist Alliance, centered in Jura, Switzerland, had outwardly but not really dissolved itself once again in August 1871. At the International's mid-

[6] Nettlau, *Miguel Bakunin*, pp. 96–100; Termes, *Anarquismo y sindicalismo*, p. 146; Hennessy, *Federal Republic*, pp. 140–141.

September 1871 London Congress, pro-Bakunin representatives had been in the minority, thus permitting the International to pass an article demanding that the Alliance cease to function once and for all. The Bakuninists, for their part, met in November 1871 in Sonvillier and called for a more representative meeting of the International than the London meeting, which had been dominated by Marx and his supporters. Spanish Internationalists were divided between Marx and Bakunin, with the group around *La emancipación* leading the Marxist forces.[7]

With the January 1872 Spanish government decree formally ordering the dissolution of the International in Spain, both Marxists and Bakuninists were forced underground, regardless of their belief in secrecy. The dispute between Marxists and Bakuninists, however, continued. The majority of the Spanish locals fell in behind Bakunin and the Jura Federation in January and February 1872. Once again in April, the Spanish secret alliance read itself out of existence. These somewhat vaudevillian disappearance acts have been well explained by Josep Termes, who has argued that "from the beginning, the Spanish alliance was a federation of small groups supporting a Bakuninist ideology, groups with few members who maintained among themselves a narrow solidarity based on the friendship, community of ideas, and animadversion to political parties. For this reason, although the bureaucratic organization might disappear, it is certain that the group functioned as before since it was impossible that the ideological and personal connections ceased to influence their conduct. Practically, there was no difference between the actions of the Bakuninist groups before their dissolution and after."[8]

Accusations filled the air in the early summer of 1872. The Marxists believed that the alliance continued to function, while Bakuninists charged that those who supported Marx and the General Council had their own secret strategy

[7] Termes, *Anarquismo y sindicalismo*, pp. 137–139.
[8] *Ibid.*, pp. 139–141.

for Spain. The alliance claimed to have dissolved and re-formed. Bakunin urged his followers in Spain to hold fast to the alliance, especially since, as he falsely charged, Marx and Engels had kept their own Communist League of 1851 and 1852 alive within the International. The effect in Spain of these charges and countercharges was that *La emancipación*, having published the list of alliance members, was expelled from the Madrid Federation on June 3, 1872. In retaliation, the Marxists formed the New Madrid Federation (Nueva federación madrileña) in early July 1872, and were immediately recognized by the General Council of the First International in London. But news of the dispute probably remained localized in Madrid and Barcelona. The Cádiz delegate to the April 1872 Zaragoza Congress, Claudio Solanes, contacted Lafargue for English-language copies of the Statutes of the First International, but there is no reason to believe that he had had any premonitions about an imminent split between Lafargue and other Spanish anarchists. Solanes wanted to distribute the statutes among fifty English mechanics who lived in Cádiz and had expressed interest in affiliating with the International.[9] His choice of Lafargue as intermediary must have had more to do with the latter's English connections than with his political principles.

During the summer of 1872, members of the alliance challenged *La emancipación* to print its entire membership list so that anarchists might judge whether or not the alliance had been loyal and efficient in furthering the goals of the International. They claimed that they were an indigenous Spanish alliance, not a branch of the association in Jura. This dispute came to a head during the International's Hague Conference of September 2 to 7, 1872, where almost all the elected Spanish delegates were members of the alliance.

At The Hague, a special commission of the General Council, assigned to investigate Alliance activities, proposed the expulsion of Bakunin and James Guillaume, a Swiss labor

[9] *Ibid.*, pp. 145–146.

leader allied with Bakunin. Affronted, their followers withdrew, splitting the International. The Bakuninists and those
mutualist organizations that looked to Guillaume recon-
vened in Saint-Imier, Switzerland, two weeks later. There
the four Spanish delegates—Tomás González Morago,
Rafael Farga Pellicer, Nicolás Alonso Marselau (from
Sevilla), and Carlos Alerini—(a French refugee in Spain),
and the leading Italians—Fanelli, Errico Malatesta, Carlo
Cafiero, and Andrea Costa—joined Bakunin and Guillaume
in formulating an international anarchist program destined
to last for a decade. The Bakuninist branch now stood alone
and united. They called for the destruction of all political
power without compromise with bourgeois political groups
and without transitional governmental forms such as vanguard parties. They urged the formation of pacts and communication networks among all the different national federations, which were invited to support one another.[10]

No Spanish delegate at Saint-Imier directly represented
Andalusia. Although officially calling themselves Internationalists until 1876, Spanish anarchists had gone over to
Bakunin; but the issue had yet to be resolved locally, where
many were understandably confused about the conflict and
suspicious of the alliance. In November 1872, an investigat-
ing committee of the anarchist local council in Cádiz reported to the FRE's Federal Council that the work of local
alliance members was compatible with the goals of the International as they understood them. This must have come as
no surprise to the Federal Council of the FRE that included
the Andalusian García Viñas, whose role as an agitator
should never be underestimated. The Council's three leading Andalusian contacts were the journalist Navarro Prieto;
the anti-clerical professor of canon law at the University of
Córdoba, Augustín Cervantes; and Trinidad Soriano. Soriano and Navarro were members of the alliance, as were
most of the members of the Federal Council itself.[11]

[10] *Ibid.*, p. 149.
[11] *Actas* I, 351; Maestre Alfonso, *Hechos y documentos*, p. 38.

Others in Cádiz Province were more wary about what the Marxist-Bakuninist split might mean for them and their autonomy from the Federal Council. Sometime in November 1872, the Puerto de Santa María local apparently issued its own denunciation of the Federal Council, attributing the division in the international workers' movement to the expulsion of the editorial board of *La emancipación* from the Madrid Federation. The Council, which had moved to Valencia, then to Alcoy the previous spring, replied that this was absurd. They argued that the split at The Hague was due to far-reaching conflicts affecting Italians, Swiss, French, Belgians, and Americans as well as Spaniards committed to "anárquico-colectivista" principles. They had all signed a solidarity pact defending the autonomy of each local and national federation.[12] The Santa María local evidently accused the Federal Council of authoritarian practices, of acting without the consent of the locals. Santa María's spokesmen seem to have been eager to defend their own liberties against the creeping power of the Council rather than to protect the Marxists. At the local level, in Cádiz at least, anarchism continued to represent the mutualist practices of local peasants and workers. The Third Congress of the FRE, meeting secretly in Córdoba between December 25, 1872, and January 2, 1873, adhered to the Saint-Imier accords, thus cementing the rift between Marxists and Bakuninists in Spain.

At the same time as the Federal Council struggled against the Marxists, they also had to contend with continued alliances between Intransigent Republicans and anarchists in Cádiz Province. In late 1872, after nearly a year of persecution by Sagasta's government, the anarchist Federal Council reminded supporters that their goal was to destroy all government and all authoritarian power, not to substitute Federal Republicans, who wanted a weak central state, for Republicans who wanted a strong one. Anarchist leaders also warned Andalusian constituents that armed struggle

[12] *Cartas* II, 270.

was not necessary to achieve anarchism, but that Intransigents would use workers as cannon fodder to achieve their own ends. In a fit of temper, the Federal Council, in December 1872, called Puerto de Santa María's anarchists "idiots" for not recognizing that Federal Republicans were bourgeois who, unlike the anarchists, were more interested in governmental form than in overcoming exploitation. Exasperated, the Council also excoriated Jerez' vinetenders for continued association with bourgeois politicians.[13] The Council feared that continuing alliances with Intransigent Republicans would provide the state with opportunities to smash the anarchists; these premonitions were borne out.

VARIETIES OF INSURRECTION

Insurrectionary politics, promoted by the Intransigents and by the Federal Council of the FRE for different ends, were diametrically opposed to a syndical program upheld by large numbers of Andalusian anarchists. Andalusia was never an easy place to organize workers and peasants. Local authorities, whether monarchist or Republican, generally regarded labor unions as seditious organizations. Even when rights of association and assembly were guaranteed, workers throughout Spain were legally required to present authorities with membership lists. Since blacklisting was all too easy under these circumstances, most workers preferred to keep their unions clandestine. But secrecy was specifically forbidden by law, making trade unions, whether anarchist or not, subject to repression.

Power relations within individual cities became the crucial factor in anarchist politics during 1873, following the ten-month monarchy of King Amadeo of Savoy and his abdication on February 11. The next day, the Cortes declared itself a National Assembly and proclaimed a republic. It was, however, a republic only by default since, as most historians acknowledge, the majority of the representatives

[13] *Ibid.*, pp. 43–44, 227, 293.

believed that the preservation of order required the strong hand of a monarch. But since one monarch had been overthrown in 1868 and the other, in the words of Frederick Engels, was the first king in history to go on strike, there was nothing for the legislators to do but to declare the First Republic in 1873.[14]

Another hungry winter, following yet another bad harvest in 1872, did nothing to impede anarchist syndicalist organizing. In fact, the threat of social upheaval similar to the Paris Commune had haunted Spain and had helped cause the king's resignation. As the unions grew, Jerez' local ruling class became increasingly anxious, and in January 1873, authorities raided anarchist butchers' and agricultural workers' headquarters. Angry anarchists planned a general strike to depose the city council and replace it with the local council of the FRE, but the government arrested the strike leaders. Later that spring, the bakers' union went out on strike and the mayor, in turn, outlawed the First International. Carlos Martos, leader of the left Monarchists or Radical party, dominated the legislature, while the Federal Republicans controlled the government until Martos staged an unsuccessful coup on April 24, 1873. Elections for a republican constitutional convention had already been scheduled for March 11, and were finally held on May 10. The Cortes itself met on June 1. The Federal Republicans were strong in Cádiz Province, where they attempted to keep their followers in line, and to consolidate municipal power in their own hands. The Federalists in Puerto de Santa María, for example, gave parties to which workers and employers were invited. All Andalusian Federalists repeatedly called for "social harmony," which leftists regarded as a call for class collaboration.[15]

Jerez' anarchists, caring nothing for Federalist hopes,

[14] Engels, "The Bakuninists at Work: Notes on the Spanish Uprising in the Summer of 1873," p. 211.

[15] Actas I, 44; II, 80; Nettlau, La Première Internationale I, 192; La federación andaluza, 19–v–1873.

were eager to capitalize upon the first good grain and bean harvests in years to demand the abolition of piece work and reestablishment of day wages for agricultural laborers in June 1873. They therefore began organizing chickpea and wheat harvesters, and threatened to strike. All workers in Jerez became suspect. A rumor circulated that suspicious-looking harvesters were massing in the Caulina plains, to the northeast of Jerez. Since the Caulina vineyards, a center of anarchist vinetenders' mobilization, were nearby, the area was viewed as a troublespot. These vineyards were among the oldest in the district, some dating back six hundred years. Many of the most militant peasant proprietors and tenants—those who after 1863 had increasingly been squeezed by falling prices for their luxury sherry and by encroachments by the large sherry merchants who bought their land when they could not pay taxes, mortgages, or rents—lived, worked, and joined the local anarchists there. The mayor dispatched the rural police to the area where the agitators were reputedly gathered, but all the police found when they arrived were two or three hundred sleeping harvesters, who normally retired to groves or secluded places in fields to pass the night.

Two weeks later, on Jerez' northern border with Lebrija, striking harvesters went into the fields to prevent scabs from working. Backed by Jerez' municipal council, the Guardia Civil went to the center of the labor agitation, the farm called "La Vizcaína," and arrested thirty men, charging them with "tyranny" for trying to "enforce their will" upon others. At the end of June, demonstrators tried to take their grievance to the mayor. Forcing their way into his office, they naively asked for his authorization to go into the fields, where scabs were the virtual prisoners of their employers. Quite rationally, the striking anarchists argued that, with the mayor's protection, they could convince the scabs to give up working at piece rates and persuade them to join the strike. When the mayor refused permission, the strikers grew angry, spilled into the streets, and aroused the crowd. In an attempt to prevent a riot, the mayor had four men who had been singled out as leaders arrested. This incensed the crowd, which surged past the municipal police in the hope of freeing the captives. When the police could no longer preserve order against the strikers and their supporters, the mayor called on the local cavalry unit, which was successful in dispersing the crowd.

Here and in subsequent rebellions two issues became clear. In provinces such as Cádiz, dominated by one or two single industries, labor struggles almost invariably turned into community struggles since "the people" and "workers" were self-identified as one. Because this was true, and because local authorities envisioned insurrection in every labor struggle, police provoked the unions, thus precipitating insurrection.[16]

Local workers also carried out offensive actions. Within three days of King Amadeo's resignation in February 1873, disorders had broken out in Sanlúcar de Barrameda. A revolutionary committee composed of the local anarchist council, perhaps including men such as Trinidad González, who directed both the shoemakers' and masons' unions, had replaced the city council, imprisoned the police, and destroyed notarial records. This attack upon the government, clearly orchestrated by local anarchists, attempted to transform social relations in one town, and represented a sharp break with the Intransigent Republican pattern of insurrection, which limited its goal to mere political autonomy from the state, leaving social relations intact.[17]

---

[16] *La federación andaluza*, 15-VI-1873, 28-VI-1873; *El guadalete*, 27-VI-1873. This theory of how repression promotes rebellion has been studied by Arno J. Mayer in *Dynamics of Counterrevolution in Europe, 1870–1956: An Analytic Framework*. Coletti's *Anarchici e questori* specifically correlates police provocation and anarchism.

[17] *La legalidad*, 14-II-1873, 15-II-1873; Barbadillo Delgado, *Historia de la ciudad de Sanlúcar de Barrameda*, p. 795; *Cartas* I, 102, 197. Carlos Martínez Shaw's *El Cantón sevillano*, which was brought to my attention by Josep Fontana after this book was completed, essentially makes the same argument for Sevilla that I make for Sanlúcar.

The crisis in legitimacy brought about the king's resignation in February 1873, and the instability and weakness of national parties had called into question social and political arrangements. Local anarchists had tried to replace political bodies with representatives from producers' syndicates. However, five days after the February 9 coup, Lieutenant Colonel Rosales and his seventy excise police, who were as often employed to put down urban rebellions as to track smugglers, had arrived in Sanlúcar. They arrested the revolutionary committee and reinstated the city council. The Sanlúcar Cantonal Uprising the following June began with an attack on the workers by municipal officials. On June 28, 1873, a Sanlúcar judge closed the FRE's municipal council. Backed by the police, the judge himself crossed town, up the long narrow street that divided the established authority from the *menu peuple*, to the International's headquarters. He dramatically entered the workers' center and declared all its members outlaws on the grounds that they violated sacred rights to work.[18] A hush fell over the town. The streets emptied. Municipal officials, fearing violence, sent to Sevilla and Cádiz for arms, which arrived the next day. Meanwhile, enraged by the judge's provocation, large groups of vinetenders, agricultural wage laborers, shoemakers, barbers, and other syndicalists assembled in the Plaza, surrounded on three sides by government offices.

By 10 P.M. that night, all was quiet. Terrified city councilors, large landowners, estate stewards, and the thirteen British merchants who lived in town vanished, leaving the city to those who dared to keep it. Even the Guardia Civil and the excise police, fearing themselves outnumbered, had withdrawn. At around 10 P.M. that evening, dinner time, the city's silence was broken only by shouts of "Long live the Revolution"; "Long live the International"; "Down with the city council." One man, a barkeeper, was accidentally

---

[18] Accounts from *El correo de Andalucía, El guadalete, El estado andaluza,* and *La federación andaluza,* cited in *El porvenir* (Seville), 3–VIII–1873; and *La federación andaluza,* 30–VI–1873, 1–VII–1873.

shot. The Provincial authorities in Cádiz sent Sanlúcar's representative, Gutiérrez Enríquez, home to set matters straight, but the local petty bourgeoisie and working class, including the peasants who resided in town, were united against him and against Republicans of all kinds.[19] The International was in charge.

It is lamentable that the Sanlúcar anarchists wrote no histories of their own. The historian is left with contemporary newspaper accounts, some reports by outraged bourgeois who returned after the terror, and with Thermidor itself. But scattered evidence seems to indicate that periodic repression by authorities, followed by public recognition that the state was unstable, led Sanlúcar's anarchists to believe that they could seize and hold their town, establishing producers' control of production and administration. The local FRE leaders therefore seized the town hall and constituted themselves a Committee of Public Safety. Clearly democratic in intent, the committee's first act was to hold elections to choose a permanent revolutionary commission. Not wishing to usurp power longer than necessary, they held the elections at 2 A.M. on the morning of June 30. It has not been recorded how many of Sanlúcar's citizens were willing or able to overcome fear or sleep to get out and vote, but the newspapers reported that those FRE members who had been deposed by the judge were elected by acclamation. Aware of the consequences of their act, between 1,000 and 1,500 armed townspeople began to erect barricades throughout the city, digging in to defend themselves against the army that would certainly come to depose them.[20]

Government troops, which arrived from Sevilla on July 2, restored the traditional ruling class, but the barricades remained standing. The rebels received arms by sea, according to official reports. It is almost certain that they did receive reinforcements because the populace, led by the FRE,

[19] *El porvenir*, 3-VII-1873.
[20] *La federación andaluza*, 3-VII-1873; *El porvenir*, 3-VII-1873; Barbadillo Delgado, *Historia de la ciudad*, p. 796.

was able to drive off the army and regain power, which they held for a month. Not until August 4, 1873, when government troops under Colonel Soria Santa Cruz assaulted the city, was the International forced to cede power and flee. During their thirty-three-day reign, the Revolutionary Committee, composed primarily of anarchists, suspended Mass, turned out the Escolapian Fathers, favorites of the dukes of Medina Sidonia, from their school and the Franciscan Mother of God nuns from their convent, and declared a property tax to replace the hated *consumo*, previously the town's leading source of revenue.[21] They destroyed no property. One person was killed accidentally. And perhaps to their discredit, they never got around to distributing land either to workers' associations or to individuals. What happened to the wheat crops, which were generally harvested in June and July, remains a mystery. The wine grapes would not ripen until mid-September, in time for the return of the local ruling class.

As punishment for their relatively mild acts, 150 men and women were imprisoned by the victorious army. An additional 200 rebels were hunted down in the surrounding countryside where they had fled. Counterrevolutionary terror lasted until the fall. Many of the insurgents, all of whom were assumed by authorities to have been anarchists, were transported to the Philippines and Mariana Islands, where several died of tropical diseases. Others rotted in dungeons without ever coming to trial.[22]

Elsewhere in Spain and Andalusia, uprisings took a similar form, but were more easily coopted by the bourgeoisie or repressed by the state. General strikes had swept Alcoy and Barcelona on July 8 and July 13. Under pressure from the right to put down the revolts in which many Intransi-

[21] *Ibid.*, pp. 796–805; *El guadalete*, 8-VII–1873; Nettlau, *La Première Internationale* I, 192.

[22] *Actas* II, 99–100, 105, 149–150; "Carta de Sanlúcar," *El condenado*, 11-IX–1873; "Carta de los trabajadores en las prisiones militares del Castillo de Santiago de Sanlúcar a la comisión federal española," *El condenado*, 6-XI–1873.

gent Republicans were engaged, Pi y Margall, the second president of the First Republic, resigned on July 18. The day before, the draft Republican Constitution drawn up by Emilio Castelar had been presented to the assembly and its drafter became the third president, the one responsible for the repression of the Cantonalist Revolts.

Jerez' ruling class latifundists were able to keep order and turn the town into a staging base for government forces because they had declared martial law and placed the city under the military command of General Tomás Bousa as a result of the harvesters' strike.[23] On July 19, having heard that Sevilla had declared itself an independent canton, Fermín Salvochea, Mayor of Cádiz, summoned his followers in the local militia. They seized the local garrison, distributed arms, and occupied strategic positions. Under Salvochea's direction, local Intransigents constituted themselves a Committee of Public Safety.[24] This type of struggle, typical of Cantonal uprisings throughout Andalusia, made no attempt to reorder social relations. The secession by most southern cantons represented the Intransigents' desire to gain their political independence from the centralists, but it did not entail the radical social changes that would improve the lot of the small producers or day laborers. The one exception to this pattern in Cádiz Province occurred in Sanlúcar de Barrameda, where the relative weakness of the Federal Republicans and the strength of anarchist secular schools, and bakers' and shoemakers' cooperatives, made the class antagonisms much clearer and added a social dimension to Sanlúcar's cantonal insurrection.

Following the 1873 uprisings, 15,000 workers throughout

[23] *La federación andaluza*, 23–VI–1873; *El guadalete*, 9–VI–1873, 23–VII–1873. The best account in English of the political issues at stake in the Cantonalist uprising can be found in Hennessy's *Federal Republic*, pp. 196–243. Our views differ chiefly on the issue of what social forces were at work during the spring and summer of 1873. Martínez Shaw's account of the Cantonalist uprising in Sevilla supports my interpretation.

[24] *El porvenir*, 22–VII–1873; Hennessy, *Federal Republic*, p. 225.

Spain were rounded up and jailed. Having temporarily broken the back of the anarchist labor movement in Sanlúcar, the ruling class cut all wages fifty percent.[25] As a result of his revolutionary activities during the period 1868 to 1873, Salvochea was sentenced to life in the penal colony of Gomera, where he served more than a decade until his escape in 1884. During his long exile, he seems to have read Bakunin, studied the proclamations of the First International and the FRE, and begun to consider himself an anarchist. In Andalusia, the terror, which had begun in August, continued throughout the fall and winter. In Jerez the local hall of the FRE was invaded by the police in October 1873. The women meeting there were insulted and the place was ransacked.[26] At such times, political repression was so intense that it was impossible for the FRE to function. The unions went underground. Since the early anarchist movement in Cádiz coincided with petty bourgeois, worker, and peasant culture itself, authorities could do little to repress it once they had corralled all those whom they could possibly designate as leaders.

If the thirty-three-day anarchist revolution in Sanlúcar de Barrameda in 1873 is any indication, Andalusian anarchists believed that institutional change would occur automatically, and that power would be destroyed during the revolutionary process. This is one explanation for why the Committee of Public Safety in Sanlúcar did nothing to reorganize local power or to establish new political structures for the future revolutionary community; the unions and sections as they were already organized, seemed to suffice. However, the Sanlúcar uprising marked the culmination of

---

[25] Lorenzo, *El proletariado militante* I, 165, 175; Soledad Gustavo (pseud. Teresa Mañé), "La mano negra," *Tierra y libertad*, 8–II–1902; Nettlau, "Zur Geschichte der Spanischen Internationale und Landsföderations 1868 zu 1889," p. 62 (hereafter, "Zur Geschichte"). "Carta de los trabajadores en las prisiones militares del Castillo de Santiago de Sanlúcar a la comisión federal española," *El condenado*, 6–XI–1873.

[26] "Política republicana," *El condenado*, 29–X–1873.

the first phase of Spanish anarchism. Never again would the Andalusian commercial bourgeoisie, organized as Republicans, be able to win support from Cádiz' masses. The Sanlúcar anarchist revolution differed from the bourgeois Federalist Cantonalist revolts insofar as it was dedicated to placing local control in the hands of workers and peasants, not in shifting class domination from the agricultural bourgeoisie to the commercial bourgeoisie. Despite its ultimate defeat, Sanlúcar stood as a beacon for Cádiz' anarchists, just as the Paris Commune remained a symbol for all European socialists of what revolutionary community might be like. The image of collective rule of the masses over themselves was one that even government repression and terror could not obliterate.

CHAPTER V

Repression and its Fruit, 1873 to 1883

Andalusian anarchists have frequently been viewed as terrorist fanatics who acted out of frustration rather than according to a political strategy. A good deal of that interpretation focuses on their actions during the decade from 1873 to 1883, and particularly on the Black Hand trials and the crime wave of 1883. Close examination reveals, however, that Andalusian anarchism underwent a basic organizational change during that period. The region as a whole resisted the insurrectionary exhortations of the Federal Commission. On the other hand, anarchists in Cádiz Province, faced with extreme local repression, attempted to fight against the established order, even by supporting violence as a calculated tactic.

The Cantonalist Uprisings of 1873 brought the house down upon anarchists throughout Spain, and altered relations between the Federal Council and Andalusian anarchists. Anarchists had been visibly involved in the Sanlúcar and Alcoy insurrections, and were blamed in part for the rest. Severino Albarracín, a leader of the FRE Federal Council, which had moved to Alcoy in the spring of 1872, led the uprising there in 1873. By the end of the year, when the Murcia Canton, organized by sailors from Cartagena and supported by the Federal Council, was subdued, the Council and hundreds of other militants were either jailed or in exile. When the FRE met secretly in Córdoba in December 1873, it chose a new Federal Council, changed its name to Federal Commission, and underlined that body's role as a coordinator of statistics and information rather than as a vanguard party.

On January 3, 1874, General Manuel Pavía, who had

led the avenging army of the south the previous summer, overthrew the Republic and established a provisional government. A week later, he turned upon the unions. A government decree of January 10, 1874, outlawed political associations that "conspired against national interests, public security, constituted authority, or the territorial integrity of the country." Since anarchist activity fell into all four prohibited areas, the law effectively reduced anarchist freedom to associate, and forced anarchist unions and sections to reorganize secretly. Local councils, mutual aid organizations, and women's groups that continued to meet in effect became secret societies. Their clandestinity was a matter of necessity rather than of strategy.

The principal weapon of Andalusian anarchism, the general strike, had already come under attack from within the international anarchist ranks. Farga Pellicer and José García Viñas, and the Frenchmen, Carlos Alerini and Paul Brousse, then resident in Barcelona, had represented Spain at the Geneva Congress of the Bakuninist Wing of the First International in September 1873. Without previously consulting their own beleaguered constituency, the Spanish delegates had agreed with other European anarchist leaders that they would abandon the general strike as a tactic because it was too easily coopted by bourgeois republicans. The principle of the general strike had given a political content to union organizations and to all strikes, since any such collective action could have been a potential catalyst to other workers, provoking united attacks upon the capitalist ruling class and the government. If there was to be no general strike, then anarchist revolutionaries needed another tactic. Insurrection was chosen by the leaders of Spanish anarchism, ratifying the Geneva accords at the December FRE Congress in Córdoba.[1]

[1] Lorenzo, *El proletariado militante* II, 124–125. The minutes from the Geneva Conference of September 1873, at which the general strike was rejected after being strongly opposed by José García Viñas of the Spanish delegation, is given in James Guillaume, *L'Internationale:*

Andalusian anarchists did not directly defend the general strike when they met in June 1874 at the Secret Madrid Congress of the FRE, but rather joined other delegates in asking what right the old Federal Council, the new Federal Commission, or even they themselves had to act in the name of others. They argued that no single body among the anarchists was sovereign. Each local was independent, and each trade union was autonomous. They alone could decide whether or not to strike.

The Congress of June 1874 instituted a system of bilateral contracts between local councils or trade organizations.[2] In order to guard against any further erosion of local autonomy, the Congress decided that they themselves and future delegates to anarchist congresses could not make decisions to which their constituents would be bound, and could not make any agreements without prior permission from home. Such decentralization promoted the authoritarianism it tried to prevent. Lacking institutional means through which to make decisions, powerful individuals, especially those united in the secret alliance, could try to rule the entire movement. As long as the locals were strong and open, the Federal Commission merely collected dues when it could, and corresponded with members about local conditions. Once the movement was repressed and the underground movement refused to act collectively, extraordinary ideological power rested with the Commission.

The Commission leaders were dedicated men, but by experience and circumstance they were far removed from their constituents in Andalusia. The Commission was dominated by José García Viñas, Tomás González Morago, and Francisco Tomás, all members of the alliance. Anselmo Lorenzo, the typographer who became the major anarchist

Documents et souvenirs (1864–1878), III, 116–118; letter, October 1929, José García Viñas to Max Nettlau, Nettlau Correspondence, International Institute of Social History, Amsterdam, Holland. See also Morato, *La sección española de la Internacional*, p. 167.

[2] Lorenzo, *El proletariado militante* II, 123.

chronicler, was distrusted because of his closeness in 1872 to the expelled Marxists in Madrid, and unheeded because of his hostility to García Viñas, remained nevertheless on the Commission until 1881, virtually powerless. González Morago, who, like Lorenzo, was a typographer, lacked the latter's common touch, but drew a great deal of prestige and power from his close connection to Bakunin and his leadership of the alliance in Spain.

García Viñas became (according to Lorenzo) the virtual dictator of the Commission during the seventies, when Morago left for France. Anselmo Lorenzo, who despised him, and Peter Kropotkin, who liked him, agreed that García Viñas was temperamentally elitist, aristocratic, and authoritarian. Like many who are intellectually committed to spontaneity, he was compulsive and rigid. Born in Málaga, a physician in his late twenties, García Viñas seems to have been estranged from his Andalusian brothers and sisters. He was outraged by poverty, but like many who have not suffered it, he appears to have been supercilious about workers and peasants' ability to overcome their own exploitation and oppression.[3] García Viñas and his fellow commissioners distrusted the poor because they suspected them of being prepared to sell out to anyone who would pay them a living wage. But this attitude seems to have been shared by many members of the alliance and was, in fact, its reason for existing. They believed that it was their mission to channel and guide popular revolutionary fervor.

ANARCHISM'S CLANDESTINE STRUCTURE

After 1874, the connections between the Federal Commission and any regional chapters other than those in Barcelona and Madrid were tenuous. At least one member of the Commission was supposed to attend each regional secret

[3] The personalities of García Viñas, González Morago, and Francisco Tomás are discussed in Termes, *Anarquismo y sindicalismo*, p. 239. Stafford, *From Anarchism to Reformism*, pp. 84–96.

congress, but Cádiz Province was far away. There is no evidence that the Commission, which continued to be represented in European anarchist congresses that attempted to maintain the First International's Bakuninist wing, had any influence at all in Andalusia.

Spanish delegates from the Federal Commission attended the 1873 Geneva Conference, the 1874 Brussels Meeting, the 1876 Berne Congress, and the 1877 Verviers Meeting, where the Bakuninist wing finally dispersed. They also went to the General Workers' Congress in Ghent, immediately following the Verviers meetings. Remnants of the First International met in Paris in 1878, and again in London three years later, attempting against odds to recreate the unity of the early seventies.[4]

The 1877 Congress of Verviers, the second such meeting following the death of Bakunin in 1876, marked a low point in anarchist affairs. The entire organization was in disarray when González Morago and García Viñas defended the Italian anarchists' theory of "Propaganda by the Deed" to an international organization that seemed incapable of either propaganda or deeds. The following year saw a rupture among international anarchists, between individualists such as Paul Brousse, Peter Kropotkin, González Morago, and García Viñas, against the Swiss syndicalist James Guillaume and the trade union militants he represented. The bankruptcy of the individualist trend in European socialism may have been responsible for persuading many European anarchists, including some Spaniards, of the need to form broad alliances, based on some kind of working-class rather than terrorist organization. For this reason, many from Verviers moved to Ghent for the General Workers' Congress, where socialist and anarchist workers met to try to resolve differ-

---

[4] Termes, *Anarquismo y sindicalismo*, p. 280. A good general study of the development of Italian anarchism in this period can be found in Pernicone, "The Italian Anarchist Movement" (Ph.D. dissertation, University of Rochester, 1971). Lorenzo, *El proletariado militante* II, 211.

ences in the hope of reuniting the socialist and anarchist wings of the First International.

Guillaume and the Italian Andrea Costa argued that some form of political trade unionism was necessary to maximize the power of the world's workers; but Brousse, Kropotkin, García Viñas, and the other Spanish delegates complained that union organization was necessarily reformist. They urged controlled insurrection or "Propaganda by the Deed" as a means of tutoring the will of the oppressed. An early version of this notion was first expressed at the 1874 Brussels Congress, where a Spanish delegate had boasted that "some infamous exploiters will never again insult workers now that houses, factories, and the like have been consumed by flames. . . . This class war will be more costly to the exploiters who will lose their property than to us poor folk who have nothing to lose since they have robbed us of everything."[5]

From 1874 on, Spain's anarchist Commission advised anarchist locals to organize Revolutionary Action Groups or War Committees, to manufacture ammunition, distribute arms, and carry on reprisals against capitalists and oppressors. Throughout the clandestine period, the Commission, located underground in Barcelona, chided the anarchist masses with being insufficiently militant. García Viñas wrote jeremiads for the most important clandestine newspaper, *La revista social*. In May 1879, at the height of famine, he reminded starving workers, "You do well to demand 'bread or work.' But you do little. You must do more. Whatever fills the granaries is yours. It is the sweat of your brows. And since it is yours, you ought not beg, you ought to seize it. . . . Now choose what is preferable: To die slowly, without dignity or courage, watching your children expire, or

[5] Lorenzo, *El proletariado militante* II, 212–218; Tuñón de Lara, *El movimiento obrero*, p. 271. For discussions of "Propaganda by the Deed," see Termes, *Anarquismo y sindicalismo*, p. 234; Stafford, *From Anarchism to Reformism*, pp. 84–96; and Nettlau, *La Première Internationale*, I, 257.

to die with head held high, among your own, with the immense satisfaction of having crushed so many infamies and injustices."[6]

As early as 1872, when anarchists were repressed by Sagasta, the Federal Council had threatened to incite class war. Documents almost certainly belonging to the clandestine period called for all-out war between the oppressors and the oppressed. They demanded that the poor destroy property records in order to reclaim their own rights to land. They incited followers to cut vines, burn orchards, and destroy grain. They argued that since the International was frequently blamed for violence against property, anarchists might as well carry on with destructive works. The rhetoric was very much that of leaders divorced from the ranks—or, what amounted to the same thing, the voice of the alliance far removed from local conditions. It can be argued that, after 1875, the Federal Commission, and García Viñas in particular, was a vanguard without followers. This is not, however, inconsistent with the 1880 assertion by the Federal Commission, composed primarily of members of the alliance, that it had never ceased to function, had never stopped fighting for collective property, and had never given up the hope of creating a federation of independent workers' communities united by pacts.[7]

Unions and sections developed by the FRE in the period before 1874 persisted in Andalusia even after they were banned. The most important structural modification made in 1874 was the division of Spain into decentralized districts called *comarcas*. These district commissions, many of which, like the western and southern Andalusian districts, overlapped, allowed maximum decentralized control. The con-

---

[6] Tuñón de Lara, *El movimiento obrero*, p. 271. The entire document is reproduced in Clara Lida's *Antecedentes y desarrollo*, pp. 418–421.

[7] *La Andalucía*, 26-III-1872, cited in Lida, *Anarquismo y revolución*, p. 255; *Le Révolté*, 29-VII-1879, 3-IV-1880; Nettlau, *La Première Internationale* I, 299–300.

tinued strength of Andalusian organization is evident in the fact that in 1875, when Catalonia had only 33 sections remaining affiliated to the FRE, Andalusia had 42.[8] Representatives from Cádiz, Arcos, Lebrija, Jerez, and Puerto Real attended the Comarcal Convention in July 1876. Subsequent district meetings were held between 1877 and 1880. Delegates from Cádiz, Jerez, Arcos, and Sanlúcar attended the September 1880 meeting. Even with the International underground, some Andalusian anarchists maintained their former agricultural and craft societies. Workers in Cádiz were arrested in the summer of 1874, allegedly because they belonged to an outlawed society. Many such societies survived as workers' circles like the Jerez Workers' Center, and others posed as the consumer cooperatives or mutual benefit associations, out of which they had in fact grown.

But in order to organize political programs, carry out demonstrations, and debate doctrinal issues, Andalusian anarchists often employed a cell organization such as that earlier used by the Democratic party between 1856 and 1866. Cell members knew only each other and possibly one member of a neighboring cell.[9] Whenever a District Commission issued a report, cell meetings were held. The cells also carried on work such as winning increased wages, reduced hours, and improved piece rates, which had previously been the work of the unions affiliated with the FRE. The existence of clandestine anarchist branches presented problems to both contemporaries and to subsequent histori-

[8] Nettlau, "Zur Geschichte," p. 58.

[9] Lorenzo, El proletariado militante II, 143; Termes, Anarquismo y sindicalismo, p. 280; Eiras Roel, El partido demócrata, pp. 176–179; Zavala, Masones, comuneros y carbonarios; "Espagne," Bulletin de la fédération jurassienne (Sonvillier), 10–x–1875, 16–VII–1876. The best evidence for this cell organization comes from the works dealing with the Black Hand trials. Bartolomé Gago de los Santos, one of the defendants, admitted to belonging to 10-person cells. See Los procesos de la mano negra II. Audiencia de Jerez de la Frontera, p. 182 (hereafter Los procesos, II); Soledad Gustavo, "La mano negra," Tierra y libertad, 8–II–1902.

ans. Were the cells secret societies or underground anarchist sections?

In 1877, for instance, a broadside called *The Popular Revolution* (*La revolución popular*) appeared, claiming to represent the views of the Committee of Revolutionary Action. It is not clear whether this was one of the Revolutionary Action Groups' War Committees developed in response to the Federal Commission's 1874 call, or simply some other group that emerged for a short period and disappeared. Nor is it clear whether the Popular Nucleus, which allegedly attempted to organize Jerez workers to build anarchism through whatever means necessary in 1879, was an anarchist cell or merely a figment of authorities' imagination. The year before, in 1878, the Jerez authorities had tried members of a secret society accused of having formed a war committee to promote terrorism.[10] The evidence indicates that the Federal Commission promoted the formation of secret societies, but only through rhetoric. There is no evidence that the Commission ever supplied Andalusian anarchists with arms, advisers, or money. Except for the fact that some of the Andalusian secret societies performed deeds admired by the faraway Commission, there is nothing but rhetoric and perhaps some personal contacts to link the two. Terrorist organizations in the south may have been organizationally independent of anarchism. Some anarchist cells seem to have engaged in incendiarism from time to time, but most of the anarchist cells diligently kept alive pre-1874 unions and cultural organizations.

When the official anarchist organization was driven underground and collective labor activity was outlawed, independent attacks on the ruling class became common, especially during periods of high unemployment, when those workers who were organized were unable to strike. In August 1873, following the repression of Sanlúcar de

---

[10] Nettlau, "Zur Geschichte," pp. 61–62; Waggoner, "The Black Hand Mystery: Rural Unrest and Social Violence in Southern Spain, 1881–1883," pp. 169, 176–177.

Barrameda's communal insurrection, uncontrolled fires swept the countryside. Olive groves burned on Jerez' border with Lebrija, and hay ricks burned in the east.[11]

Foreclosures were as important as general starvation in uniting the petty bourgeoisie in Cádiz Province with the famished mass of unemployed. Between 1874 and 1883 there were bread riots and attacks on property that cannot be accounted for simply by referring to starvation. In bad years, when there was general crop failure, the small proprietors could not pay their mortgages or direct taxes. Many lost their land; others, such as peasants who produced luxury sherry, could not pay their pruners and other hired help. Sharecroppers and tenants were thrown off their plots because landlords of grainfields did not want to pay for seed and credit in years when the crops were certain to fail. The emiseration of all, including the wine-producing peasants, had ramifications in the villages and towns where marginal tradespeople found the majority of their customers too poor to buy food or hard goods. Since the skilled workers, peassants, and shopkeepers were recognized as leaders of anarchism in the locality, the authorities persecuted them. Police took advantage of social disorder to "get" those known to be union men. In late January 1878, the Commander of Sanlúcar's Municipal Police went to the door of Teodoro Chía, a worker who, as a "known anarchist," had been arrested following the 1873 Cantonal revolt. They took him from his home on an icy January day, but instead of carrying him to jail, they brought him to the El Palmar woods. The Police Chief gave the signal to have him beaten, and he was left for dead in a ditch. As he passed out, he heard the Commander say, "I won't be content until all you Internationalists are dead." Chía dragged himself home, where he shared his outrage with fellow workers.[12]

[11] El guadalete, 17-VIII-1873, 29-VIII-1873.

[12] "Espagne," L'Avant-Garde (Berne-Chaux-de-Fonds), 10-III-1878, 20-V-1878; El imparcial, 13-IV-1878; "Carta de los trabajadores en las

Unemployed laborers, unable to carry on political strikes, may have taken to the fields or streets in order to retaliate, but they certainly did not need the exhortations of the Federal Commission. In the spring of 1878, when many from Sanlúcar and the surrounding towns went to Jerez seeking jobs on the grain latifundia, eight thousand field hands discovered that there was no work. On May 8, 1878, field workers divided into groups of twelve and thirteen and went to the central Plaza de Arenal, where they invaded butcher shops and bakeries. Others went into the countryside to requisition animals. They returned to the city and distributed meat. The city placed armed guards at food shops and called the army. That summer, as in 1873, fires swept Jerez' fields, leading authorities to indict workers allegedly responsible for the attacks.[13] In one trial in the summer of 1878, the judge indicated that authorities believed that unrest was not simply sporadic, but was well organized by a secret society. Shortly after the trial, local authorities claimed that they had acquired "a manuscript notebook, of poor penmanship and worse spelling, which stated the aims of a society called *The Upright Poor against the Tyrannical Rich*." By 1879, officials had begun to gather dossiers about illegal political associations.[14]

January, when even those who had been employed were often out of jobs, was a favorite time for preemptive police roundups. Jerez' police imprisoned seven men in January

---

prisiones militares del Castillo de Santiago de Sanlúcar a la comisión federal española," *El condenado*, 6-XI-1873.

[13] *L'Avant-Garde*, 20-V-1878; *El imparcial*, 13-IV-1878; Lida, *Anarquismo y revolución*, p. 248; *Antecedentes y desarrollo*, pp. 441-451; *Revista social*, 1-IX-1881, 8-IX-1881.

[14] Lida, *Anarquismo y revolución*, p. 250; Lida, "Agrarian Anarchism in Andalusia: Documents on the Mano Negra," pp. 321-322. Lida's article is the outstanding work on the Black Hand and its background in class struggle in Cádiz Province. I am indebted to it. Her essay has been translated and reprinted as *La mano negra: Anarquismo agrario en Andalucía*.

1879, claiming to have found documents and attack plans for subversive activities. Nearby in Cádiz and Puerto de Santa María, workers continued to demand work and attack bakeries. The troops were called to Sanlúcar a month later because of looting of markets. The elite of Ronda, on the eastern border, distributed money and shelter to a working class they feared. Troops were kept moving around Andalusia that winter by demonstrations in Granada, Jaén, Ronda, and Arcos, including further attacks on bakeries and granaries. Local officials ordered permanent guards on bakeries and butcher shops. With poverty so widespread, the provincial government distributed funds to the municipalities and imposed extraordinary taxes, which forced the rich to pay so that the poor might eat.[15] Whether officials were in search of scapegoats for the summer riots, or because they held anarchist labor leaders responsible for all rural and urban unrest, known trade union leaders throughout Spain were arrested and accused of subversive activities in June 1879. In Madrid, anarchist assassination attempts on King Alfonso XII contributed to hysteria among the ruling class.

The police tried their hand at provocation. Manuel Sánchez Álvarez, a local field hand in the Jerez area, claimed that Tomás Pérez de Monteforte, captain of the rural police, urged him to act as an *agent provocateur*, organizing others to cut vines and burn grain fields. He was told that if he refused, he would be arrested. Sánchez demurred. Shortly after, in June 1880, Sánchez was arrested along with sixteen others who were allegedly found destroying rural property. They were accused of attacking orchards, vineyards, and fields belonging to large proprietors around Arcos. Sánchez was also said to be a clandestine member of the First International and the author of a handwritten underground anarchist newspaper, *El movimiento social*, which circulated in Jerez and environs. Sánchez must have remained on police

[15] *El imparcial*, 3–I–1879, 12–I–1879, 13–I–1879, 15–II–1879, 19–IV–1879, 24–IV–1879; *Le Révolté*, 17–V–1879, 29–VII–1879.

lists; twelve years later, after the 1892 Jerez Insurrection, he was arrested because he was "a known anarchist."[16]

Despite provocation and repression, associational life in Andalusia remained surprisingly strong, especially after February 1881, when Sagasta returned to power. As part of his liberal program, workers were once again permitted to associate, although the law guaranteeing that right was not effective until the following September. In July 1881, Spanish delegates to the London Congress, organized in order to resurrect the First International, reported that the Andalusian sections not only continued to exist but were more numerous than the Catalan sections. Twenty-four of the forty-eight remaining anarchist locals affiliated with the FRE were in Andalusia. Catalonia had only fourteen.[17] And the number of sections underrepresents Andalusian anarchist strength during the clandestine period, since many unions, cooperative societies, and mutual aid associations, which had once affiliated with the FRE, had long since dropped that connection without discarding what would have to be considered anarchist principles. Bakers, carpenters, masons, coopers, vinetenders, and field hands formerly associated with the First International had continued to coordinate local activities even after the anarchists were outlawed.

Whatever such workers and peasants considered themselves, government officials in Andalusia simply assumed that any organized worker was an anarchist. For instance, Olvera's consumers' cooperative was accused as early as 1879 of being an anarchist front organization. A Jerez cooperative suspiciously calling itself "Legality" in 1879 was believed by the authorities to be an anarchist cell, as was "Anarchy," a Jerez mutual aid association formed in May

---

[16] Núñez de Arenas, *Historia del movimiento obrero español*, p. 131; *Le Révolté*, 24-VII-1880; Nettlau, "Zur Geschichte," p. 63; AMJF 3302:7595.

[17] *Le Révolté*, 22-II-1879, 17-V-1879, 29-VII-1879; Termes, *Anarquismo y sindicalismo*, p. 269.

1881. Their cooperative warehouse, which was active in the summer of 1881, may have been a descendant of the earlier anarchist consumers' cooperative. Sanlúcar's libertarian elementary school, established in October 1872, still seemed to be functioning nine years later—further evidence of the continuity of anarchist life.[18]

Despite the fact that unions were essentially interdicted between 1874 and 1881, Andalusians, especially in the Province of Sevilla, nevertheless carried on some remarkable strikes against wage reductions, for higher piece rates, and for more breaks. When five hundred factory workers in Cambrós faced fifty percent wage cuts in the spring of 1879 they struck, even though there was high unemployment in their region and unions were illegal. The two-month-old strike was put down only when the Guardia Civil began escorting unwilling workers to the factory floor. In nearby Sevilla, electrical workers struck for five weeks that same spring. In September 1881, agricultural workers in Carmona refused to work for low wages and bad food, even though throughout the region, in the neighboring towns of Lebrija, Marchena, and Trebujena, unemployed workers were demanding food or work.[19]

Further support for the argument that anarchist sections persisted locally comes from examining the rapid rebirth of anarchist locals following the founding congress of the Workers' Federation of the Spanish Region (Federación de trabajadores de la región española, FTRE) on September 24, 1881 (see Table 5-1). Salt miners in the Cádiz Bay towns formed a federation of syndicates in December 1881. By 1882 in western Andalusia alone, the FTRE had 19,168

[18] *Le Révolté*, 22-II-1879; AMJF 8:12,627; "Antecedentes de sociedades que se enviaron al Gobierno Civil de la Provincia por tenentes reclamados," AMJF 579 (1923).

[19] *Actas* I, 256–257, 368; *Cartas* I, 148, 305; *Revista social*, 7-VII-1881, 1-IX-1881; *Le Révolté*, 17-V-1879, 29-VII-1879; Quirós, "El comercio de los vinos de Jerez," p. 35; Lida, *Anarquismo y revolución*, p. 252.

Table 5–1

Sections of the FTRE in Northern Cádiz Province, 1881 to 1882

Town	No. of sections in Sept., 1881	No. of members in Sept., 1882	Population in Dec., 1877
Towns centered around Jerez			
Las Cabezas de San Juan	—	10	4,821
Lebrija	1	—	12,859
Trebujena	—	25	3,974
Sanlúcar de Barrameda	2	—	22,770
Chipiona	1	—	2,784
Jerez de la Frontera	3	1,079	64,535
Rota	—	15	8,009
Puerto de Santa María	3	706	22,122
Cádiz[a]	9	687	65,028
Puerto Real	1	129	9,632
San Fernando	—	50	26,836
Medina Sidonia	—	46	12,394
Chiclana de la Frontera	—	25	2,444
Towns centered around Arcos			
Montellano	—	—	5,726
Villamartín	1	—	6,761
Bornos	1	429	5,157
Arcos de la Frontera	2	656	16,283
San José del Valle	—	—	1,006 (Oct. 1877)
Algar[a]	—	—	1,766
Paterna de Rivera	1	25	3,082
Alcalá de los Gazules[a]	—	185	9,294

Table 5-1—*Continued*

Sections of the FTRE in Northern Cádiz Province, 1881 to 1882

Town	No. of sections in Sept., 1881	No. of members in Sept. 1882	Population in Dec., 1877
Towns centered around Ubrique, between Arcos and Ronda			
Olvera	—	—	8,289
Alcalá del Valle	—	180	3,690
Prado del Rey	—	—	3,594
Arriate[a]	1	628	3,330
Grazalema[a]	—	225	8,046
Montejaque	—	—	1,778
Benaocaz[a]	2	203	2,433
Ubrique[a]	4	1,017	4,868
Ronda	—	1,160	19,181

[a]Represented at the Organizational Congress of the FTRE in Barcelona, September 1881.

Sources: Max Nettlau, *La Première Internationale* I, 681-682; II, Tableau II; AMJF *Archivo memoranda 10*, p. 76.

members in 179 sections and 61 local councils, a number large enough in proportion to the working population to terrify the rulers.[20]

THE BLACK HAND TRIALS

Increased union activity was accompanied by widespread violence in the second half of 1881 and 1882, though they were often at cross purposes. Cereal crop failures due to drought in the summer of 1881 ensured widespread poverty in the winter of 1882, although sherry exports remained relatively high. During the summer and winter of 1882, the FTRE national leaders repeatedly begged workers to resist

[20] Lorenzo, *El proletariado militante* II, 233-235; *Le Révolté*, 24-XII-1881; Nettlau, *La Première Internationale* I, 367, 373, 376.

precipitous action.[21] Their fears that terror against adversaries would beget further repression proved correct in the late winter and early spring of 1882 and 1883, when a series of murders, seemingly common crimes, provided an excuse for the police to attempt to stifle the entire organized workers' movement. The authorities claimed the killers belonged to a secret society that was associated with the FTRE and its agricultural workers' union, and attempted to assign blame equally to all workers, peasants, and trade union members. Merely reading an anarchist newspaper was grounds for suspicion after the autumn of 1882.

A tavern keeper, Juan Núñez, and his wife were murdered on December 3, 1882. The preceding day, authorities had arrested seventy-five local workers in connection with violent acts that police attributed to trade unionists. The police claimed that workers suspected that Núñez, in whose tavern they often assembled, was an informer, and considered his murder a lesson to others. A small boy, supposedly a witness to the murders, identified the gang leader as Juan Galán, a field hand who belonged to the FTRE. Galán and his friends were arrested shortly afterwards and charged with murder. Two months later, Jerez police announced that Galán had been ordered to commit his crime by a secret society of anarchist assassins they called the Black Hand. By the time he came to trial during the summer of 1883, political charges were dropped, and he was convicted of attempted burglary and murder, for which he was executed.[22]

Prior to the local government's announcement that Galán belonged to the Black Hand, the Guardia Civil Commander,

[21] *Crónica de los trabajadores de la región española*, Libro I (2 diciembre, 1882), p. 4, cited in Waggoner, "The Black Hand Mystery," p. 189.

[22] *Ibid.*, pp. 162–163, 181; *El guadalete*, 27–II–1883. In late May 1883, reports from Jerez claimed that there was voluminous evidence linking the Núñez murders to secret societies. See *El imparcial*, 28–v–1883. Constancio Bernaldo de Quirós claims in his "El espartaquismo," p. 20, that Galán was thought to be taking the blame for a personal crime committed by his father.

José Oliver, arrested sixteen men, possibly members of the 110-person San José del Valle branch of the FTRE's Union of Field Workers (UTC), for the murder on December 4, 1882, of a former comrade. Continued attacks on property, thefts of food, and ordinary crimes that winter left the Cádiz ruling class in a state of panic. Brawls and murders of agricultural workers were blamed on the Black Hand. The discovery of a skeleton in a remote field, the death of a watchman six months earlier—any unusual occurrence—was attributed in the winter of 1882 to 1883 to the Black Hand or to the UTC or to the FTRE, all of which were taken to be identical. One of the major centers of the Federation was said to be the town of San José del Valle, but its reputation as a movement center must have rested with its relatively large fieldworkers' union and its hunger for anarchist literature, since it had no documented FTRE section in 1882 or 1883.[23]

Several different crimes were blamed on the Black Hand, but most came to trial as criminal, not political cases. Three murder trials were known officially as Black Hand trials. In these, even more than in the others, the prosecution tried to link the murders to the alleged existence of a secret society, the Black Hand. The first trial, for the Crime of the Crossroads Tavern (Crimen de la posada de cuatro caminos), began on May 26, 1883. Four men were accused of having met on April 1, 1883, in the Evora vineyard in Sanlúcar and of having plotted to rob the tavern keeper, Antonio Vázquez. That night, carrying out their plan, they killed Vázquez. The men were convicted of murder and given

[23] Nettlau, *La Première Internationale* I, 681; II, Tableau II, p. 3, col. 6 shows that in October 1882, the San José del Valle anarchist section of the UTC had 110 members, roughly one-tenth of the entire population of the village. Col. 16 shows that 300 copies of the proceedings of the 1882 FTRE Sevilla Congress were distributed in San José between December 1882 and July 1883, at the height of the repression. In June 1883, Enrique Martínez, correspondent for *El imparcial*, claimed that San José was an FTRE center. *El imparcial*, 11–VI–1883; Waggoner, "The Black Hand Mystery," pp. 173–174, 190.

life terms in jail, but the prosecution was unable to prove the conspiracy charge. The verdict set off large but peaceful demonstrations in Jerez' central plaza.[24]

In early March 1883, two 28-year-old agricultural workers were arrested in Arcos in what was to become the second Black Hand trial. Cristóbal Durán Gil of Arcos and Antonio Jaime Domínguez of El Bosque were charged with murder for the August 13, 1882, beating of Fernando Olivera, who died several weeks later. Police claimed the two beat Olivera, a watchman with whom they often worked, for refusing to join the Black Hand, of which they were members. Under torture, Jaime admitted membership in the Black Hand. Cristóbal admitted only to being a member of the International. The trial took place at the end of May 1883, and although the prosecutor could prove neither that the Black Hand existed nor that Fernando Olivera had died as the result of being beaten, Durán received a life sentence for murder and Jaime Domínguez was sentenced to seventeen years in prison for being an accomplice.[25]

The third trial filled the newspapers for weeks; its defendants came to be known and feared by bourgeois citizens throughout Spain. Amid an atmosphere of terror, Jerez' authorities organized a show trial of sixteen peasants and agricultural workers from San José del Valle and its hamlet, Alcornocalejo. Pedro Corbacho was described as the head of the Black Hand secret society, to which all the defendants belonged; he was accused of ordering the execution of his 24-year-old hired hand, nicknamed Blanco de Benaocaz, for quitting their organization.

Nothing about the case is clear. Blanco had left San José del Valle in November 1882 to get seeds from his parents in Benaocaz, and was never seen again. A decomposed corpse was found in a remote field in San José del Valle in

---

[24] *El imparcial*, 28–v–1883, 29–v–1883.

[25] *Ibid.*, 31–v–1883, 2–vi–1883; Waggoner, "The Black Hand Mystery," p. 173; *Los procesos de la mano negra I. Audiencia de Jerez de la Frontera.*

February 1883, which the police claimed to be his, but an autopsy was inconclusive. Some of the accused men confessed to having participated in murder, but all had been tortured. Most admitted membership in the FTRE, which was legal, but all denied ever having heard of the Black Hand secret society. Pedro Corbacho, his brother Francisco, the anarchist school teacher, Juan Ruiz, and a local anarchist union organizer, Roque Vázquez, were charged with masterminding the crime, though it was never alleged that any of these four had actually taken part in it. They were, however, widely believed to be the directors of the Alcornocalejo section of the FTRE, a renowned center of anarchist organizing in the Arcos-Jerez area. Some of those who confessed argued that the Corbachos owed Blanco the substantial sum of 150 pesetas in back wages, and that they had him killed to avoid repaying him. Others said that Blanco had been given a piece of land to cultivate in exchange for part of the debt. Still others implied that Blanco's attempt to seduce the Corbachos' young female cousin caused a vendetta that resulted in Blanco's death.[26]

The prosecution resurrected memories of earlier secret societies, such as the Popular Nucleus, and frequently referred to a document that the indefatigable commander of Jerez' rural police claimed in 1883 to have found under a rock in the hinterland—an unlikely hiding place, to say the least. The document, said to be the statutes of the Black Hand Society, described the structure and goals of an organization of "the poor against thieves and executioners." During the trial, the police "discovered" other secret cabals throughout the south. For instance, toward the end of May 1883, the Guardia Civil of Grazalema uncovered in the village of Benamahona a secret association said to have three hundred members, of whom they arrested twenty-two. The police claimed to have found records that the association had expelled a woman thought to be an informer. All this

[26] Waggoner, "The Black Hand Mystery," p. 169; Lida, "Agrarian Anarchism in Andalusia," pp. 321–322.

took place against a background of anarchist-led harvest strikes, which were going on before and during the trial.[27]

The trial provided insights into the life of agricultural workers in the hill towns around Arcos. Pedro Corbacho, for example, was 34, with a wife and three children. He and his brother and his family were cereal-producing, land-owning peasants who seem to have suffered severe economic decline by the early eighties. Corbacho and most of the other defendants were well educated, and Corbacho was singled out by reporters as being very perceptive and articulate.[28] The story he told the court of his relationship with the deceased indicates the cooperative spirit that may have prevailed among poor wage laborers and poor peasant proprietors. Corbacho claimed that Blanco had been a hired hand for ten months and had proved himself an assiduous worker. Blanco, who was said to have been ambitious, asked Corbacho to hold his salary for him. Since the 1882 crop had been bad, the Corbachos, small grain farmers, lacked cash with which to repay Blanco, and offered him a plot of land to rent in lieu of back wages. Blanco began to plow in late summer, 1882, but unseasonable rains interfered, and Blanco spent nearly seventeen days doing the job, which usually took half that time. Undaunted, he kept working. Then he left on his fatal trip to his parents.

The trial focused on the political allegiance of the defendants rather than on evidence of murder. The prosecution alleged that the Corbachos often met with other defendants at the Parrilla flour mill, on the nearby Barea farm, where anarchist sympathizers read *La revista social*, the official organ of the FTRE.[29] This newspaper was at the time legally printed and distributed, but that fact never came up at the trial. The prosecution implied that to read the journal was to be a murderer. Almost all the defendants conceded that they were members of a workers' society, described

---

[27] *Los procesos* ii, 174; Bernaldo de Quirós, "El espartaquismo," p. 21; *El imparcial*, 6-vi-1883 to 19-vi-1883 covers the trial.

[28] *Los procesos* ii, ix, 250.　　　[29] *Ibid.*, p. 180.

by the shepherd, José Fernández Barrios, as a mutual aid association, the rules of which prohibited whoring and drinking. Only two defendants, the gypsy Cayetano Cruz and the school teacher Juan Ruiz, were positively identified as members of the FTRE. Cayetano, according to most of the defendants, had falsely accused them to authorities; thus he was kept apart from them in jail. Ruiz had attended the 1882 FTRE Congress of Sevilla. Ruiz admitted that he and Pedro Corbacho, for whom he sometimes acted as watchman to supplement his meager school teacher's wages, had read *La revista social*, agreed with the ideas it presented, and organized the Alcornocalejo section of the FTRE in April 1882, which was legal. But they denied that the Black Hand existed or that they had murdered Blanco. Primarily on the basis of their anarchist sympathies, Ruiz, the Corbachos, Roque Vázquez, and three others were convicted of murder and garroted on June 14, 1884.[30]

All socially conscious workers were suspect in Andalusia in 1883. Isabel Luna, the 23-year-old daughter of a Benaocaz laborer, was arrested in early 1883, apparently for being an anarchist school teacher. The local rulers were tormented by fears of secret societies. In places like San José del Valle, remote villages near Arcos where repression was greatest, anarchist workers retained the cell organization of the clandestine period even after 1881. Juan Ruiz himself admitted having read about a terrorist organization, "The People's Tribunal," mentioned in *La revista social*.[31]

The defendants seem to have been feared by the ruling class as working-class leaders more than as terrorists. The Black Hand trial and subsequent arrests of Spain's major

[30] *Ibid.*, pp. 25, 53, 63, 109–110, 117, 132, 177, 364; Bernaldo de Quirós, "El espartaquismo," pp. 23–24; *El guadalete*, 8–III–1883. Alcornocalejo was a hamlet of 41 people in 1877. San José del Valle, the nearest city, had 1,006 people at that time. AMJF *Archivo memoranda 10*, p. 76; Waggoner, "The Black Hand Mystery," p. 180.

[31] Bernaldo de Quirós, "El espartaquismo," p. 20; *Los procesos* II. 64.

trade union leaders demonstrates that even though unions were legal after 1881, the right to read anarchist newspapers, to discuss social issues, and to organize in order to bring about more humane conditions were by no means guaranteed. Local police, the ruling class, and even the British commercial agent in Cádiz took labor organization and crime to be synonymous. Finding one, they always expected to encounter the other. On June 6, 1883, British consul in Cádiz, Gerald Raoul Perry, wrote that "the trials of the 'Mano Negra' or Black Hand Association (Spanish Socialists) are now going on at Jerez de la Frontera, and the general feeling among the well disposed and better classes is, that unless those found guilty of murder are condemned to death and actually garroted, the security to life and property will be but slight in the future, as the association is said to be, in great measure, composed of Andalusian Workmen." Agricultural workers and latifundists realized that improved agricultural conditions, promising a bumper crop in June 1883, would permit workers to use strike threats to demand better conditions and increased wages. The Black Hand trial indicated that the government could execute any worker who might be a union leader. The number of prisoners in Cádiz and Jerez grew from about three hundred in February 1883, when the roundup began, to about two thousand in Cádiz and three thousand in Jerez barely a month later. Remarkably, despite the extraordinary repression, Jerez and San José del Valle workers formed new sections of the FTRE during the spring and summer of 1883.[32]

Recent studies of the Black Hand have tended to focus upon whether such a society in fact existed. Glen Waggoner's "The Black Hand Mystery," taking up traditional Spanish liberal arguments, has effectively argued that the society was a chimera conjured up by local officials. He shares contemporary anarchist arguments that Monteforte

[32] Letter, June 6, 1883. FO 72/1654; Lida, *Anarquismo y revolución*, p. 253; Nettlau, *La Première Internationale* II, Tableau II, p. 3.

and Oliver, with the complicity of state and local officials, fabricated the conspiracy in order to crush the rapidly growing anarchist labor movement. Clara Lida disagrees. In her "Agrarian Anarchism in Andalusia: Documents on the Mano Negra," she describes the long tradition of secrecy in Andalusian social organizations. She argues that the strategy of disciplined syndicalism promoted by the FTRE based in Barcelona was incapable of confronting the widespread and excruciating misery of Andalusian workers. She masterfully documents the existence of associational life in Andalusia. But her thesis that terrorist cells were more appropriate to the Andalusian situation than union organization cannot be substantiated one way or the other until Spanish police archives are opened, and perhaps not even then.

The reconstruction of anarchist organizational strategy must include an examination of anarchist collective behavior. The widespread incidence of strikes even in the clandestine period indicates that some kind of workers' organizations persisted. The defendants in the Black Hand trials readily admitted belonging to unions, mutual aid societies, or to the FTRE. Even under torture, the majority of defendants denied knowledge of any secret society, although undoubtedly many of their FTRE sections had been clandestine in the period between 1874 and 1881. Scattered evidence thus far seems to indicate that the Alcornocalejo and San José del Valle sections of the UTC were centers of Andalusian anarchist trade union organization and were repressed precisely because, as relatively visible branches of a national association, they were particularly threatening to local officials.

CHAPTER VI

Collectivism versus Communism: Unions and Community, 1881 to 1888

The challenge to anarchism in Andalusia was to organize those who were working while, simultaneously, winning solidarity from masses of women and the unemployed. Ideological splits over how this might be accomplished, and about whether workers or the poor community ought to be given priority in the struggle to win anarchism, plagued the FTRE throughout its history in Andalusia. Theoretical issues took political form at the Second National Congress of the FTRE in Sevilla in 1882, when anarcho-communists and anarcho-collectivists split over long-range goals and short-term strategy, a division that reflected fundamental differences between reformist trade unionism and terrorist-prone communalism. The Black Hand trials added pungency to this struggle, but they were probably less significant than the growth of the Union of Field Workers (Unión de trabajadores del campo, UTC) and their Jerez harvesters' strike in June 1883. Though less dramatic, that strike and abortive attempts by anarchist bakers to achieve unity across municipal lines pointed to internal contradictions among Andalusian anarchists, and led them back to promoting mass mobilizations to seize regional power. The strategy of the general strike that had been rejected by Bakuninists at the Geneva Congress of 1873 reemerged in the eighties.

Spanish anarchism had always been two movements. It was partly communalist, in that its potential constituency was the entire community of the poor, including self-employed craftsmen, peasant tenants and small landholders, rural and urban proletarians, housewives, children, and the jobless. But whether or not one uses the term, the fundamental structure of anarchism had always been syndicalist. General organizations such as cooperative bakeries, anarchist schools, and women's societies fit awkwardly into a structure which, in the eighties as in the seventies, organized people primarily by occupational group. The conflict was as old as anarchism. The First International's 1868 Brussels Congress had declared its goal to be the creation of collective property controlled by workers' organizations. After 1868, the French Internationalists had formed trade unions and local federations in Paris, Lyon, Marseille, and Rouen. In Paris, at least, the International's organization was identical to that of the local trade federation.[1] When the FRE held its First National Congress in 1870, it too adopted the federated union structure as its political and economic base. During the clandestine period from 1873 to 1881, the Federal Commission abandoned political trade union strategy in favor of insurrection, though in Cádiz Province unions continued to function locally and carry on strikes. While previously organized workers, especially in the south, defended political union organization, the basis of collectivism, the Federal Commission tried to promote community solidarity through insurrection.

Until 1880, the Commission continued to maintain the fiction that a national Spanish anarchist organization existed. Finally in 1880, demoralized by political impotence and what he considered the reformism of Spanish anarchists, the 32-year-old José García Viñas, who had dominated the Commission, retired from the anarchist ranks, although he maintained personal contact with anarchists such as Peter Kropotkin. García Viñas went home to Málaga and then to Melilla, where he took up his medical practice. A few months later, in February 1881, the FRE dissolved itself.[2]

Scarcely five months later, two Spanish delegates attended

[1] Stafford, *From Anarchism to Reformism*, pp. 9, 17.

[2] Termes, *Anarquismo y sindicalismo*, pp. 256, 269; Morato, *Historia de la sección española*, p. 79.

the London Congress, where some old European trade unionists and Bakuninists attempted to recreate an anarchist international. The July 1881 meeting was a watershed between anarcho-collectivism and its inadvertently reformist tendencies of using trade unions to win immediate improvements in wages and working conditions, and anarcho-communism, the program Peter Kropotkin, Errico Malatesta, and many Italian anarchists hoped to promote.[3] Malatesta and Kropotkin tried to orient the London Congress away from urban working-class problems toward the plight of European peasants and rural workers, who were suffering in one of the worst agricultural depressions in living memory. Calling themselves anarcho-communists, they argued that peasants should expropriate uncultivated land, hold the property communally, and employ the tactic called "Propaganda by the Deed" as a strategy of community warfare against the bourgeoisie through the destruction of property. Their model was what they perceived to be common practice among workers in Russia, Italy, and southern Spain, and differed little from the strategy the Federal Commission in Spain had tried to promote during the clandestine period. However, unlike the old FRE leaders, Kropotkin's and Malatesta's stress upon rural rather than urban conditions made them sympathetic to the need for local anarchists to have complete political autonomy in deciding, on a day-to-day basis, what tactic would inflict the most damage on the local ruling class.[4]

The FTRE, founded in September 1881 from the rem-

[3] Morato, *Historia de la sección española*, p. 176; Cascales y Muñoz, *El apostolado moderno*, pp. 195–196; Pernicone, "The Italian Anarchist Movement," pp. 78–80; Nettlau, *La anarquía a través de los tiempos*, pp. 189–190. For collectivist views about the future, see *Revista social*, no. 81, cited in Urales, *La evolución de la filosofía en España*, p. 109.

[4] Cascales, *El apostolado moderno*, p. 196; "Manifiesto de 'Los Desheredados' (1885)," *La revolución social*, 5-IV-1885, reproduced in Lida, *Antecedentes y desarrollo*, pp. 451–456; *Le Révolté*, 23-VII-1881, 6-VIII-1881.

nants of the old FRE, was dedicated to building solidarity among Spanish workers, but it avoided the issues of casual laborers, the unemployed, and women. Since the organization was formed in Barcelona, the majority of the delegates were also from northern Spain, which skewed political decisions in favor of those who were familiar with factories, urban workshops, and the relatively prosperous peasant agriculture of Catalonia. At its First National Congress in Barcelona, the FTRE adopted anarcho-collectivism as their goal, calling for collective ownership of the means of production, communication, and transportation, but union control of what they called "the integral product" of work.[5] To women and casual laborers in Andalusia, such a proposal may have seemed like the tyranny of unionism over the community.

The issue as it developed in the eighties turned upon the collectivist belief that individual workers' commissions, not society as a whole, had the right to whatever wealth was created. This was a view that skilled workers and peasants in Andalusia might accept, but it would not appeal to the great masses. The unskilled and unemployed in Andalusia gravitated to a program by which the entire community, regardless of occupation, would unite against the established order. As the anthropologist Julian A. Pitt-Rivers has argued, "The concept of the pueblo as the unique political unit was so deeply embedded in the outlook of the peasants that it became a cornerstone in anarchist policy. The anarchists sought, in fact, not to break this political monopoly, but rather to become empowered with it."[6] This community consciousness could be expanded from identification with the pueblo to focus upon the oppressed in the broader socioeconomic network, roughly the province. Such feelings, often expressed in religious terms, were often stronger for the most impoverished anarchists than for the relatively

---

[5] Lorenzo, *El proletariado militante* ii, 233–235.

[6] Pitt-Rivers, *People of the Sierra*, p. 17.

more prosperous skilled workers and peasants, who had provided the leadership for early Andalusian anarchism. In the eighties, peasants, cooperage workers, and bakers increasingly used their unions to win reforms in their own workplaces. In so doing, they came into political and social conflict with anarcho-communists, whose first allegiance was to the community.

1882 CONFLICT IN SEVILLA

The Second National Congress of the FTRE in September 1882 in Sevilla witnessed the development of what amounted to an ideological class war among the anarchists. It demonstrated that there were tremendous discrepancies between the collectivist theory of the majority in the FTRE and those who represented the poor. Fifteen hundred delegates, mostly from the south, attended the Sevilla meetings, which took place against the background of a serious drought. The tensions between those who had work and were organized in unions and the desperate community led an Andalusian group, calling themselves anarcho-communists, to split from the FTRE. They attacked the collectivists for holding bourgeois notions of property and social organization, and for focusing exclusively on the organization of work, while overlooking the unemployment that afflicted the vast majority of Andalusians. Miguel Rubio, a longtime Andalusian militant, took the offensive. He accused the Catalans, especially their leading spokesman, José Llunas, of being petty bourgeois politicians who were blind to the needs of rural proletarians. Where collectivists stressed the importance of individual freedom and "respect for property acquired by individual work," Rubio opposed division of property into small units or parcels of land. He wanted all workshops and land, whether property of latifundists or small producers, to be held collectively. Vicente Daza, an anarcho-communist from Madrid, continued the attack, arguing that community decisions should take precedence over union autonomy.[7]

Although neither collectivism nor communism was a systematic philosophy, they each had some notions appropriate to the class they represented. While the debates between 1882 and 1888 often revolved around how anarchist society might be organized in the future, they had profound implications for contemporary politics. Collectivists promised community ownership of the means of production, communication, and transportation, and union control over the goods produced. The more inventive, skilled, or industrious the workers, the more prosperous they and their unions would be. Each individual workers' commission would make its own political and economic decisions on the basis of its own needs. In the eighties, this collectivist ideology tended to attract the most skilled workers and peasants, especially those engaged in sherry production, because it promised economies gained from collective labor, but individual union ownership of whatever was produced.

Anarcho-communist doctrine was generally associated with Peter Kropotkin's theories; it proclaimed that not only would there be collective ownership of all productive resources, but also common ownership of everything produced. Each person, whether worker or housewife, healthy or infirm, young or old, should have whatever he or she needed from the common storehouse.[8] Decision-making power would be based on full democratic participation rather than representation; it would rest with each individual acting as part of the community of the poor, and could not be delegated to the labor union or social section of which one was a part.

Collectivists, on the other hand, wanted the benefits of

[7] Urales, *La evolución de la filosofía*, pp. 112, 116; Nettlau, "Impresiones sobre el desarrollo del socialismo en España," p. 405.

[8] Ricardo Mella, *Diferencias entre el comunismo y el colectivismo*, cited in Urales, *La evolución de la filosofía*, pp. 116–117; Cascales, *El apostolado moderno*, pp. 245, 281–287.

production to be allocated only to those who had contributed and in proportion to that contribution. This meant that each separate local union would own what it produced. Each individual in it would receive certain shares of the proceeds. In theory, syndicates would trade with one another, with those producing more valuable items profiting from the exchange. The workers' commission would make all decisions unrestricted by the needs of nonproducers such as the aged, the disabled, women, and children, or the needs of the community as a whole. Whoever wanted food had to trade something for it. If they had nothing to trade, because individually or as a group they produced no commodity, they could try to secure aid from those who worked. According to a leading collectivist spokesman Ricardo Mella, writing in 1888, anarchist society would not even be responsible for the care of children or the aged, who would remain the sole charge of their individual families.[9]

Anarcho-communists, on the other hand, wanted communal consumption as well as production. They contended that by temperament, talent, intelligence, strength, and good fortune, people were intrinsically different. But these differences did not mean that some were better than others or more deserving of food or life's other pleasures. True equality, they argued, meant that everyone should get what he or she wanted or needed, whatever his or her abilities or contributions. And true political liberty required that each individual be the final arbiter of what he should do, when he should do it, and what, if any, were his obligations to the union or the community. Anarcho-communists rejected coercion of any kind, and argued that even the principle of majority rule was tyrannical. For them, complete liberty entailed rejecting the authority of any individual or group over any other. They rejected collectivist union politics in favor of a vague notion of community. Their faith that each person was born benevolent and with an innate social con-

[9] Ricardo Mella, *La solidaridad* (Seville), 9-XII-1888.

science made any institutional protection against greed or competition unnecessary. It also precluded the need for any individual to subordinate his wishes to any other individual or group. The attraction of this form of anarchism for the seasonal workers, especially in the hill towns to the east of Jerez, made the anarcho-communist version of anarchism popular among the poorest people.[10]

The debate between collectivism and anarcho-communism at the 1882 Sevilla Congress also covered the issue of violent tactics. The collectivists feared that violence would provoke government repression of unions, while advocates of terrorism argued that the unemployed could effectively use terrorism against landlords and oppressors during the contemporary economic crisis, since the Andalusians themselves knew who the worst exploiters were. Miguel Rubio claimed that there were 30,000 unemployed workers in Andalusia, of whom 14,000 were anarchists. A handful of people or even a single individual could strike a blow for all workers. Rubio argued that "Propaganda by the Deed" warned the wealthy that the poor community as a whole held the rich responsible for their poverty. It also provided poor peasants and agricultural workers with the opportunity to take aggressive action against the ruling class.[11]

Such talk did not endear Rubio or his supporters to the FTRE national leadership or to Andalusian trade unionists struggling for the right to associate. The communists among Andalusian anarchist leaders began to see themselves as marginal to the FTRE because that organization was concerned primarily with the needs of trade unionism at a time when so many of the unemployed poor were facing starvation. The FTRE's own district commission that was centered in Arcos rejected the moderate proposals of the mother organization. Shortly after the Sevilla Congress, the

[10] Cascales, *El apostolado moderno*, pp. 246, 324; Pitt-Rivers, *People of the Sierra*, pp. 220–221.

[11] Nettlau, *La Première Internationale* i, 407; Cascales, *El apostolado moderno*, pp. 241–245.

commission was expelled by its own local council, dominated by syndicates of agricultural workers and vinetenders. Members of the commission were not themselves necessarily terrorists, but they upheld the right of reprisal. The district commission and some supporters, primarily from Jerez, Sanlúcar, and Arcos, in turn expelled members who continued to support the FTRE and to oppose terrorist violence in favor of union organization. The communists, led by Miguel Rubio, Francisco Gago, and Manuel Pedrote, agitator in Sanlúcar and Cádiz between 1873 and 1888, held a secret meeting of their own in Sevilla in January 1883, known as the Congress of the Disinherited (Congreso de los desheredados). They met again in Cádiz in December 1884, and they may have held other local meetings. But their commitment to decentralization, to each community's right to decide what to do, meant that there was very little coordination. It is not clear whether all those who split over the issue of reprisals actually joined the Disinherited Ones, a secret revolutionary anarchist, terrorist group around Jerez and Arcos, or whether the latter considered themselves communist and were synonymous, in fact as well as in name with the group in Cádiz led by Pedrote.[12] Anarchocommunists' policy of support for terrorists does not mean that they were responsible for even a part of the violence aimed at the elite. They merely accepted the validity of a popular tactic already being used by the poor against the rich.

THE UNION OF FIELD WORKERS

The most important organization in Andalusia in the eighties was the Union of Field Workers (UTC), refounded in 1881 just after the Organizational Congress of the FTRE.

---

[12] Nettlau, *La Première Internationale* I, 402, 423–430; Nettlau, "Impresiones," p. 454; Lorenzo, *El proletariado militante* II, 233–239; Lida, *Anarquismo y revolución*, p. 235; Lida, "Agrarian Anarchism in Andalusia," p. 334.

An unfortunately ambiguous name for a labor confederation that organized vinetenders, peasants, cooperage workers, carters, and bakers, the Union of Field Workers had first been founded in April 1872, shortly after the Second National Congress of the FRE. Independent locals had been formed as early as June 1870, and some had affiliated directly with the First International. When the UTC met for its Second National Congress in late May 1873, there were sections of vinetenders, agricultural workers, bakers, and even cobblers and seamen in Sanlúcar, Lebrija, and Jerez.

Initially, the Federal Council of the UTC, seated in Sans, Catalonia, had been independent of the FRE, though they maintained close contact with its leaders in Barcelona. UTC branches had affiliated with FRE locals at will. Finally, at the May 1873 meeting of the UTC, the organization voted to join the FRE. The two organizations shared a single view about strikes. The UTC favored "dignity strikes," which permitted workers to defend themselves against the increased exploitation of such abuses as wage cuts. But the first UTC also tried to promote "scientific strikes," general strikes designed to unite all workers for political goals. By the spring of 1874, clandestine sections of the UTC had been organized in Lebrija, Chipiona, Jerez, Medina Sidonia, San Fernando, and Sanlúcar.[13]

The Agricultural Workers Union had been as crucial to the FRE as it was to be to the FTRE. Seven months before the first UTC affiliated with the FRE, Francisco Tomás of the FRE Federal Council reminded the UTC Federal Council about the importance of uniting all agricultural workers, regardless of skill or relation to production. Recognizing differences among tenants, small peasants, and landless laborers, he still believed that there was room for solidarity among them. He advised them to "let the day laborers demand increased wages and the tenant farmers lower rents

[13] Molnár and Pekmez, "Rural Anarchism in Spain and the 1873 Cantonalist Revolution," pp. 173, 175–176, 180–181; Nettlau, *La Première Internationale* ii, Tableau i.

or that they be permitted to pay one-quarter or one-fifth share of their harvest instead of half. The small farmers in their turn will benefit when the price of their produce goes up. Once solidarity has been established between agricultural workers, the fight against the robbers may begin. These last will be the only ones to suffer the consequences, while all workers will obtain an improvement in their living conditions. To attain this result, all must be fully aware of the situation. Knowledge of the facts will help us to reach our goal."[14] Clearly the FRE Federal Council conceived of the agricultural workers' union as a means of achieving broad-based political solidarity.

Shortly after the First National Congress of the FTRE in late September 1881, the new UTC was formed (see Table 6–1). Between February 1881, when Sagasta regained power, and September, when the right to organize was guaranteed, official pressure against labor unions was somewhat diminished. Eight hundred vinetenders in Sanlúcar (where the UTC had had a 200-member vinetenders' union in 1872) struck during the summer of 1881, at the time of the last pruning before harvest. Spanish representatives to the International Anarchist London Congress of July 1881 had claimed that there were still anarchist locals, presumably including UTC members, in Arcos, Benaocaz, Cádiz, Jerez, Puerto de Santa María, Puerto Real, Sanlúcar, and Ubrique. At the organizational meeting of the new UTC the following September, there were branches of the union in Arcos, Arriate, Bornos, Benaocaz, Chipiona, Jerez, Lebrija, Paterna de Rivera, Puerto de Santa María, Sanlúcar, Ubrique, and Villamartín. It seems more than likely that in at least some of these towns, the UTC had enjoyed an unbroken organizational history. By September 1882, when its official rules and regulations were approved at the Second National Congress of the FTRE in Sevilla, the UTC, as distinct from the FTRE, had 104 sections with 20,915 members in Spain. Of

---

[14] *Cartas* I, 117, translated and cited by Molnár, "Rural Anarchism," pp. 182–183.

Table 6–1

Anarchist Organizations in Northern Cádiz Province, 1881 to 1882

| Town | September 1881 | | September 1882 | |
	UTC sections	Total sections[a]	UTC members & sections	Total members & sectio
Towns centered around Jerez				
Las Cabezas de San Juan	—	—	— (1)	10 (1
Lebrija	1	1	103 (1)	— (1
Trebujena	—	—	25 (2)	— (1
Sanlúcar de Barrameda	2	2	530 (1)	— (1
Chipiona	1	1	50 (1)	— (1
Jerez de la Frontera	2	3	850 (2)	1,079 (7
Rota	—	—	— (1)	15 (1
Puerto de Santa María	1	3	391 (1)	706 (7
Cádiz	—	9	40 (1)	687 (14
Puerto Real	—	1	15 (1)	129 (5
San Fernando	—	—	— (1)	50 (1
Medina Sidonia	—	—	— (1)	46 (1
Chiclana de la Frontera	—	—	— (1)	25 (1
Towns centered around Arcos				
Montellano	—	—	200 (1)	— (1
Villamartín	1	1	230 (1)	— (1
Bornos	1	1	425 (1)	429 (2
Arcos de la Frontera	1	2	617 (3)	656 (4
San José del Valle	—	—	110 (1)	— (1
Algar	—	—	110 (1)	— (1
Paterna de Rivera	1	1	22 (1)	25 (2
Alcalá de los Gazules	—	—	175 (1)	185 (2

Table 6-1—*Continued*

Anarchist Organizations in Northern Cádiz Province, 1881 to 1882

| Town | September 1881 | | September 1882 | |
	UTC sections	Total sections[a]	UTC members & sections	Total members & sections[a]
Hill towns entered around Ubrique, between Arcos and Ronda				
Olvera	—	—	720 (1)	— (1)
Alcalá del Valle	—	—	160 (1)	180 (2)
Prado del Rey	—	—	— (1)	— (–)
Arriate	1	1	566 (1)	628 (3)
Grazalema	—	—	200 (2)	225 (2)
Montejaque	—	—	50 (1)	— (1)
Benaocaz	1	2	196 (2)	203 (3)
Ubrique	1	4	770 (2)	1,017 (8)
Ronda	—	—	1,125 (3)	1,160 (5)

[a]Includes local councils, cooperatives, mutual aid societies, schools, unions, and women's sections.

Sources: Max Nettlau, *La Première Internationale* I, 376, 681–682; II, Tableau II; MJF *Archivo memoranda 10*, p. 76.

these, 3,000 members were in Cádiz Province alone, with another 2,000 in the towns on the eastern border.[15]

[15] Nettlau, *La Première Internationale* I, 273, 376, 610, 612; II, Tableau I, II; *Revista social*, 7-VI-1881, 7-IX-1882; *Le Révolté*, 4-II-1882; *La autonomía* (Medina Sidonia), 18-II-1883. The UTC was not the only Spanish labor confederation whose importance has been overlooked. Few historians have noted the high degree labor organization in Spain in the eighties, but anarchists themselves were aware of their labor history. Manuel Buenacasa, a twentieth-century militant, author of *El movimiento obrero español: Historia y crítica, 1886–1926*, had planned to write on the FTRE and its unions between 1881 and 1885. His notes are in his 1928 manuscript in the Nettlau Collection of the Institute of Social History, Amsterdam. I am grateful to Rudolf de Jong for permission to consult Buenacasa's writings.

The UTC was exceptionally strong in Arcos, Grazalema, and other hill towns east of Jerez, where salaries were generally one-half those paid in Jerez or Cádiz. In July 1882, Andalusian UTC branches held a regional meeting in Cádiz, where they affirmed the collectivist principles laid down by the FTRE the previous autumn. They appointed their own regional commission to coordinate syndical activities in the Jerez-Arcos area, and specifically excluded workers who favored violent tactics. By the autumn of 1882, cities such as Arcos and Ronda each had three sections of the UTC. In Arcos, one section was devoted to vinetenders, and another, about three times as large, to agricultural workers. The remainder were bakers, carters, and coopers. In the hill towns around Ubrique, almost half the UTC branches had several sections. Multiple sections may be due to a variety of causes, but large numbers is the most likely. Workers in these isolated and oppressed mountain towns were organizing themselves relatively openly into trade unions. The ruling class may have been frightened about their numbers, but they certainly had no reason to imagine that these were *secret* societies. There was even a UTC newspaper, *La autonomía*, which commenced publication in February 1883 in Medina Sidonia. Following the Black Hand trials and the harvesters' strike, it was moved to Sevilla in October 1883.

Some groups of local workers preferred to work outside unions, perhaps to join the anarcho-communists. Others refused to join anybody. Government repression against organized workers intensified in December 1882 and throughout the spring and early summer of 1883, during the Black Hand scare. Since it is plausible that rapid growth in the UTC caused the authorities to imagine conspiracies among their workers, it is equally plausible to imagine that workers under duress might choose to maintain a low profile. Quite the contrary. Despite the threat from authorities, UTC members around Arcos openly used their syndicates to defend workers' interests. In May 1883, the Arcos section of the UTC announced that it had expelled an old comrade, Antonio Guerrero Capote, who had become a foreman and had been exploiting workers on behalf of the boss. This minor incident indicates that despite the numbers of militants jailed by late spring 1883, trade union activities and the day-to-day struggles of workers against employers continued, albeit in localized ways.[16]

THE 1883 HARVEST STRIKE

The first major test of the UTC in Cádiz Province came in the spring of 1883. Weather and cereal growth indicated by February that, barring unusual winds or rains, grain production in June would be the best in a decade, thus providing anarchist workers an opportunity to demonstrate their right to organize and strike for better wages. Agricultural workers might show how they viewed the production process in their trade, and what wage rates they wanted for each task. They might also attempt to establish their right to determine who should work.

The British vice consul in Jerez, himself a leading sherry merchant, described traditional harvest practice in Jerez: "from time immemorial the reaping has been done by squads of men from the North [sic] of Portugal or from the Alpuharras [sic], coming here under the leadership of Capataces or manijeros who contracted on their behalf with the farmers for the reaping of the Beans, Barley, and Wheat produced in this district. These contracts were made on the basis of so much per acre and on the conclusion of the work, in the event of any dispute arising the ground was measured by an expert, or land surveyor, the party losing having to pay the expense of such measurement. This system seems to have worked well for a long series of years but the Portuguese, of whom there are supposed to be more

---

[16] Nettlau, *La Première Internationale* I, 367, 452, 601; "S.A.F. y F.J.T., secretario de sección, Arcos," *La autonomía*, 3-VI-1883.

than two thousand (2,000) hanging around the Town, influenced no doubt by the Trade Unionists or Secret Societies, refuse to adopt this form of labour and demand exorbitant daily wages insisting on say 12 reales for Beans, 16 for Barley and 20 reales for Wheat. They allege that the area reaped has always been understated by the Farmers, and that when measurements have been made he has even bribed the experts against them, this evidently a futile pretence for in more than fifty years during which I have known this neighborhood there has been no dispute not amicably settled, and though some abuses may have been committed, the Capataces or manijeros [foremen] are all practical men not likely to allow themselves to be deceived to a serious extent. The fact is that the actual Cereal Crop is unusually abundant, and that these men besides looking to their own interests, are instigated by the Unionists, and have succeeded in placing the Farmer in a dilemma from which he will with difficulty extricate himself, except by a heavy loss. Fortunately the weather has been moderately cool and has not prematurely ripened the grain, but the Beans are beginning to drop from the pod, and in a few days the Barley will be fully ripe, the Wheat will also shortly follow and unless soon reaped must inevitably perish."[17]

Piece work, which had been employed in Jerez agriculture for at least twenty years prior to 1883, was one of the crucial issues over which latifundists and workers struggled. In 1883, a piece worker could harvest about 14 acres in 40 days, for which he would earn 125 pesetas, possibly his total income that year. At daily wages, however, it would take him sixty days to harvest the same area, for which he would receive 150 pesetas.[18] Employers argued that increasing the harvest pace on the latifundia helped workers and management, since the risk of losing unharvested crops

[17] Letter, June 6, 1883 signed by Vice Consul George William Suter, FO 72/1654.

[18] "Un agricultur explotado," *La autonomía*, 12–VIII–1883.

through inclement weather was reduced if the ripe grain was brought in quickly. But Andalusian field hands preferred to work an additional 20 days for 25 pesetas more, since they could expect enforced leisure the rest of the year.

The strikers demanded the reintroduction of day wages, which would vary according to the crop picked or harvested. The demand for a daily wage for Portuguese as well as the local laborers was, in effect, an attack on the contract labor system by which foreign migrants undercut local wage rates. But it was also an attack upon the latifundists, whose surveyors undoubtedly cheated the agricultural laborers. Their alternatives were to accept the expert's judgment, paying him out of their own pockets if they lost, or to lead other workers out on strike. A successful agricultural strike entailed persuading the indentured Portuguese, either through inducements or threats, to join the struggle.

A contemporary journalist sympathetic to the landowners assessed the situation in Jerez. He claimed that "in this district there are a large number of workers always disposed to provoke and support conflicts of every kind. The worker of Jerez is, above and before all, a vineyard worker or, as some say, an 'oficial de viña.' Among these it is impossible to speak of agricultural work other than work on vines. They have no desire to work as domestics, nor to be sales people, nor transporters, nor anything else. Thus their families live in the greatest misery." He related their militance and that of the Portuguese migrants to their alleged stupidity. "The miserable workers from the Alentejo and the Algarve," he wrote, were "as crude as they were ignorant and incapable of understanding that they were being duped by skilled manipulators." He did not believe they were the organizers of the strike. The leaders, he thought, were the people from the Sierra who, though less numerous than the Portuguese, were more firm in their position. They, in turn, were supported by more than one thousand poverty-stricken Jerez workers. He blamed their resolve upon the International, especially on the stand taken at the Sevilla Congress of the FTRE against piece work.[19]

The strike was relatively well coordinated. For instance, on May 26, 1883, fifty harvesters on a farm about three miles from Jerez refused to work or to leave the fields. Troops were brought in to push them out. This strategy was repeated, thereby drawing in troops and police. The proprietors increasingly pleaded with the government to provide troops to bring in the harvest. The growers, supported by Mayor Bertemati of an old Democratic party sherry vinting family, repeatedly urged the Portuguese to accept increased piece wages. The Portuguese Consul in Cádiz was brought in to urge his compatriots to return to the fields. But the Portuguese and their supporters in Jerez and the hills held out for daily wages. Unable to force their men to accept a compromise, Portuguese contractors began to speak of "invisible forces" that were at work.

The Spanish FRE Federal Council had been exiled in Lisbon in the summer of 1871. They took their forced vacation from Spain as an opportunity to organize in Portugal, and succeeded in founding a Portuguese anarchist organization, which may have had an influence on contract laborers traveling to southern Spain. Although in 1883 the migrants were dependent upon their Jerez wages, each time they were rounded up in the central plaza and escorted to the fields, they fled and returned to town. Local authorities blamed the International, and there is some reason to believe that the strikers' solidarity was organized by the UTC. Authorities blamed the strike on the FTRE which, it was said, even supplied the striking Portuguese with food to sustain them during the strike.[20]

The government responded with repressive decrees and finally with troops. Allegedly to prevent terrorist acts that

[19] Nettlau, *La Première Internationale* I, 373; *El imparcial*, 27–v–1883, 28–v–1883, 29–v–1883, 5–vi–1883.
[20] *El imparcial*, 8–v–1883, 1–vi–1883, 5–vi–1883.

strikers might use to support their demands, the governor of Cádiz Province stepped in and issued ordinances to defend property against possible attacks by strikers, in effect limiting the mobility and civil rights of the entire working-class community. Any worker found walking or riding on a back road would be fined. Carters were required to have licenses stipulating what they were carrying and to what destination, clearly a government attempt to limit the dissemination of anarchist literature, often carried up from Cádiz by wagon. Overseers were to present authorities with lists of those they employed, and especially with lists of those they fired. Workers with past police records could be rounded up if there was any property destroyed in their neighborhoods. And "persons found in the proximity of fire, or destruction of property, *which is not proved to be accidental*, shall be regarded as the supposed authors of such damage, and in default of any suspects, the blame shall be attached to those persons composing the Local Committee of the so-called Workingman's Association." Such stringent laws were, of course, too inclusive to enforce. But if the third Black Hand trial, which was going on simultaneously with the strike, was not sufficient to persuade workers that they ran tremendous personal risks challenging the agricultural bourgeoisie by unionizing, the new decrees made it clear that when workers acted collectively they forfeited their civil rights.[21]

As a last resort, when they failed to crush the strike through political repression, the state openly supported the latifundists by bringing in the army to act as scabs and harvest the crop. The government brought in about two

[21] This proclamation by the governor of Cádiz, Eduardo de la Loma, issued on June 4, 1883, was included in a report made by the British consul in Cádiz and sent to his government. FO 72/1654. In their book on French strikes, Charles Tilly and Edward Shorter argue that the state was concerned with public order rather than with repressing the working-class movement. *Strikes in France, 1830-1968,* p. 39. The evidence for Spain indicates that the state presumed that the organization of workers was synonymous with political disorder.

thousand soldiers, paid them lower wages than the strikers were demanding, and attracted other laborers fearful that their one annual job opportunity would be lost if they did not go back to work. The troops and the beaten laborers, some of whom decided to return to the fields once the strike had been lost, brought in one of the finest wheat harvests in living memory. But breaking the strike cost the growers a great deal. A discussion of the Jerez strike in the Cortes revealed that sending two thousand soldiers to the harvest was actually more expensive than paying workers the daily wages they desired.[22] But the issue, as both sides recognized, was not money, but control over work. The proprietors won the first round of struggles with the UTC, but following 1883, possibly due to the strength of organized labor, field workers' wages maintained a comfortable margin over bread prices (see Figure 1–2 on p. 26).

The issue of the harvesters' strike takes on added importance when juxtaposed with the Black Hand trials taking place simultaneously. Although official after official claimed that workers had the right to organize to improve their working conditions, they purposely tended to confuse militant unions with secret societies allegedly dedicated to robbery and murder. Troops occupied in the fields would not be able to pursue criminals. Strikers congregating in towns menaced the established order. The rapid and visible growth of the UTC in late 1882 and early 1883 was further cause for alarm. Those convicted in the third Black Hand trial, for which the verdict was handed down in the middle of the strike, were leaders of the FTRE in San José del Valle. Some may also have been directors of the UTC there. With a population of just over a thousand in San José, the UTC chapter there had 110 members in 1882.

Cádiz' Union of Field Workers was weakened by the Black Hand trials, by the arrest of thousands of union men, and finally by losing the Jerez strike. Even as they met in

[22] *El imparcial*, 13–VI–1883.

Valencia after the FTRE's Third Congress in October 1883, trade union members, including members of the UTC, were being jailed throughout Spain. Nevertheless, representatives from Montellano, Medina Sidonia, Prado del Rey, Paterna de Rivera, Villamartín, Ronda, and even from San José del Valle and Benaocaz attended the October 1883 UTC meeting in Valencia. Undaunted, the delegates went on with their work, discussing whether as an organization they should attack the practice of sharecropping and how they would organize general strikes in the future.[23] They did, however, take the precaution of moving the UTC's Western Andalusian Commission headquarters, as well as *La autonomía*, from Medina Sidonia to Sevilla, where it was undoubtedly safer.

The year 1883 marked a turning point in political activity among Cádiz agricultural workers. The possibility that secret societies continued to exist alongside the FTRE provided an opportunity for contemporary authorities to blur the difference between *carbonari*-type plots and trade union activities, and to repress any attempt of labor to organize. If both terrorist societies and unions were secret, it was because even during so-called legal periods, workers in Andalusia were prevented from organizing. Even when labor activities were permitted, unions were required to present the governor with membership lists, which he generally passed on to the police.[24] The governor demonstrated that he believed that so long as unions did not act collectively, so long as organizers did not try to persuade workers to join them, unions were legal. But the governor seemed to think that union organizers' attempts to win others to their position was tantamount to interfering with latifundists' rights.

[23] "F.T.R.E. Acuerdos del congreso de la unión de los trabajadores del campo celebrado en Valencia los días 9, 10, 11 de octubre de 1883," *La autonomía*, 14–X–1883. The debate about sharecropping ran in *La autonomía*, 2–XII–1883 through 18–III–1884.

[24] Waggoner, "The Black Hand Mystery," p. 182.

Bakers and Women's Problems with Collectivism

Despite repression, labor activity increased in Cádiz Province between 1885 and 1888. The UTC continued to emphasize workers' discipline and control over the work process. But as the unions grew, so did reformist tendencies to improve wages and working conditions rather than build power for social revolution. Bakers were extremely important in this process. In small cities such as Puerto de Santa María, San Fernando and Sanlúcar, numerous bakeries employed hundreds of workers. Since the majority of the population ate little else than bread, and since bread was often part of the salaries paid to agricultural workers, its quality and price were a crucial issue to the entire population.

Bakers were the cutting edge of the UTC, between the more numerous agricultural proletarians, whose services were required only two or three months of the year, and the highly skilled coopers and vinetenders, who formed an elite among the anarchist working class. During the summer of 1881, before workers' associations were formally legalized, Puerto de Santa María's bakers union had struck for over two weeks, demanding a one peseta wage increase and thirty-six ounces of bread. They also had proposed that the number of workers in a given crew be increased from four to six. Scarcely eighteen months later, in February 1883, just as workers throughout the area were being jailed in connection with the Black Hand trials, Santa María's UTC bakers' syndicate had attempted to coordinate a strike among all the bakers in Cádiz, San Fernando, Jerez, and Sanlúcar. They demanded better working conditions and more power over bakery work. One hundred forty members of the UTC bakers' section complained of twelve- to eighteen-hour shifts through the night. Most of all they complained that the machines that were being introduced would rob them of their jobs. Before that happened, they wanted clearly defined rules about what rights they had and what obligations their employers had toward them.

While they issued reformist demands concerned with control over the specific job situations, rather than revolutionary calls for the transformation of work, given the level of repression at this time the mere presentation of collective proposals was usually seen as a revolutionary act by employers and authorities. Nevertheless, many of the demands were inconsistent with anarchist egalitarianism and revolutionary ideology. They were clearly designed to improve conditions of workers in a single trade and to improve conditions of skilled workers more than those of the unskilled. For instance, the bakers established sliding wage scales. They stipulated nine different job categories ranging from the master of the bakers' peel (the shovel upon which the loaves were passed into the ovens) to second-level apprentices. The workers in each category were to receive money, in declining amounts, from 4 pesetas a day at the top to 1 peseta a day on the bottom. In addition to money, each worker was to receive 36 ounces of bread. These demands were not exorbitant. At the time, the government considered 1.6 pesetas a day to be the minimum daily sum required to feed a family in Andalusia. An adult male generally ate 12 ounces of bread a day, leaving 24 ounces for the rest of the bakery worker's family.[25]

Santa María's UTC bakers also asked for control over hiring, claiming that they did not wish to work with individuals who did not respect their union. They demanded a closed shop, in which anyone who wanted a job had to join the bakers' union. The bakers required, in effect, that the union function as a hiring hall through which syndicate members would determine who would work. Between mid-

[25] *Revista social*, 11–VIII–1881. The detailed discussion of bakery practice in Cádiz Province in 1883 comes from "Reglamento de la sección de obreros panaderos para el año de 1883: Dictamen," *La autonomía*, 18–II–1883. Report on agricultural workers' wages was made by Victoriano Doctor to the Commission on Social Reforms, 1883, and is cited in Tuñón de Lara, *El movimiento obrero*, p. 265. Rate of consumption is given in *Revista social*, 28–VII–1881.

October and mid-November 1888, Cádiz bakery employees struck. The Santa María bakers had requested a 1-peseta daily wage plus 36 ounces of bread for the lowliest bakery employees; nearly six years later, neighboring bakers in Cádiz demanded only 1.25 pesetas daily wage plus 35.2 ounces of bread. The employers' association broke the strike that followed by having the governor arrest the strikers. Then they signed a contract with nonunion bakers for a 1-peseta daily wage. Since the highest salaries were determined in relation to the lowest, this meant the more skilled bakers also lost their demands.[26]

These bakers strikes underline some of the flaws in the collectivist UTC's strategy. Despite Santa María's valiant attempt to unify bakers throughout the Cádiz Bay towns in 1883, they could not persuade UTC sections from different municipalities to ally, even around a trade demand. The local autonomy guaranteed them by both the FTRE and by their union isolated each local syndicate from others in their trade. As relatively privileged people in towns where unemployment was so high, such exploited workers tended to be isolated from the rest of the community. Lack of unity, either among different town syndicates or between workers in the same trade in the different communities, weakened individual unions which, as a result, could be easily defeated by local ruling classes.

Another flaw in the anarcho-collectivist strategy was their ambiguous treatment of women, which also contributed to their lack of ties to the community as a whole. Collectivist practice, going back to the seventies, was to organize everyone in the community, if not into a union, then into a section or a workers' circle. The FRE had had miscellaneous sections, which had included journalists and physicians as well as groups of housewives. This practice continued among anarcho-collectivists after 1881 with the FTRE. But there was a conflict between anarchist unionism, which or-

[26] *La autonomía*, 18–II–1883; *La solidaridad*, 21–X–1888, 18–XI–1888; *Bandera roja* (Madrid), 15–VI–1888.

ganized people primarily around collective work, and feminism, which was a communalist demand for equality between the sexes. There is no question that women in Andalusia were increasingly employed outside their homes at the end of the nineteenth century. In Jerez in 1871, for example, very few women had been engaged in agriculture; but by 1883, quite a large number were employed seasonally picking beans and olives for one-half the salary paid to male harvesters. During the same period, when women were employed in offices or in shops, they were paid one-quarter the salary paid to men for the same work.[27] This was obviously a union issue. Anarchists were made aware of the problem of working women when two young female textile workers from Sevilla, Manuela Díaz and Vicenta Durán, addressed a session of the 1882 Sevilla Congress of the FTRE. They asked that the congress issue a statement about the rights of women. One representative who supported them argued that recognizing the rights of women would lead female workers to form unions within the FTRE. And the 1882 Congress unanimously declared their support.

The ensuing growth of women's sections paralleled the growth of UTC locals in the hill towns east of Jerez (see Table 6-2). Female school teachers such as Isabel Luna of Benaocaz must have been responsible for initiating some of the women's sections that emerged throughout Cádiz Province between 1881 and 1884. Arcos' female group seems to have been among the most active, but there were also women's sections in Benaocaz, Jerez, Grazalema, Villamartín, and Arriate. Even Algar, the entire population of which was 1,766 in 1877, had a women's group. It was quite rare at the end of the nineteenth century for women to work alongside men; therefore UTC locals, which organized around specific jobs, were probably sexually segregated. Since women's sections seem to have arisen in and around Cádiz Province only where the UTC was strong, it is likely that many of the women's groups were unions of female agricul-

[27] AMJF 199:10,506:73, 81.

Table 6–2

Some Collectivist Sections around Northern Cádiz Province,
1881 to 1884

Town	Number in UTC chapter	Women's section
Towns centered around Jerez		
Lebrija	103	unknown
Trebujena	25	unknown
Sanlúcar de Barrameda	530	yes
Chipiona	50	unknown
Jerez de la Frontera	850	yes
Puerto de Santa María	391	unknown
Cádiz	40	unknown
Puerto Real	15	unknown
Towns centered around Arcos		
Montellano	200	unknown
Villamartín	230	yes
Bornos	425	unknown
Arcos de la Frontera	617	yes
San José del Valle	110	unknown
Algar	110	yes
Paterna de Rivera	22	unknown
Alcalá de los Gazules	175	yes
Hill towns centered around Ubrique, between Arcos and Ronda		
Olvera	720	unknown
Alcalá del Valle	160	yes
Arriate	566	yes
Prado del Rey	—	yes
Grazalema	200	yes
Montejaque	50	unknown
Benaocaz	196	yes
Ubrique	770	yes
Ronda	1125	yes

Sources: Max Nettlau, *La Première Internationale* I, 681–682; II, Tableau II.

tural workers rather than sections that united all poor women. There is no evidence that collectivists created associations of the poor women who usually raised chickens and goats, sold eggs or milk, and kept a little garden to feed the family.[28] Such women could not be organized into unions around their work. Although in the seventies the FRE seems to have tried to organize women around such practices as infant initiation into anarchism, there is no evidence of this kind of activity in the eighties. However, since failure to baptize one's child was tantamount to admitting anarchist membership at the time of the Black Hand trials, women may have continued their anarchist rituals in secret, while conforming to church demands in public.

Women contributed to the growth of anarchism by providing community spirit and support. Lyrics sung in and around Arcos in 1883 at the time of the bakers' and agricultural workers' union campaigns indicate that women did support the unionization of men. For instance, one song laments, "I asked my dark-haired girl why she scorned me, and she calmly told me to join the union." Another demonstrates that more militant workers made better husbands. "If you want pleasure in life with rights assured, marry a worker who is a union man."[29] It is not clear that these songs were sung by women. Even if women supported unions

[28] Describing the situation in Grazalema in the 1950s, Julian Pitt-Rivers wrote, "In Alcalá [pseud. Grazalema] women do not normally work in the fields for hire, though it is common in the plains of Andalusia for girls and even elderly women to go out in parties to weed upon the large farms. They are most commonly seen there working separately from the men. . . . On the other hand, it is quite frequent for wives or daughters of poor families to help in work upon the family plot of land, weeding or harvesting, or sowing the seeds. Women are most commonly seen working in this way in the *terrazos*, and the spraying and harvesting of grapes is mainly women's work." *People of the Sierra*, p. 86.

[29] These lyrics were recorded by Leopoldo Alas (Clarín), who was the correspondent for *El día* in Jerez covering the Black Hand trials. They are reproduced in Bernaldo de Quirós, "El espartaquismo," pp. 18–19.

and union men, that does not mean that the unions gave the vast majority of women any power over their own work or their life situation. Women required something other than syndicates to tie them to the broader community. Nor were the unions, as such, appropriate for the majority of men in the hill towns who, for most of the year, derived their income from the occasional labor that included making charcoal, collecting esparto grass, or poaching. Unions could improve the conditions of their own members, but did not appreciably alter the lives of the people outside.

Disintegration of the FTRE

The FTRE was brought down by a combination of repression and reformism. Reformism weakened the unions, separating them from each other and from the community as a whole, thereby making repression easier. What appeared to be purely theoretical debates about the ideal allocation of community resources were, in fact, crucial issues in everyday life during the eighties. Collectivist federations like the UTC were loose associations of separate locals of bakers, vinetenders, agricultural workers, carters, and coopers. Whereas the communists had argued that everyone, regardless of age, sex, or ability was entitled to equal economic benefits, the collectivists, as demonstrated in the wage scale demands, believed the more skilled should get more money, thus reinforcing old hierarchies. Another problem was that collectivist syndicates tried to win improvements for workers in particular occupational groups in particular places, further splintering the communal movement.

Conditions in the late eighties were little better than they had been in the early eighties. In Grazalema's judicial district, comprising Ubrique, Benaocaz, El Bosque, and Benamahoma as well as Grazalema itself, people were so desperate that prisoners begged to remain in jail, where they were fed, rather than return home to starve. The strength of capitalist latifundist grain producers in Cádiz Province could not be fought piecemeal. The political and economic power of the dukes of Montpensier and the Ponce de Léon family were extraordinary around Arcos, Bornos, Villamartín, and Prado del Rey.[30] It required mass workers' organizations united for common benefit rather than individual unions seeking piecemeal gains to confront the political and economic power these latifundists wielded. Better still, in the view of some thoughtful anarchists, would be a strategy that united the collective power of the unions with the massive power of the community.

The importance of violence as an anarcho-communist tactic has been overemphasized. The communists were, it is true, preoccupied with the might of the state and the ruling class, and approved the use of terrorism against them, but they were relative amateurs. In towns like Arcos and Ubrique, where daylight robberies and murders were common, the rich were under siege even without anarcho-communist organizing. Virtual class war was part of the daily life in the eighties; communists hoped it would continue as long as oppression continued. Communists believed this kind of resistance should be encouraged so long as it was impossible to channel the united power of the community into broader social revolutionary organizations.

The Black Hand murders were part of a general crime wave in Cádiz Province in 1882 and 1883; but the FTRE's response to them is demonstrative of their divorce from the remote areas of Andalusia and the desperation of collectivists for the right to organize. In March 1883, as the roundup of Andalusian workers was at its height, the FTRE issued a statement reasserting its collectivist principle that everyone should receive the "integral product of his work." After the trials were over, and after the Jerez harvesters' strike had

[30] A moving report written in 1888 by a judge who had been in Grazalema first appeared seven years later, during a subsequent depression. Juan J. García Gómez, "La miseria en Andalucía," El corsario (La Coruña), 21-II-1895; Madoz, Diccionario geográfico, II, 484.

also been defeated, the FTRE held its Third National Congress in October 1883 in Valencia. While the accused murderers of Blanco de Benaocaz were appealing their sentences, the FTRE denounced the members of the Black Hand association as criminals, assassins, and robbers, and dissociated itself from them. The FTRE seems to have accepted authorities' allegations that the Black Hand organization actually existed. They assumed that Andalusian renegades such as the Disinherited Ones or the communists were among its ranks.[31]

The FTRE continued to hold national congresses. But the Barcelona meeting in 1884 had only sixty-four delegates present, instead of the fifteen hundred who had attended the Sevilla Congress two years before. No one but the Federal Commission bothered to attend the 1885 Barcelona Congress, and a pitiful sixteen delegates came to the 1887 Madrid meeting. The FTRE finally gave up and dissolved itself in September 1888 in Valencia.

But this dissolution of the national organization did not mean that anarchism was dead in Andalusia; on the contrary, it opened the door to greater regional autonomy among Spanish anarchists. Representatives from twenty-five Andalusian cities and nine other areas had come to the secret congress in Cádiz in December 1884. Once the FTRE ceased to be a factor with which they had to contend, the Disinherited Ones asked in 1886 to be readmitted to Jerez' local council, which had remained strongly collectivist despite the many secret societies and communist groups there and in the surrounding hill towns.[32] They were accepted back.

Whatever power skilled workers had over employers would have been significantly reduced without the solidarity of people in the locality. Solidarity was particularly im-

[31] Lorenzo, *El proletariado militante* II, 250–251; Nettlau, "Impresiones," p. 455.

[32] Tuñón de Lara, *El movimiento obrero*, pp. 282–283; Lida, *Anarquismo y revolución*, p. 258; Nettlau, *La Première Internationale* I, 453, 455.

portant to organizations of unskilled workers whose neighbors were the chief potential strikebreakers. Trade union consciousness would not have sufficed in such situations to keep hungry laborers in neighboring towns from breaking strikes of locally organized workers. Only the anarchist communal strategy was successful in convincing people to support organized workers in their struggle against their employers and against the state.

As the FTRE was disintegrating, anarchist trade unionists met in May 1888 in Barcelona to form the Spanish Federation for Resistance to Capitalism (Federación española de resistencia al capitalismo), a weak labor confederation generally called the Pact of Union and Solidarity (Pacto de unión y solidaridad). Grazalema was the only town in Cádiz Province represented at the meeting, which called for solidarity pacts between workers in different trades and among workers in the same trade in different localities. To a certain degree, this proposal represented a return to the traditional collectivist structure first delineated in 1870. But the Pact organization added a new twist; the association was to unite all workers' groups, whether anarchist or not. The final Valencian 1888 meeting of the FTRE the following autumn broadened the definition of anarchist to include all individuals, societies, groups, circles, and journals that accepted anarchy as their goal, whatever their tactics. Thus the FTRE attempted to reunite collectivists with communists and other community people. Militants committed to the need for political cadres and fearful of reformist inclinations of organizations based on unions created a direct political successor to the FTRE called the Anarchist Organization of the Spanish Region (Organización anarquista de la región española, OARE).[33] Many belonged to both the Pact and the OARE, since one was a general labor confederation and the other a political group.

[33] Tuñón de Lara, *El movimiento obrero*, p. 335; *La solidaridad*, 19-VIII-1888; *La Révolte* (Paris), 25-X-1888; Elorza and Iglesias, *Burgueses y proletarios*, p. 18; Woodcock, *Anarchism*, p. 368.

The conflicts of the eighties were resolved through the evolution of a new theory, a compromise between anarcho-communism and anarcho-collectivism, known later as anarcho-syndicalism. It attempted to combine union strength with community organization. By placing increased stress on workers' centers, cooperatives, mutual aid associations, and women's sections, collectivism and communism were able to overcome the localism of the former and the willful dissociation of the latter. In the late eighties, anarchists in Cádiz Province tried to forge a new movement by rejecting reformist economic strikes or terrorism in favor of the general strike, a tactic designed to unite organized workers of the entire province with people in the community against capitalism and the state.

The tactics that united workers and the jobless were mass demonstrations and boycotts, many of which were organized through mutual aid associations, cooperatives, and workers' circles. The Pact was used by Andalusian anarchists to help build a regional alliance of the poor, whatever their class. The Pact's main activity was to unite all the oppressed, whether or not they were employed, around May Day demonstrations calling for the eight-hour day. Tacticians argued that while strikes could be beaten by importing strikebreakers, it took the army to defeat a massive community uprising. They also attempted to educate people about the boycott as a tactic to put community pressure on individual oppressors. The boycott, Andalusian anarchist newspapers explained, was a technique developed in Ireland, where it prevented a tyrannical landowner, Captain Boycott, from getting laborers to work for him and thus forced him to give up his land. This method, as the anarchists noted, had already been effective in the United States. The boycott enabled people of different classes to unite against a single oppressor without jeopardizing their individual jobs.[34]

[34] Philip Rodney, *Captain Boycott* (Dublin, 1966); *La huelga general*, 25-XII-1901; Brecher, *Strike!*

If the unions and the sections established the organizational preconditions for anarchist revolution, the tactic designed to unite them was the general strike. The general strike as developed in Andalusia was a tactic that relied on community support of organized workers. Unemployment for so large a portion of the population made strikes of any kind difficult to carry off. The anarchist combination of workers' commissions and sections such as women's groups, workers' centers, and cooperatives therefore filled the gap created by the high rate of unemployment. Only by coordinating all the poor organized in their sections, and keeping them informed by pamphlets and newspapers, could the Andalusian anarchists even hope to challenge the government and capitalism. The general strike, really a mass mobilization of the community, could take advantage of the weight of numbers rather than of particular workers' strategic positions in industry and commerce. The general strike as it developed in Cádiz Province enabled militant unions and equally militant community people to march together against an oppressive system rather than fight alone against individual capitalists.

CHAPTER VII

We the Workers of the Fields

The general strike periodically resolved the contradictions between reformist trade unionism and communalism, tendencies that had plagued the Andalusian movement in the eighties. The three most important general strikes in Cádiz Province were in Jerez in January 1892, the Cádiz Bay area in 1902, and Alcalá del Valle in 1903. Very little was spontaneous about them. In all three, workers and peasants, by uniting community associations around the leading trade unions, were able to attack the ruling class and the government with at least some success. These attempts to seize and hold key areas for anarchism used old community organizations, but also began what would become a new regional insurrectionary tradition that became synonymous with Andalusian anarchism.

Anarchist militants who had devoted themselves to union activity attempted to establish some coordinating body that might give workers leverage over political authorities. In November 1888, representatives from Jerez and Alcalá del Valle met to discuss a unified committee for organizing agricultural workers, since the UTC had officially been dissolved along with the FTRE the previous September. They planned to call a congress before the first of the year to consider creating a new agricultural workers' federation and to discuss strategies of social revolution. To that congress they would invite all collectivists and communist agricultural workers. The Alcalá del Valle group described themselves as "socialist without adjective" while these Jerez workers now considered themselves communists. But they were concerned with devising a unified regional strategy.[1]

---

[1] "El congreso comarcal de Andalucía del oeste a todos los traba-

By May 1890, anarchists in Jerez, Puerto de Santa María, and Cádiz employed May Day demonstrations for the eight-hour day to unite workers and community people. As anarchists noted, the tactic had been developed in the eighties to demonstrate international solidarity among workers. Agricultural laborers joined with other workers and the poor in these community efforts to transcend the reformist unionism that had previously characterized Andalusian anarchism in key centers such as Jerez. Fermín Salvochea, the former Federalist who had been jailed for nearly a decade, during which time he became an ardent anarchist, returned to Cádiz in 1886, founded *El socialismo*, and attempted to reunite communists and collectivists. Salvochea used his paper to build support for the 1890 May Day demonstrations in Cádiz. For Spanish anarchists, such demonstrations were political strikes designed to show the ruling class how powerful the poor community was. Anarchist journalists claimed that Spanish strikes had reached revolutionary proportions in the spring and summer of 1890.

Authorities made a determined effort the following year to suppress the May Day activities. On April 28, 1891, Salvochea was arrested along with his aides, Juan José García and José Ponce. The anarchist rank and file refused to be intimidated, and 5,000 people attended a protest meeting on April 29. The police responded by arresting another leader. In spite of the arrests, 6,000 people marched in Cádiz on May 1, shouting "down with the bourgeoisie!" and "long live anarchism!" Several days later, explosions rocked Cádiz, killing a worker and four young people. The police blamed the still incarcerated Salvochea and his newspaper. They organized a midnight raid on the newspaper's offices and claimed to have found bombs. Those who were present at the time of the raid were arrested, the paper was closed, and several weeks later Salvochea was rearrested.[2]

---

jadores, abril 1887," *El socialismo* (Cadiz), 15-VI-1887; D.V.R., "Remitido," *La solidaridad* (Seville), 4-XI-1888.

[2] "La jornada de ocho horas," *La alarma* (Seville), 12-IV-1890; "La

The struggle for the right to organize continued to be a principal activity of the anarchists. Repression enhanced communalism in the nineties, and increasingly workers in one area came to the aid of others through mass demonstrations and solidarity strikes. Mobilizations in Cádiz and neighboring towns in the province continued, and may even have accelerated despite mass arrests. In August 1891, authorities accused 157 Jerez workers, many of whom probably belonged to the agricultural workers' union, of being members of the Black Hand. The government intentionally confused the UTC local in San José del Valle with the Black Hand in 1882 and 1883 (see Chapter V); it is probable that they also did so for the Jerez agricultural workers' cell in 1891.

The first congress of the Agricultural Workers of the Spanish Region (Organización de agricultores de la región española, another OARE), apparently the organizational successor to the UTC, met in Córdoba in December 1891, just five weeks before the Jerez de la Frontera insurrection. Peasants and agricultural workers from twenty-one different places, reputedly representing thirty thousand constituents in Andalusia, called for coordinated uprisings. They claimed that the government had created a news blackout on strikes and demonstrations in an effort to discourage coordinated labor activity. They urged members to communicate directly through anarchist newspapers, which were still reporting labor insurgency. But they knew that without a specific strategy, the "idea" of revolution was not enough to win the masses. The congress therefore discussed how to unite sharecroppers and rural proletarians, how to clarify peasant ideas, and how to develop revolutionary propaganda.[3]

---

huelga general," *La alarma*, 27-IV-1890; *La Révolte*, 24-V-1890, 28-VI-1890, 9-VIII-1890, 30-V-1891; "Las huelgas," *El socialismo*, 16-VI-1890; Rocker, *Fermín Salvochea*, p. 28; (Ricardo Mella, anon.), *Los sucesos de Jerez, 8 enero 1892-10 febrero, 1892*, p. 9.

[3] "Congreso de agricultores de la región española celebrado en

But, having discussed all this, one-third of the delegates refused to put peasant organization on a permanent footing by forming a solidarity pact among agricultural workers in different localities. All the organization could agree upon was that they should, once again, organize massive May Day demonstrations that spring. Anarchists were hampered by their deep commitment to democratic principles and their opposition to majority rule. A clear majority wanted to carry on coordinated action around the issue of agricultural employment. But a large minority refused.

Those who wanted to act apparently proceeded with their plans. While neither Jerez nor Cádiz was represented at the December 1891 congress, Bornos, Benaocaz, Lebrija, Ubrique, and Arcos, from which many of Jerez' agricultural workers came, were represented, and there was a great deal of organizational activity in the entire region. *El productor* of Barcelona, the voice of Spanish anarchism once the FTRE had dissolved, circulated widely through the countryside. Just as workers had met to read *Revista social* in the early eighties, they gathered in sheds and in cafes to read *El productor* in the late eighties and nineties. Almost every little anarchist town in Cádiz Province had its correspondent who reported upon social conditions and indignities suffered by workers and the poor. Each town had a distributor—often a barber—who collected money for subscriptions, distributed copies, and held discussions in his shop. It is also likely that in towns such as Alcalá del Valle, where there was a strong women's section of agricultural workers, the women took at least one subscription.

In the winter of 1891, one of those charismatic organizers dreaded by local authorities appeared in Andalusia. Félix Grávalo Bonilla, a bricklayer from Madrid, settled in Jerez. Supported by passing the hat whenever he spoke, he traveled to anarchist sectional meetings in and around Jerez.

Córdoba los días 30 de noviembre y 1 de diciembre de 1891," *El corsario*, 31–1–1892.

Through his sharp intellect and his practical experience he seems to have clarified anarchist ideas and contributed to unifying different local groups. He probably attended the OARE (henceforth these initials refer only to the agricultural workers' union) Córdoba Congress in early December. Shortly after that conference, a group of Jerez anarchists, possibly with Grávalo among them, met in Lebrija, about sixteen miles to the north of Jerez, to plan a coordinated uprising in the two cities. The Guardia Civil broke up the assembly. Fearful of revolt, Mayor Valverde of Jerez conferred with Brigadier General Castillejo, commander of Jerez' army garrison. In late December or early January they arrested sixty-five radical workers, mostly known anarchists. On January 8, representatives from Arcos, Lebrija, Sanlúcar, Puerto Real, Puerto de Santa María, Bornos, Montejaque, and Grazalema allegedly met in a barbershop on Arcos Street in Jerez.[4]

The Jerez Insurrection that occurred on the night of January 8 may at last have been what the local authorities had feared, a revolution to seize the entire Jerez region and establish an anarchist community like that the Sanlúcar workers tried to create in 1873. There were, in fact, simultaneous uprisings in Arcos, Lebrija, and Ubrique the night of the Jerez Insurrection, and rumors of aftershocks in Bornos, Benaocaz, Montejaque, and Grazalema in successive weeks. On the other hand, the 1892 Jerez Insurrection may have been intended primarily to free the prisoners. It is also possible that, as in so many earlier uprisings, workers may simply have been using violent political means to assert the right to associate. There is no evidence that the Italian anarchist Errico Malatesta, carrying out a propaganda tour near Jerez at the time of the insurrection, had prior knowledge of the event, but he must have been delighted by the show of force.

Compared to the May Day marches in which thousands

<hr/>

[4] Bernaldo de Quirós, "El espartaquismo," p. 25; *La Révolte*, 20-II-1892; *El imparcial*, 10-I-1892, 19-I-1892, 23-I-1892.

demonstrated to authorities their allegiance to anarchism and their open hostility to the established order, the Jerez Insurrection was rather small, but extremely well organized. The specter of the peasant masses brandishing sickles and pitchforks as they marched into town had haunted the "better classes" in Europe since the peasant wars of the sixteenth century. Five to six hundred such peasants, not all of them landless laborers, attacked Jerez at 11:30 P.M. the night of January 8. Coming from the east and north, they poured down Calle Larga, Jerez' fanciest street, where the rich shops and cafes spoke of the town's extraordinary wealth. They headed for the army barracks, the government buildings, and the jail, where many of their comrades from the previous May and August were held captive. Some observers reported that the rebels attempted to win over the troops at the garrison, regulars who came primarily from the surrounding towns of Bornos, Lebrija, and Arcos. Arriving at the barracks, anarchist workers such as Antonio González Macías called upon the soldiers to hold their fire, since they were brothers. The army did not join the insurrection, but they shot at the anarchists only reluctantly, one reason why only one worker was killed and why so many of the rebels escaped unharmed. Had the army gone over to the anarchists, their insurrection might have been at least temporarily successful. As it happened, the police were able to defend the jail and the city hall, and drive the rebels back before large numbers of people from Jerez came to their aid. Immediately after the insurrection three anarchist leaders allegedly met in the Ducha vineyard and grain-producing district to plan future activities.

Official reports claimed that some people from town did participate in the rebellion, but not according to anarchist plan. A group drinking in a tavern heard the shots. They shouted, "A Republic has been established tonight. It must survive. Down with the bourgeoisie!" As they staggered from the bar, they pounced on Manuel Castro Palomino, a young clerk returning from a late night at the tax office.

173

Shabbily dressed but wearing the gloves that distinguished the bourgeoisie from those with calluses on their hands, Palomino was mauled by the mob. One man nicknamed Busiqui allegedly struck him in the face with a sickle, shouting, "Die, Bourgeois!" Another man, said by authorities to be the 34-year-old el Lebrijano, a friendless agricultural worker who lived in town with his wife and child, then attacked and beat Palomino; eventually the corpse was mutilated by the mob. Another man, José Soto, a traveling wine salesman, was also found in the streets, his body torn limb from limb. This crime was blamed upon the shoemaker Antonio Zarzuela, who had previously been arrested for violent behavior.[5] One worker, caught in the crossfire as he went to work, was killed, probably by the soldiers in the garrison, but no one was brought to trial for his murder. The killings reveal the high level of class rage among the poor, which was usually repressed but was discharged periodically in Spanish towns during revolutionary upsurges.

But there was also a more distinctively anarchist political aspect to the insurrection, which seems to have been planned as a seizure of the town by organized peasants and workers. According to the forced testimony of Zarzuela, local anarchists had been organizing a massive demonstration since the previous May. Allegedly, fourteen thousand workers from all over the district had been scheduled to assemble at 7 P.M. on January 8. One thousand were to meet at a place in Caulina and four thousand in Tablas, about four miles from the city of Jerez. Because of heavy rains, many stayed

[5] Bernaldo de Quirós, "El espartaquismo," p. 27; AMJF 3302: Telegramas. AMJF 3302 contains the police reports on individual suspects and correspondence about the Jerez events. Although individual documents are numbered, and those numbers are given here, the section is in nearly complete disarray. The account of the uprising itself and some of the "confessions" said to be deposited are not now in this section. It is, nevertheless, an extremely rich source of information on several hundred local workers arrested or questioned in connection with the insurrection. The best general coverage of the Jerez Insurrection can be found in *El imparcial*, 10–1–1892 to 12–11–1892.

away. Others were afraid. The contingent from the Sierra did not arrive on time, and only the Caulina group, diminished by half, actually entered Jerez at 11 P.M. that night.

Other observers reported that a well-organized band of peasants and field hands entered Jerez from the direction of the ancient Caulina vineyards and the Caulina and Tablas plains, the richest wheat and truck gardening district in Jerez. The agricultural workers of the plains, the tenants and proprietors, "masterless men" who worked the irrigated plots or *huertos* in stream and river beds or below water mills, and the pruners and tenants on the vineyards, had been highly organized by the UTC in the eighties and probably by its successor, the OARE, in the early nineties. According to police reports, disciplined troops dressed in farm workers' clothing came from the direction of the farms and vineyards of Huertas de Cabra Coja, Huerta Vista Alegre, Ducha, and Vico. As authorities reconstituted events, men like the 24-year-old José Vázquez Escalante, a worker in Ducha, had helped organize others to march on Jerez as part of an intricate battle plan. Luis Jacuarto from Jerez, and his friend Juan Barea Domínguez from Ubrique were regularly employed on the Vico farm. They and others in the hill towns were said to belong to an anarchist society called "The Pines" which may well have organized this march of hill people into Jerez. Once inside the city, they were met by the 18-year-old baker José Crespo Sánchez, who, according to plan, led them to steal guns and two cannons. Crespo, who was to become one of the leading militants of twentieth-century Andalusian anarchism, seems already to have been a well-known anarchist leader in Jerez. In 1892, his activities were used by the government as evidence that the insurrection was a relatively well-coordinated political attack upon legitimate government.

Despite the planning, the uprising was put down by the police, who seized some people that night and spent the succeeding months scouring the countryside for the rest. The organizers almost certainly expected local masses to rise up to support them by attacking government offices and building barricades as they had done in 1868 Cádiz, 1869 Jerez, and 1873 Sanlúcar de Barrameda. But the earlier insurrections had occurred either in direct response to government repression or in response to the disintegration of the state. Had the organized anarchists been able to hold on longer in 1892, or had they prepared the ground more thoroughly, many might have come to their aid. As it was, the insurrection did not take. Most of the militants escaped, but only for a short time.

The revolt provided authorities with a legitimate excuse to go after those they believed to be responsible not only for the insurrection but for the labor militance of the previous six months. For that they needed a case against Salvochea, who had been safely in Cádiz jail during the uprising. After being threatened with torture, the anarchist labor organizer Félix Grávalo agreed to cooperate with the police and testify as a witness to conspiracy. Grávalo was not arrested until January 14, nearly a week after the insurrection. Within days of the uprising, others, including two barbers, José Fernández Lamela and Manuel Díaz Caballero, had been charged with organizing the assault upon Jerez. According to Grávalo's testimony, probably derived from police intelligence, Lamela, Díaz, and José Sánchez Rosa had gone to visit Salvochea in jail and had then hatched the plan for the insurrection. Lamela was standing outside his Arcos Street barbershop, where local workmen often congregated, at 4 P.M. on the afternoon after the fighting, when the police came to arrest him. They charged him with leading the revolt. At the time of arrest, the police listed his political beliefs as "unknown," but the admitting officer associated barbers with anarchists, since the Barbers Union had always been one of the most important local anarchist sections.[6]

Sánchez Rosa was also a logical choice for the police.

[6] AMJF 3302: 1473, 6142, 6323, 6363, 6677, 9537; *Los sucesos*, pp. 15–16; *El imparcial*, 12–11–1892.

Destined to be one of the most active labor leaders in the south, this native of Grazalema lived most of his life in Jerez and Alcalá del Valle, each of which was a hotbed of labor agitation when he was around. Although nothing is certain about his 1892 activities, he was arrested on January 11 and charged with being an anarchist leader. Apart from Grávalo's testimony, there was no evidence linking Crespo, Sánchez Rosa, or Díaz the barber with secret plots by Salvochea or with the uprising. Nevertheless, all three were given life sentences (which were later reduced). Salvochea, who was accused in a secret letter written by Grávalo, was condemned to twelve years at hard labor. His living conditions in jail were so bad that this saintly man, who had already spent fully half his life in prison and in penal colonies, tried to commit suicide. He was saved and released in 1899 under a general amnesty. Between then and his death in 1907 at 88, he was repeatedly forced to flee from police in Spain and North Africa.

Others less famous also suffered terrible injustice as a result of the terror following the insurrection. Grávalo was again the key witness. The police were not content merely with locating a plot, apprehending murderers, and putting away Salvochea. In an attempt to destroy the labor movement, they marched Grávalo through town and the fields; he picked and chose, pointing out people who had allegedly participated in or had been leaders of the movement. Grávalo admitted in 1893 that he had falsely accused many of the anarchists because he was threatened with torture if he refused to act as the police demanded.

The government focused on the anarchist newspapers as the key means by which the rebellion was organized. The barber Lamela described how he came to be designated by the police as "director" of the insurrection. According to his official statement the "24-year-old barber, son of Alonzo Fernández and María Lamela, native of Benaocaz, citizen of Jerez . . . declared that on January 9 at four in the afternoon, I was detained in my establishment by a pair of rural police and was brought before a judge who asked me if I recognized a package of *El productor* and another of a new journal, I think the *Boletín oficial* [the newspaper to which he referred was the *Boletín oficial de los trabajadores en hierro de la región española*, the anarchist iron workers' journal] which was found in the mail by the authorities with my address on them. I said that although the packages came in the name of M. Ramírez Díaz, they were for me. At once I was carried off to jail and put in solitary. So I remain today. (January 25, 1892)"

Several months later, the rural police tracked the suspected anarchist newspaper correspondent Manuel Ramírez to the vineyard on which he worked, but they could discover no complaints about his conduct. A year later, in January 1893, a judge in Jerez claimed that Manuel's brother, Juan Ramírez, was reporting on conditions in Jerez' jail to the anarchist newspaper *El productor*. The municipal police finally unraveled their problem. They claimed that Juan Ramírez was really Manuel Ramírez Díaz, who had two brothers, José and Domingo. Manuel was the regular correspondent of *El productor* and sent daily dispatches. The brothers were from Bornos, but they lived and worked in Jerez most of the year. Manuel was in prison, so José had become the correspondent and signed J. Ramírez.[7] The reports he was sending dealt primarily with hygienic conditions and lack of medical treatment for those arrested in connection with the 1892 uprising.

The government continued even a year after the rebellion to investigate the networks through which anarchist news was disseminated in Jerez, for these same networks were responsible for the spread of the labor movement. Authorities probably knew that anarchist newspapers were generally sent to one person in a city for distribution. In fact, the police had probably known about the system for a long

---

[7] AMJF 3302: 6142, 8832, 8893, 9177; *Los sucesos*, pp. 22, 33–34; *La Révolte*, 22–IV–1893; Rocker, *Fermín Salvochea*, pp. 29–31; *Tierra y libertad*, 4–III–1904.

time but, since the publication and distribution of anarchist literature was legal at that time, they waited until the insurrection to haul in anarchist journalists, who could be charged with no specific crime.

To find out more about the anarchist network, the police and the Guardia Civil introduced the widespread use of torture. On the night of January 22, Lamela was dragged from his cell and forced to *listen* to them torture Manuel Díaz. Then he himself was tortured. José Sánchez Rosa was also taken from jail to the barracks and tortured until he begged for death. He was told that death was too easy for him. Díaz, who had had the misfortune of having taken in Grávalo as a lodger when the latter was an important trade union organizer, suffered for his mistake. Possibly because Grávalo knew his movements so well, Díaz was viewed as another important link in the anarchist news network. A week after the insurrection, he claimed that the police entered his home and asked what kind of periodicals were read in his barbershop and if he knew Grávalo. The police left and then came back a few days later and arrested him. He was taken to jail. In late January, he was brought to the Guardia Civil barracks, where again Félix Grávalo was present. Díaz too was beaten until he pleaded for death. But they continued to question him about an alleged meeting at Ducha. He said he had attended no such meeting. The police lieutenant then said he would kill him if he denied having been there. Díaz was taken to a cell where Lamela lay in chains. Next they took Lamela and forced Díaz to listen in turn to his friend's shrieks of pain. Díaz and Lamela were then taken, along with Grávalo, to a farm in Ducha and to the Sangarriana farm nearby. The police chief Revilla ordered the shed at the Sangarriana farm opened and asked Grávalo whether the meeting had taken place there. He answered affirmatively. He also volunteered that the men had often come to this shed to read *El combate*, another important anarchist paper. Díaz and Lamela denied any association with the place. They were then returned to prison, kept in dark cells, and intermittently tortured for another fourteen days.

On February 5, Díaz was asked if he knew José Sánchez Rosa; he claimed he did not. He was only then told that Grávalo confessed that Díaz, Lamela, and Sánchez had gone to Cádiz prior to the uprising to receive orders from Salvochea. Díaz admitted that they had gone to Cádiz, but for a pleasure trip, not for a meeting. Grávalo further claimed that on his way back from Cádiz, on January 8, Díaz had stopped in Caulina, possibly to make final arrangements with the vinetenders and farmworkers. Díaz again denied everything and was returned to the Guardia Civil barracks that night for another session of torture. Many of the other unionists suffered under similar conditions. Manuel Caro Clavo who, like Díaz, had been condemned to life imprisonment, died in February under mysterious circumstances, possibly by his own hand; his body was so mangled that officials refused to allow the corpse to be viewed before burial.

Since the events of January 8 were considered an insurrection, they fell under military jurisdiction. Speedy trials were held during the first week of February 1892. The findings were no harsher than people had expected. Dozens received life sentences. Four men were sentenced to die as the leaders of the revolt: Manuel Fernández Reina, known as Busiqui, Antonio Zarzuela Granja, and Manuel Silva Leal, known as El Lebrijano, were convicted of the murders of the salesman and the clerk; Zarzuela said that he would be happy to die if Grávalo, the informer, went with him. Lamela was the fourth; he was guilty of nothing more than being an anarchist barber in whose shop local workmen undoubtedly met to complain about their lives, their wages, and the oppressive conditions under which they lived.

The day before the February 10 execution, all the condemned men refused visitors. Zarzuela, since he claimed to have been framed, planned to end his days showing with continuous acts of defiance just how disorderly he could be;

he planned to get drunk. The 34-year-old El Lebrijano, friendless in Jerez, also maintained his innocence to the end. Lamela discussed anarchist doctrine all morning, refused the confessor, claimed they were all martyrs to the cause, and waited for the executioner in relatively good spirits. He ate a huge meal to demonstrate that he was still full of life, and he and the resigned Lebrijano slept well. The irascible and frightened Zarzuela and Busiqui stayed up all night talking. Zarzuela begged to die by sword or bullet rather than the garrot, but the authorities denied his request. At 6:30 P.M. all four were taken from their cells and placed on separate benches with partitions between them. Zarzuela for one last time protested his innocence and cursed his executioners; the guards took him by force only after half an hour of struggle. Busiqui also claimed he was not guilty. He was the first to be executed; then Lamela, who had not said a word; then Lebrijano, and finally Zarzuela. He proclaimed as their epitaph, "Children of Jerez, Martyrs of Labor."[8]

Aftermath

The men condemned to life terms or to fifteen- or twenty-year sentences were people against whom there was almost no evidence linking them with the insurrection. Díaz, Crespo, and Sánchez Rosa were all actively involved in labor organizations, but an 1887 law had made it legal for workers to associate so long as they petitioned the government. The condemned men had different histories, but a common connection to the anarchist trade union movement. When the police first arrested Juan Gómez Correa, for instance, they did not even know whether he was an anar-

---

[8] AMJF 3302: 6142, 7038, 7694, Telegramas, February 10, 1892; *Los sucesos*, pp. 13, 19, 34–40; *La Révolte*, 26-III-1892; *La tramontana*, 20-VII-1893, cited in *La Révolte*, 25-VIII-1893; Bernaldo de Quirós, "El espartaquismo," pp. 28–29; "A los anarquistas de Jerez: Antonio Zarzuela Granja, José Fernández Lamela, Manuel Fernández Reina, Manuel Silvo Leal, Caro Clavo," *El corsario*, 14-II-1892.

chist. His place of residence, Huerta Vista Alegre, an important farm district where the OARE was organizing, may have made him a suitable target for the police. When he was tried by a civil jury, they dismissed all charges. Then the case went to a military tribunal, and he was condemned to twenty years' hard labor. José Barea Moreno's case is a variation on the theme. When he was first arrested in April 1892, living in the Barrio de la Plata, his accusers said he was an anarchist, but no charges were made about any activities on the night of January 8. A few days prior to the insurrection, however, workers in the La Plata and Las Mesas districts had struck for wage hikes of one-half real and for rest periods. And the rural police, consulted in May 1892, said that he was widely known to be an anarchist, but he was not guilty so far as they knew of any misconduct. Yet the military tribunal gave him a life sentence. Essentially the same was said about and done to José Márquez Fernández, who was lucky to get only twelve years on no evidence. Manuel González Guillén seems to have received twenty years in jail simply because he was employed by Manuel Díaz, the barber. Juan Agis was accused of being a man of "bad character" and an anarchist; the military tribunal condemned him to fifteen years.

The inquisition continued for over a year after the insurrection. In May 1892, 121 prisoners, many of them peasants, were still awaiting sentencing for their part in the uprising. The men were subjected to harassment from the priest, who spoke of Christian charity and divine forgiveness, and warned them that anarchism was a fantasy opposed by religion. In effect, he accused them of heresy. An anonymous Jerez worker reported that the priest's discussion took place under conditions where the air was so foul the men could hardly breathe. The men were not permitted to question or argue with the priest. When they refused to go to Mass, they were forced into solitary confinement. On June 10, the remaining prisoners were marched from Jerez to the Arcos jail, a distance of eighteen miles. Many suffered from exhaustion and thirst. Once there, it was impossible for them to get any medical care; needless to say, anarchist literature was forbidden, although some managed to receive publications through circuitous means.[9]

The authorities had good intelligence on anarchist activity in the Jerez area. They knew, for instance, that the *hortelanos*, peasants whose plots were on the irrigated *huertos*, were independent men, and many were anarchists. The Hortelano Society had probably been a section of the UTC and was almost certainly affiliated with the new anarchist agricultural workers union, the OARE. Authorities also knew that "Workers' Hope," a cooperative society that dated back at least to 1872, was a workers' center, possibly the anarchist local council in Jerez. Bakers who continued to be affiliated with the agricultural workers were also suspected of anarchist activities, and Crespo provided the link between the bakers and the agrarian workers.

Soon after the insurrection, the police seized the records of the Hortelano Society office, on Calle las Cruces in Jerez. They accused many of the *hortelano* peasants of being anarchists, of using their so-called cooperative society as an anarchist center, and of joining Crespo in stealing arms and cannons. Anyone who held a plot in the *huerto* districts was assumed guilty since the peasant brigade, according to government witnesses, had marched from the direction of Huerta de Cabra Coja. On these grounds, José Requera Garrido was given a fifteen-year jail sentence although no one positively identified him either as a participant in the rebellion or as an anarchist. Gallardo, whom the local police claimed was often drunk and belonged to Workers' Hope, was brought back from Tarifa, near Gibraltar, where he was working in February 1892.[10]

[9] *Los sucesos*, pp. 41–46, 55; AMJF 3302: 6142, 6406, 7655, 7729, 7879, 9376, 9531, 9537, 9570; "L'Insurrection en Andalousie," *La Révolte*, 16–I–1892.

[10] Letter, May 19, 1891. AMJF 8: 12,627 claimed that "Workers' Hope" had been founded in November 1872 as an anarchist workers'

In the aftermath of the Jerez uprising, all associations were suspect. The authorities arrested reporters of the French paper *L'Avenir–anarchiste*, who had come to Jerez to cover the trials, and charged them with being foreign agitators. Yet, despite the worsening economic situation between 1892 and 1896 and the police repression that lasted at least a year after the insurrection, the local workers' associations and anarchists remained alive. On May Day 1892, Jerez witnessed a massive one-day strike for the eight-hour day. And on February 10, 1893, Lamela's brother José led a peaceful demonstration to the cemetery on the first anniversary of the executions. Similar mobilizations in honor of the "Jerez Martyrs" were carried on throughout Spain and Europe. The Union of Agricultural Workers of the Spanish Region (Unión de agricultores de la región española, UARE), probably a new name for the OARE, held a congress in August 1893 from which they sent a message to Andalusian workers: "As capitalism is strong, so too labor must be united in order to provide the necessary force to overcome capitalism."

Barcelona workers who rose up in defense of the Jerez victims were themselves incarcerated and tortured at Montjuich prison. Between 1892 and 1893, over twenty thousand Spaniards were held for a considerable time under preventive arrest. Many of these people had been tortured in an attempt to get them to reveal the names of anarchist labor leaders. This wholesale repression between 1892 and 1897 drove individual anarchists to engage in terror and assassination. It was at this point that the anarchist bombthrower

---

cooperative. It also notes that "Legality," described as an anarchist workers' association, had been founded in September 1879, during the clandestine period. The date of the letter, before the Jerez Insurrection, demonstrates that following the May Day demonstrations in 1891, Jerez' authorities carried out investigations into local workers' organizations and tended to view them all as anarchist cells. J. A. Pitt-Rivers gives an excellent description of *hortelanos* around Grazalema in his *People of the Sierra*, pp. 40–41; AMJF 3302: 6720.

emerged as a familiar figure in Spain. He was, however, considerably less important to the Andalusian anarchist movement than those who attempted to maintain newspapers, associations, and unions to promote the struggle for the overthrow of capitalism through united action by organized labor and the poor.[11]

PHYLLOXERA

The fortunes of the sherry industry had some effect upon the continued involvement of vinegrowers and pruners in the forefront of anarchist activities around Jerez. Patterns elaborated for the period up to 1873 continued for the decade thereafter, but were severely modified by the exogenous factor of phylloxera, a plant louse that destroyed the major French vineyards. The phylloxera plague seems to have come to Europe on American vines that were resistant to its effects. It first appeared in France in 1853, reducing must production and attacking the wine stocks themselves. The only known way to combat the louse was to graft old shoots onto American stalks, a costly enterprise that only vinegrowers with a great deal of capital could afford. Though resistant to phylloxera, the new vines were more susceptible to mildew and fungus than the old; thus they required more spraying and dusting, all of which cost money. Since they were hardier in structure, they seldom required skilled pruning. Therefore the demand for skilled labor declined still further, while demand for unskilled labor increased. Whereas the European vines had produced after four years and had a lifespan of sixty to a hundred years, the new vines lasted fewer than forty years.

[11] *La Révolte*, 12–III–1892; "Manifiesto que el congreso de la unión de agricultores de la región española (celebrado los días 13 a 16 agosto de 1893) dirige a los campesinos y a los demás trabajadores," *El corsario*, 8–X–1893. Superb accounts of the late nineteenth and early twentieth-century anarchist labor movement in Catalonia can be found in Joan Connelly Ullman, *La semana trágica* and Joaquín Romero Maura, *"La rosa de fuego."*

The worst period of phylloxera in France came between 1868 and 1887. Initially, all wine producers in Spain benefited from increased demand for their products and from reduction of French and English tariffs on Spanish wine. The French tragedy was a windfall for the bourgeoisie in Jerez, completing trends in the sherry industry that had begun before mid-century. Demand for cheap sherries increased, but the price of Spanish wine remained low. Quantity, not quality, was required to transform cheap sherries into more common drinking wines. But while overall demand for inferior sherries increased, sherry prices, and thus the prosperity of vinegrowers on the prestigious *albariza* soils, continued to decline. As the fortunes of one portion of the industry improved, those of skilled vine dressers and the peasant vinegrowers for whom they worked grew worse. Still, the long-term trends of Jerez wine for the late nineteenth century were generally good, as exports reached their height between 1867 and 1873 and again, at a slightly lower level, between 1889 and 1891 (see Figure 7–1).

After the seventies, the local bourgeoisie became buttresses of the Spanish monarchy. Opposed to an unresponsive state before 1874, the sherry producers and the monarchy mended their fences after the Restoration, largely because the government attempted to lower wine duties. Wine was Spain's major export and its chief source of foreign exchange in the latter part of the nineteenth century. Alfonso XII took cognizance of sherry producers' contributions to national prosperity by ennobling members of the González-Byass family. Manuel González was named marquise of Bonanza and his brother Pedro, who directed the company until 1935, was named marquise of Torre Soto de Briviesca. Sherry producers broke with their Republican past. Manuel González served as a Monarchist Cortes representative. Manuel Bertemati, long-time mayor of Jerez and scion of a Republican sherry-producing family, had by 1887 become the marquise Bertemati.[12]

[12] Harvey J. Smith, "Village Revolution," pp. 125–136; González

FIGURE 7–1

JEREZ WINE EXPORTS (1822-1905)

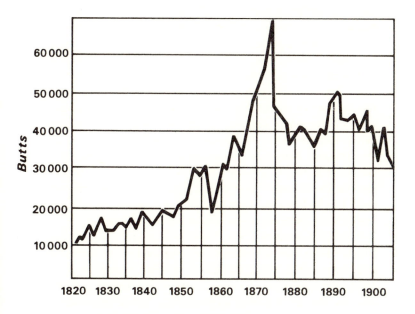

(A butt is between 108 and 113 gallons.)

Source: Francisco Quirós, "El comercio de los vinos de Jerez," *Estudios geográficos*, 23, no. 86 (1962), 35.

However progressive they had appeared in comparison with the grain latifundists before 1873, the big sherry producers were, in fact, traditionalist in their business practices. The British consul in Cádiz claimed that they, like other Spanish investors, were notorious for their unwillingness to

Gordon, *Jerez*, pp. 134, 221, 246; Croft-Cooke, *Sherry*, pp. 127–129; letter, April 13, 1876, FO 72/1493; letter, February 12, 1883, FO 72/1654; *Accounts and Papers* (1897), XCIII, 403.

invest money in their own country and for "their craving after high interest." The same witness reported that even in the drought and depression years of 1881 to 1883, investors were receiving 30 to 34 percent returns.

Yet it seemed evident to all observers that the wine industry in Jerez was undergoing dramatic changes. In 1883, Manuel Carvajal, an old Republican member of the Cortes, argued that export prices in Jerez were declining because of infiltration of the sherry market by grapes grown in Córdoba and the county of Niebla in Huelva. To a certain degree he was correct. It has already been demonstrated for the earlier period that the large sherry producers had begun to undercut their own product by introducing cheap sherries produced on *barro-arena* soil. While no place in the world could compete with wines produced on *albariza*, the counties of Niebla, Montilla, and Moguer, to name just three wine districts in Huelva, could produce cheaper musts, as could Yugoslavia, Hungary, and South Africa, all of which began to export sherry in the eighties. The shippers who had promoted low-priced sherries had increased their general markets, while undermining the luxury product over which they had held a monopoly. The late nineteenth-century depression also hurt Jerez by reducing the prosperity of the European bourgeoisie whose earlier growth in numbers and wealth had initially promoted the demand for expensive sherry. Sherry producers suffered from "the scanty demand for high class wines in England," and increasingly they cultivated markets in the United States. By 1907, the United States had replaced the United Kingdom as the major importer of Jerez' wines.

Moreover, it was clear to all wine producers that they were not immune to the phylloxera, and that it was only a matter of time before Spain's grape crops would be affected. Even though Spain dominated international wine sales until 1892, the blight, brought to Spain by Catalan spademen who worked in the Languedoc vineyards, struck northern Spain in 1870. It began to move south and west, carried in the clothing of vinetenders and grape harvesters. By 1892, it had reached almost all Spanish vineyards outside of Cádiz Province. In the south, vineyards in Sevilla and Málaga Provinces were affected. Cádiz Province enjoyed two more years of prosperity, because sherry producers secured most vineyard workers locally. These laborers had not been in blighted areas, and thus did not carry the phylloxera louse. (Grain harvesters came from the hill towns near Málaga and from southern Portugal.) The second sherry export boom from 1889 to 1891 almost certainly created a demand for grape pickers that could not be supplied sufficiently from local labor resources.

The phylloxera first struck Jerez on July 21, 1894, via Lebrija from Ronda, according to González Gordon of the González-Byass family. Phylloxera first hit the Ducha vineyards to the northeast of the city, where some peasant vinegrowers, cultivators of *albariza* soils, had continued to persist. Next the infestation moved to *barro-arena* vineyards.[13] Until 1897, the proportion of the vineyards affected by the phylloxera was still small, and even where the phylloxera was serious, the quantity but not the quality of musts was affected. By 1899, however, the full force of the blight had struck Jerez. Scorching winds and intense heat just prior to harvest exacerbated the damage done by phylloxera, resulting in a low vintage of unsatisfactory flavor. The plant louse took its toll. A vineyard that had "produced 100 to 140 butts [11,000 to 16,000 gallons] per harvest until 1897, produced 56 in 1898 and only 6 in 1899." To encourage growers to introduce American vines, the government granted tax exemptions on vineyards suffering from phylloxera and a 10-year exemption from future taxes to those who agreed

---

[13] González Gordon, *Jerez*, p. 223; *El imparcial*, 13-VI-1883, 17-I-1892; Gumersindo Fernández de la Rosa, Domingo Lizaur y Paúl, and M. G. Pérez, *Informe sobre la invasión de la filoxera en la provincia de Cádiz y el plan de defensa* (Jerez, 1894), cited in Muñoz Pérez and Benito Arranz, *Guía bibliográfica para una geografía agraria de España*, p. 640; *Accounts and Papers* (1908), CXVI, 264.

to plant American vines. Few peasant proprietors could afford the costs, however. As the consul in Cádiz reported, "only the wealthy among the vine owners have been able to replant their vineyards and wait for better times." Many peasants in the area simply planted grain, ill-suited to the soil, upon their devastated vineyards. The 1903 grape harvest was the first the newly planted vineyards yielded, and was said to be of good quality. Demand was still high and the selling price increased a hundred percent over the previous year. By 1907, the plague was over, having completed the transformation of the sherry industry begun in the early nineteenth century. The vineyards had become large, consolidated factories in the fields, owned and operated by forty major shipping companies, and the formerly independent small vineyard owners had become wage laborers in the fields they had once owned.[14]

Syndicates, Mutual Societies, and General Strikes

Between 1892 and 1901 severe droughts reduced grain production in Cádiz Province, causing high unemployment and suffering among the people. But in bad years the propensity to strike declined. 1896 marked a nadir for peasants and agricultural laborers in Cádiz Province. Decline in grain production, due to insufficient rains, and the Cuban War of Independence between 1895 and 1898 also exacted their toll in Cádiz Province. In the spring of 1896 very little planting was done, and those who did work earned less than one-half peseta per day, a 30 percent cut in wages since 1886. The governor of Cádiz Province received telegrams from mayors and city councils in Grazalema, Arcos, and Villa-

[14] *Accounts and Papers* (1900), CVI, 93–96; (1902), CX, 164; (1904), CI, Part A, 343. Barrington Moore, Jr. has captured the political sensibility of people like the anarchist vinegrowing peasants and pruners, describing movements such as theirs as "the dying wail of a class over whom the wave of progress is about to roll." *Social Origins of Dictatorship and Democracy*, p. 505.

martín, indicating that mobs of workers in their towns were roaming the streets looking for bread. The local officials said they were penniless and powerless to help. The governor proceeded to establish public works projects, probably with the image of the Jerez Insurrection in mind.

The situation the following year was no better. Cádiz Province was forced to import grain from the Canary Islands, but bread prices remained high. Trade was at a near standstill. The winter of 1897 to 1898 promised to be even worse than the previous winter, since bread prices would be high and supplies scarce. The absence of many local youths who were with the army in Cuba seems to have diminished the prospect of social upheaval, but authorities were still worried. They raised subscriptions "to prevent begging in the streets in an imposing and sometimes threatening manner." Anarchists and government officials seemed to agree that extreme poverty might promote revolt. Miguel Rubio, active in anarcho-communist affairs since the eighties, argued in *La tribuna libre* in 1893 that hungry people had a right to revolt. But in fact the wave of bombthrowing and assassination that swept northern Spain between 1893 and 1896 never reached Andalusia. Ironically, despite continued drought, the economic situation in Cádiz improved in 1899, due to the import of foreign capital after the loss of Cuba and the Philippines.[15]

Until conditions improved, especially with the good harvests of 1901 to 1903, the people of Cádiz Province were too famished for organized political activity. There is no doubt, however, that workers' unions, resistance societies, and mutual aid associations connected with anarchism con-

[15] "Aritmética revolucionaria," *El socialismo*, 28-11-1886; "Revista semanal: Cádiz," *El corsario*, 26-111-1896, 30-1V-1896; Miguel Rubio, "Los sucesos de Jerez," *La tribuna libre* (Seville), 23-1-1892; Woodcock, *Anarchism*, pp. 369-370; *Accounts and Papers* (1897), XCIII, 320, 403; (1900), CVI, 93; (1906), CXXVIII, 557; García-Baquero González, *Comercio colonial y guerras revolucionarias*; Quijano, "El Nivel de precios en España," p. 41.

tinued to exist in the area. New legislation legalizing workers' associations in 1897, improvement in trade after 1899, and finally good harvests following 1901, contributed to the reappearance in large numbers of unions (or resistance societies against capitalism, as they had begun to be called in the eighties). Many of the syndicates, mutual benefit societies, and workers' circles that seemed to emerge full blown between 1897 and 1904 probably had been alive but dormant. Winecellar men, coopers, construction workers, masons, bricklayers, carpenters, and painters had been among the most militant anarchists beginning in 1870, when they first joined the FRE. They were among the first to form legal associations under the new laws in 1897. The Jerez Coopers Guild, supposedly founded in 1897, had 150 members by 1904. The Jerez resistance society of masons and construction workers, directed by Juan Cuarto, was legally formed on June 28, 1899, with 800 initial members. On July 5, 1899, José Sánchez Florez and his 500 carpenter friends applied to Jerez officials for a license for their society, which they claimed was dedicated to "the moral and material improvement of working conditions." The new society, called "Hope," was made up of 50 winecellar workers in Puerto de Santa María, and was probably another case of a legal incarnation of a previously clandestine anarchist syndicate.[16]

The building trades' workers are a good example of old

[16] *El condenado*, 21–VI–1873; *Cartas* I, 174–175. The most important source for the development of late nineteenth-century unions, cooperatives, and mutual aid societies was prepared for the government by the Institute for Social Reform. Like their other publications, it is based upon questionnaires distributed to officials of different localities. A comparison of their evidence with material in the liberal and anarchist press indicates that the picture the report gives of associational life in Andalusia underestimates the continuities in organizational life and the level of mobilization. Instituto de reformas sociales, *Estadística de la asociación obrera*, pp. 74–75 (hereafter, *Estadística*); AMJF 579.

anarchist crafts that remained militant as they were industrialized. The continuing relationship of this group to anarchism suggests the flexibility of the movement as it adapted to changes in capitalist production. Between 1901 and 1905, strikes by building construction workers, masons, carpenters, stone cutters, and marble cutters swept Northern Cádiz Province. While development was slow and incomplete, the rate of construction was greater in Cádiz at the turn of the century than in the two previous decades. Construction of docks, foundries, and processing plants for beet sugar provided jobs for increased numbers of skilled and unskilled laborers. Skilled masons and stone cutters, many of whom had previously been employed in small ventures with four or five assistants, began to work in large teams with numerous proletarians beneath them. Since so many of them undoubtedly associated labor unions with anarchist politics, they attempted to win over the less skilled to anarchist organizations while putting wage pressure on employers.

The new tactics employed by the turn-of-the-century workers' societies were consistent with anarchist strategy. There were, of course, economic strikes for immediate improvement in working conditions for specific trades. But workers also tried to coordinate goals and strategies across regional lines and across trades. Increasingly at the end of the nineteenth century, unions throughout Cádiz Bay tried to build mass industrial syndicates composed, for instance, of all the longshoremen and shipping workers in the entire region. Early twentieth-century Andalusian anarchism was based upon the ideal of solidarity, not just among all members of an occupational group but between all workers and all poor people. In January 1902, when capitalist employers reneged upon commitments to longshoremen in Cádiz Bay towns, other Cádiz Bay workers struck. The strike brought out 3,000 workers and members of the community in Cádiz. When Barcelona's metallurgical workers went on strike in 1900, calling out nearly 500 workers, they appealed to their counterparts in Cádiz for support, which was given to them.[17]

Anarchists in Andalusia also seem to have returned to organizing the community through social sections. The most prominent organizations in Cádiz Province were still the cooperatives, mutual aid associations, and workers' centers, some of which were undoubtedly remnants of former anarchist local councils. Typographers in Cádiz, who had organized in 1893 "to improve working conditions," founded their own shop in 1901, in which employed associates worked and divided the profits among themselves. Clear links between the anarchism of the eighties and the later movement can be seen in San Fernando's 327-member Workers Center founded in 1885. Although it described itself to officials as a mutual aid society, it was almost certainly an anarchist local council.[18] Ubrique in 1900 formed a legal Workers and Craftsmen's Center with 125 members. There were also organizations that described themselves as sections of miscellaneous workers, as did the 300-member Arcos association and the 16-member Algar Society of Various Workers, which were probably the anarchist local commissions in these towns with long histories of anarchist activity (see Table 7-1).

AGRICULTURAL WORKERS AND GENERAL STRIKES

Agricultural workers joined those in other trades in their "spirit of association," preserving their trade unions, which an old adversary had once claimed gave "the labouring classes a form of organization to many of their criminal proceedings." Like winecellar workers, coopers, and masons, agricultural laborers and peasants continued to form unions in many of the same places that the UTC had been strong. A government report prepared in 1904 severely under-

[17] *El trabajo*, 15–IV–1900, 15–VII–1900; *Tierra y libertad*, 25–I–1902.
[18] *Estadística*, pp. 74–75.

Table 7–1

Workers Organizations
in Trades Previously Associated with the FRE or FTRE

Towns	Name of society	Founding date under 1887 law (renewed in 1897)	Membership in 1904
Towns centered around Jerez			
Sanlúcar de Barrameda	Vinetenders Society	1899	800
Jerez de la Frontera	Coopers Guild	1897	150
	Guild of Agricultural Workers	1899	459
	Society of Vineyard Workers	1899	200
	Masons and Bricklayers Society	1900	115
	The Locomotive (Workers and Employees of the Andalusian Railroad)	1903	170
Puerto de Santa María	Reform (Society of Skilled Coopers)	1897	188
	Hope (Society of Winecellar Workers)	1899	50
Cádiz	Solidarity (Society of Stevedores and Sailors)	1893	983
	Society of Tool, Die, and Iron Workers	1901	15
	Union (Society of Cafe and Innkeepers)	1901	407
	Tobacco Workers Mutual Aid Society	1901	1,104
San Fernando	Workers Center	1885	327
Medina Sidonia	Society of Agricultural Workers	1903	300
Chiclana de la Frontera	Vineyard Workers Center	1900	350

Table 7-1—*Continued*

Workers Organizations
in Trades Previously Associated with the FRE or FTRE

Towns	Name of society	Founding date under 1887 law (renewed in 1897)	Membership in 1904
Towns centered around Arcos			
Villamartín	Defense (Society of Agricultural Workers)	1900	90
Espera	Society of Agricultural Workers	1900	482
Arcos de la Frontera	Society of Flour Millers	1899	22
	Section of Miscellaneous Workers	1899	300
Algar	Society of Agricultural Workers	1900	30
Alcalá de los Gazules	Redemption	1901	28
Towns centered around Ubrique, between Arcos and Ronda			
Prado del Rey	Society of Agricultural Workers	1900	140
Benaocaz	Society of Agricultural Workers	1900	20
Ubrique	Society of Agricultural Workers	1900	949
	Workers and Craftsmen's Center	1900	125

Source: *Estadística de la asociación obrera* (Madrid, 1907), pp. 74–76.

estimates the degree of development (see Table 7–2). Between 1897 and 1904 unions such as the Guild of Agricultural Workers formed in Jerez with several hundred members. On August 5, 1899, in Jerez, Francisco Cala, José Jiménez, Antonio Núñez, Manuel Gutiérrez, and Manuel

Moreno Mendera founded a Society of Vineyard Workers with 1,000 members dedicated to "the cultural and economic emancipation of workers." Smaller towns also had their associations of agricultural workers. Algar, for instance, had several dozen workers enrolled in 1900, and Benaocaz another dozen. Medina Sidonia's Society of Agricultural Workers had 300 in 1903. Ubrique's society of farm workers had 949 at that time. By 1904, the overwhelming majority of organized workers in Cádiz Province,

Table 7–2
Agricultural Workers Unions
That May Have Been Anarchist, 1882 and 1904

Towns	1882 UTC membership	1904 agricultural societies	1904 membership
Towns centered around Jerez			
Las Cabezas de San Juan	—	Union & Fraternity (Agr. Workers)	499
Lebrija	103		—
Trebujena	25		—
Sanlúcar de Barrameda	530	Society of Vine-cultivators	800
Chipiona	50		—
Jerez de la Frontera	850	Guild of Agr. Workers	459
		Society of Vine-cultivators	200
Rota	—		—
Puerto de Santa María	391		
Cádiz	40		—
Puerto Real	15		—
San Fernando	—		—
Medina Sidonia	—	Society of Agr. Workers	300
Chiclana de la Frontera	—	Society of Vine-cultivators	350

Table 7–2—*Continued*

Agricultural Workers Unions
That May Have Been Anarchist, 1882 and 1904

Towns	*1882 UTC member-ship*	*1904 agricul-tural societies*	*1904 member-ship*
Towns centered around Arcos			
Montellano	200		—
Villamartín	230	Defense: Society of Agr. Workers	90
Bornos	425		—
Arcos de la Frontera	617		—
Algar	110	Society of Agr. Workers	30
San José del Valle	110		—
Paterna de Rivera	22		—
Alcalá de los Gazules	175	Redemption	28
Towns centered around Ubrique, between Arcos and Ronda			
Olvera	720		—
Alcalá del Valle	160		—
Arriate	566		—
Grazalema	200		—
Montejaque	50		—
Benaocaz	196	Society of Agr. Workers	20
Ubrique	770	Society of Agr. Workers	949
Ronda	1,125	Society of Agr. Workers	99
Prado del Rey	—	Society of Agr. Workers	140
Espera	—	Society of Agr. Workers	482

Sources: Max Nettlau, *La Première Internationale* I (edited by Renée Lamberet), pp. 681–682; II, Tableau II; AMJF *Archivo memoranda 10*, p. 76; I.R.S. *Estadística de la asociación obrera*, pp. 73–75, 164, 207.

almost 4,000, were in agricultural workers' unions. José Crespo helped found the Society of Agricultural Workers (Sociedad de obreros agricultores, SOA) which, like its predecessors, adopted the 1882 rules of the anarchist Union of Field Workers. The new Society of Agricultural Workers probably affiliated with the Federation of Workers Societies of the Spanish Region (Federación de sociedades obreras de la región española, FSORE), formed just the year before, in October 1900, as an umbrella organization for various workers' societies that were blossoming all over Spain.

The proliferation of organizations with so many of the old anarchist leaders gives evidence that the militants of the nineties such as Crespo and Sánchez Rosa were trying at the turn-of-the-century to reunite anarchists into some kind of organization that would permit coordinated action. Attempts by the seasoned anarchist leaders to unite workers' associations and anarchist sections were relatively successful. The old problems continued—strikes by individual unions against single employers for increased wages became more frequent at the turn of the century—but the strikes were now coordinated with mass demonstrations, which ended in two general strikes in as many years.[19]

In January 1902, a workers' delegation consisting of José Crespo and Miguel Solano Núñez, among others, traveled throughout Cádiz and Sevilla Provinces, organizing protest meetings and building support for the Jerez workers who were still held in jail a full decade after the 1892 insurrection. They also attempted to form a regional anarchist commission, as suggested at the last congress of the Federation of Workers' Societies of the Spanish Region. But despite the new legalization of workers' associations in 1897, workers in Andalusia were still subject to harassment; while unions were legal, anarchism was not.

[19] Report from the British vice consul in Jerez, cited in *Accounts and Papers* (1884), LXXX, pp. 577–578. *Estadística*, pp. 74–76; AMJF 579 (1923), "Antecedentes de sociedades que se enviaron al gobernador civil de la provincia por tenentes reclamadas"; Díaz del Moral, *Historia de las agitaciones campesinas*, pp. 191–192.

The year 1902 marked a turning point in anarchist organizing in Cádiz Province. The Federation of Workers' Societies of the Spanish Region, despite its loose series of pacts between unions and localities, seems to have been able to do what the earlier national anarchist bodies and the Jerez insurrection had failed to accomplish, unite workers across local boundaries through a general strike. In January 1902, what must have been the anarchist local commissions in Cádiz, San Fernando, Puerto Real, and Chiclana went on strike.

Recognizing that local community support for anarchist workers created a potentially incendiary condition, police in Cádiz repeated past practice by arresting a labor leader, José Fernández. He was intercepted at a friend's house and held simply because he was known to be an anarchist, although there was no evidence linking him to any of the strikes under way. The 1902 series of strikes lasted six weeks and involved the whole Cádiz Bay area. Employers tried to starve out workers by pressuring merchants to eliminate credit, thus depriving the strikers of food and provisions. They and their local supporters rioted against the shopkeepers, not only stealing food but destroying the shopkeepers' property. By February 1902, strikes and demonstrations in support of strikes were so widespread that the government declared a state of war and banned all anarchist newspapers and journals.[20]

A month later, in February 1902, workers in Sevilla, Huelva, and Cádiz agreed to form a regional commission of the new national labor confederation of the FSORE. Their decision may have been helped by a visit from the Catalan anarchist labor leaders Teresa Claramunt and Leopoldo Bonafulla, who held a meeting in Jerez in 1902. The relatively good harvests of June 1902, like those of June 1883, seemed to make latifundists and their government supporters wary that labor shortages would give organized workers

[20] *La huelga general*, 5-1-1902; *Tierra y libertad*, 25-1-1902, 8-II-1902; "El trabajador y la huelga revolucionaria," *La revista blanca* (1ᵃ serie), v, 237.

too much leverage over the local ruling class. In fact, in June 1902 there were agricultural strikes throughout Cádiz, Granada, Badajoz, and Valencia. And the following October, grape pickers in Jerez also struck. They were joined by local agricultural workers organized by the Society of Agricultural Workers, the anarchist agricultural union. What the farm laborers wanted in October and November 1902 was a new sowing contract that would have paid them daily wages; they were supported by sympathy strikes throughout Northern Cádiz Province.[21]

Numerous isolated local strikes seemed to reach a critical mass in 1902, and were suddenly transformed and molded into a general strike. Sevilla rather than Cádiz Province was the center of the massive strike wave that swept all of western Andalusia in October 1902. The agricultural, textile, and coopers' strikes caused Sevilla's authorities to close down workers' centers and to arrest labor leaders. Workers' success in winning their strikes persuaded them to call a mass meeting to demand the reopening of workers' associations. They agreed to hold a general strike meeting the first week in October to protest against the persecution of anarchist leaders and newspapers. The authorities, fearing insurrection, brought police into Sevilla's factories, which itself prompted 15,000 workers in Sevilla and surrounding areas to go out on strike. When a new demonstration of workers was called, 5,000 people appeared. The city had become a battlefield. Government troops were brought in and quartered everywhere.[22] Since hundreds of working class leaders, even more than usual, were jailed, plans for a general strike were postponed, possibly to a time when harvest workers' threats might be added to those of other anarchists.

After the tumultuous events of 1902, workers and their opponents prepared for harvest time 1903, which promised to be momentous so long as the crop was good. Landowners

21 "Movimiento social," *Tierra y libertad*, 8–II–1902; "Lucha social," *El corsario* (Valencia), 28–VI–1902; "Crónica obrera," *El corsario*, 17–X–1902, 24–X–1902; Juan Mateos Moscoso, "Al director de *El eco de Jerez*," *Tierra y libertad*, 14–IX–1903.

22 "Crónica obrera," *El corsario*, 11–X–1902, 17–X–1902.

in Utrera, Sevilla, held a meeting to decide on a joint program to deal with the threat of mass strikes by agricultural workers. In advance of the 1903 harvest, they called upon the government to suppress strikers. This organization of landowners was a tribute to the success of anarchist coordination and to the strength of the new agricultural workers' unions.

The big agricultural strike that occurred in the summer of 1903 might just as easily have borne Jerez' name as that of Alcalá del Valle. The threat of agricultural strikes that summer caused the government to arrest those who had addressed a July 25 mass meeting in Jerez. By August 8, twenty-two of the twenty-nine speakers were in jail. Local leaders of the agricultural workers, Rafael Jiménez Contreras and Miguel Solano Núñez, were arrested shortly after a planning meeting, but before the strike had begun. The strikes that subsequently occurred seem to have been better organized than any since the Jerez insurrection of 1892. Unlike the eruption the previous October, the summer 1903 general strike went on despite the loss of leaders. Beginning with a strike of agricultural workers in Alcalá del Valle, a network of work stoppages developed throughout the hill towns of the Sierra and across to the plains of Jerez, running roughly down the Guadalete River basin and across the ridges. Even domestic servants, often wives and sisters of strikers, went out. The government attempted to enforce a news blackout in an effort to slow the spread of the anarchist general strike. A local journalist covering the strike in Grazalema for workers in Casas Viejas, near Medina Sidonia, was jailed in Jerez and tortured for spreading the word among various agricultural workers' groups.

Labor leaders in Alcalá del Valle were jailed on August 1, and local workers held mass demonstrations to protest the arrests. Their demonstration was suppressed, and the people of the town declared a general strike. The police arrested an assortment of strikers and sent them to jail in Ronda, where they were tortured by the Guardia Civil, who knew that a general strike had been planned and wanted to know who was involved in the conspiracy. Two workers were said to have died of genital mutilation and other wounds inflicted by the torturers. From Córdoba to Morón de la Frontera, and from Jerez to Grazalema, the leading trade union leaders were rounded up as conspirators in the general strike. There were abortive insurrections throughout the region, but the army and the police successfully repressed them.[23]

The ruling classes all over Andalusia used the strike as justification for closing workers centers, dissolving trade societies, imprisoning known trade union militants, and closing down workers' newspapers. Repression forced journals such as *Tierra y libertad* to abandon issues raised by the strike and turn their attention to defending the trade union leaders in jail. In such cases, however, Andalusian anarchism's high degree of decentralization was a source of strength. New groups with names like "Neither God nor Master" sprang up all over Andalusia. The general strike of 1903 seems to have been a community-supported agricultural workers' campaign to go beyond union organizing and seize the region for the anarchists. Ruling-class attempts to repress all forms of trade unionism to prevent the spread of the general strike ended—as many late nineteenth-century Andalusian general strikes ended—in community insurrection. The government then clamped down for a while, forcing the masses of workers and poor people to take their unions and associations underground until they could get their leaders out of jail. But the everyday organizing clearly continued. Although improved grain harvests between 1901 and 1903 had contributed to labor militancy, the last major natural famine in Western Europe, between 1904 and 1906, and police repression forced Andalusian anarchism underground until wartime prosperity and the possibility of mass strikes revived it a decade later.

[23] *Ibid.*; *Tierra y libertad*, 7–VIII–1903 to 12–VIII–1903, 3–IX–1903, 17–IX–1903.

Turn-of-the-Century Success

The attempt in 1892 to coordinate insurrections in Jerez, Ubrique, Lebrija, and Arcos appears in retrospect to have been a reasonable tactic. Only calculated insurrections or the mass demonstrations of May Day could break down the insularity of anarchist workers. By coordinating general strikes in several cities, the successive anarchist agricultural workers' unions, which were the largest syndicates in the region, might have induced workers in all trades to join in solidarity movements. The timing was important. The way to win supporters was to present workers, peasants, and the unemployed with a city under anarchist control. The other anarchist unions in Jerez would hardly have been in opposition had they awakened on the morning of January 9, 1892, to find that the city had been placed in anarchist hands. Even the case presented by the police in 1892 indicates that at least the agricultural workers, and possibly all the large unions, had returned to a strategy of insurrectionary general strike modeled upon the 1873 Sanlúcar de Barrameda events.

The great strength of late nineteenth-century Andalusian anarchism lay in the merger of communal and militant trade union traditions. In towns where the vast majority worked in agriculture, agricultural workers' unions came to be identified with the community as a whole. This was especially true of the hill towns of Grazalema, Alcalá del Valle, Benaocaz, and San José del Valle. In the eighties the UTC was synonymous with anarchism in such places; and its various successors probably maintained that distinction. Therefore the interests of the agricultural workers were genuine community interests, as in the Alcalá del Valle strike of 1903. But in 1902, anarchism had already shown that the demands of agricultural workers and proletarians could be combined with community support to create an insurrectionary situation. One day such interrelated attacks upon the government and the bourgeoisie might bring down the entire system.

It would be a mistake, then, to argue that "village anarchism" in Andalusia was distinct from militant unionism, or that the movement was a surrogate religion. The union was the community in places like Ubrique or Arcos. In the eighties, unions such as the UTC fought for improved conditions for their people, but by the nineties, the failure of that reformist strategy was probably obvious to everyone, since even the right to organize continued to be in question. Improvements won by strikes one year might be obliterated the following year. Unless they were organized regionally, unless everyone who might potentially work in the harvest was united in the same union, committed to the same principles, and, most important, unless their actions were supported by the community as a whole so that the entire mass of the poor could put political as well as economic pressure on the bourgeoisie and the government, the anarchist movement was doomed. Apparently anarchists realized this in 1892, attempted to carry out such a program in January 1902, and tried again in a more coordinated fashion in the summer of 1903.

The anarchists failed. Their strategy, however, was a good one, given their circumstances. Their belief in the power of anarchists to govern themselves and to achieve prosperity for all through egalitarian communalism lived on in Andalusia until destroyed by fascist terror during the Spanish Civil War.[24]

[24] Edward E. Malefakis' now classic *Agrarian Reform and Peasant Revolution in Spain: Origins of the Civil War* should be consulted for a general overview of Spanish agrarian conditions in the late nineteenth century. Joan Connelly Ullman's *La semana trágica* portrays Catalan anarchism of the turn of the century as viable within certain parameters, and thus supports my view of the anarchists, as does Roderick Aya's *The Missed Revolution: The Fate of Rural Rebels in Sicily and Southern Spain 1840–1950*. Those interested in early twentieth-century anarchism should consult Romero Maura, "*La rosa de fuego*"; Calero Amor, *Historia del movimiento obrero en Granada (1909–1923)*; Meaker, *The Revolutionary Left in Spain, 1914–23*; Payne, *The Spanish Revolution*; and Lorenzo, *Les Anarchistes et le pouvoir*, among others. The best treatment of early twentieth-century conditions in Andalusia can still be found in Brenan, *The Spanish Labyrinth* and Díaz del Moral, *Historia de las agitaciones campesinas*.

CHAPTER VIII

Spontaneity and Millenarianism

Popular movements challenge historians. They often seem to emerge out of nowhere, disseminate their message by mysterious means, and apparently disappear. Historians seeking to account for the forces driving Andalusian anarchists have focused on evidence of their spontaneity and millenarianism.

Anarchists were committed to building a revolutionary movement that would not coerce its members. This lack of coercion was what the anarchists meant by spontaneity. As one anarchist remarked in the eighties, "organization, the grouping of organs for a vital function, is always the result of spontaneous evolution. In plants and animals, molecules associate, dissociate, and group together again without a commander. The same is true for societies: They organize themselves by the free play of their will."[1] Anarchists argued that, like other organic processes, social change had internal laws. These laws could not be enforced by states or institutions, but operated through the spontaneous but orderly action of constituent parts. The laws were effective only when "free play" or spontaneity prevailed at every level of society.

Andalusian anarchist ideas about spontaneity were intimately related to their ideas about workers' control. Workers' control entailed the ability to make decisions about one's trade or craft on the spot, without asking advice or permission from foremen or supervisors. It was also part of their ideas about community autonomy. The local council or commission, made up of all syndicates and sections, would make decisions for the community spontaneously, not ac-

[1] *La justicia humana*, cited in *Le Révolté*, 2–VIII–1887.

cording to rigid rules. Spontaneity was thus the sole basis for what anarchists called administration, and what we like to call political and social life.

But spontaneity alone cannot explain how a group that rejected authority and organizational discipline carried on coordinated strikes, insurrections, and general strikes. Anarchists' unwillingness to submit to administrative discipline does not mean that they were not organized. From the seventies on, they formed trade unions, affinity groups such as housewives' sections, and broad cultural associations such as workers' circles, where the anarchist press was read and discussed. The different phases of Andalusian anarchism were coordinated under the FRE by local councils, under the FTRE by local commissions, and under the late nineteenth century anarchists by district commissions. But the councils and commissions were loose bodies that would not and could not act for constituents. They could only attempt to establish forums for discussion. Even when anarchists constituted a large proportion of the population, as in San José del Valle in the early eighties, they could not speak for the community, for the individuals in it, or even for all the other anarchists.

The most common explanation for anarchist mobilization has been that they were millenarian. Constancio Bernaldo de Quirós, one of the leaders of the positivist school of criminology, was one of the earliest critics to explain the power of anarchism by calling it a secular religion, based upon an apocalyptic belief in an unrealizable egalitarian society. In 1913 he wrote, "People of the Betic Mountain region ordinarily feel no drive to associate, but this time [the late nineteenth and early twentieth century] the idea of a Second Coming emerged with a great expansive force, and spread rapidly among the rural laborers, who saw in a burst of light the immanent advent of His reign."[2]

The thesis that the anarchists were driven by belief in a

[2] Bernaldo de Quirós y Pérez, "Bandolerismo y delincuencia subversiva en la baja Andalucía," p. 33.

secular Redemption sought to explain the all-embracing scope of Andalusian anarchism, the rapidity of its spread, and the staunch commitment of its followers. This kind of movement, it was argued, had emerged during times of stress in the middle ages, and during the sixteenth-century Reformation; it also had appeared during the seventeenth-century French and English rebellions, when peasants and craftsmen had risen up against legitimate authority and had attempted to create a new society, one that would be more appropriate to their needs.

Like the Andalusian anarchists, such people often used the Christian idiom, taking Biblical phrases to justify their attack upon secular authority and their claims for a more just society. Some of these movements may have been activated by delusions; the rebels may have been insufficiently acquainted with how their societies actually operated and with what kinds of repressive force were available to their enemies. Centuries of Christian hegemony had given them a language with which to express abstract ideas, but no separate language to express a new egalitarian consciousness.

These groups have been called millenarian because many of them used Christian imagery of the Second Coming, as did the early medieval millenarians, who had expected Redemption to occur in the year 1000 A.D. The basis for this belief could be found in the Apocalypse, one of the most revolutionary portions of the Christian canon. Because the imagery used in so many of the peasant and artisan revolts of the early modern period came from the Bible, scholars have argued that these movements were fundamentally religious in character.

In 1929, when Juan Díaz del Moral published his magisterial study of peasant movements in Córdoba Province, the theories of Bernaldo de Quirós were widely known in Spain.[3] Two factors—the periodicity of anarchist rebellions and the vehement passions expressed during the insurrec-

---

[3] Díaz del Moral, *Historia de las agitaciones campesinas andaluzas.*

tions—led Díaz to formulate a social-psychological explanation of Andalusian anarchism to cover the massive detail he had assembled. Díaz concluded that anarchism, like certain other pre-modern religious movements, had a magical rather than a scientific sense of time and historical development. Not only did millenarians attribute special significance to the millenia, or units of one thousand, but to decimals. Since many of the late nineteenth-century anarchist insurrections did occur at decade intervals, in 1868 to 1873, 1883, 1892, 1902–1903, there seemed to be concrete evidence for his theories.

Díaz del Moral implied that the working class and the peasants had the right to be angry about their lives, but that they were filled with irrational fury at nameless forces that caused drought, high bread prices, and high unemployment, and that because these forces could not be concretized, anarchists struck out aimlessly. The objects of their fury were the church and the latifundists, both of which seemed to be immune from the evil forces of nature that persecuted the anarchists.

Gerald Brenan illuminated Spanish social history by describing the Spanish Civil War against the background of regional history, geography, and social structure. His personal observations of life in Andalusia convinced him that the millenarian argument was correct. Taking up where Díaz del Moral left off, Brenan argued that the Andalusian poor, who had been abandoned by the church in the nineteenth century, transferred their allegiance "from the Church to the revolutionary ideologies hostile to it."[4] Brenan claimed that "the chief characteristic of Andalusian anarchism was its naive millenarianism. Every new movement or strike was thought to herald the immediate coming of a new age of plenty, when all—even the Civil Guard and the landowners—would be free and happy. How this would happen no one could say."[5] The implication was that

[4] Brenan, *The Spanish Labyrinth*, p. 290.
[5] *Ibid.*, p. 157.

the "Idea," the anarchist utopian vision of a world composed of "autonomous sections in autonomous regions," was a secular version of the Kingdom of God on earth, an unrealizable, hence irrational goal.

While Díaz and Brenan assembled massive evidence that Andalusian anarchism was a coherent social movement with leaders, organizations, and strategies, their millenarian analysis did not take their own evidence sufficiently into account. Eric J. Hobsbawm's unsurpassed *Primitive Rebels* posited an evolutionary scale of political development on which anarchism occupied a high position as a transitional political form in the growth of modern revolutionary parties. Yet Hobsbawm, despite respect for anarchists' rational perseverance against oppression, also accepted certain portions of the millenarian analysis.

The millenarian theory is too mechanistic to explain the complex pattern of Andalusian anarchist activity. The millenarian argument implies that popular religion forms the background, hunger serves as trigger, and anarchism is the result. But the millenarian theory cannot explain why anarchist movement grew as it did in Andalusia, but not in other regions of Spain that were, if anything, more pious and equally poor. Bernaldo de Quirós had an explanation of Andalusian anarchism based upon race and climate that most contemporary theorists would oppose.[6] Díaz del Moral and Brenan believed racial and national characteristics predisposed Andalusians toward anarchism. Hobsbawm would reject their theories of racial temperament out of hand.

The millenarian argument is also ahistorical in that it fails to explain ideological conflict and change among Andalusian anarchists. As capitalist development transformed social relations in Andalusia, anarchists changed their strategy from one of collectivism to one of mass communalism. The millenarian argument does not deal with the ways in which ideology was translated into political action. The collectivists built producers' syndicates that struck for workers' con-

---

[6] Bernaldo de Quirós, "Bandolerismo y delincuencia," p. 48.

trol of production; the late nineteenth-century anarchists adopted the general strike as a tactic to unite union organizations with the entire community. Nor does the millenarian argument explain how individual psychological impulses were channeled into a rational strategy. Class hatred was undeniably a powerful reality for poor people in Andalusia, but the anarchists discouraged individual outbursts of rage in favor of an organized mass movement.

In a secular age, the taint of religion is the taint of irrationality. The millenarian argument, in portraying the Andalusian anarchists as fundamentally religious, overlooks their clear comprehension of the social sources of their oppression, which, in their view, were the latifundists and the wine-producing bourgeoisie who together formed the regional ruling class. The millenarian argument assumes that the anarchists' defeat was a result of their irrationality. This view overlooks the power of the state to crush popular social movements that, in the case of the Andalusian anarchists, were more threatening because their strategy and tactics were so rational and effective at mobilizing the masses against key groups in the structure of power.

The millenarian argument also underestimates the ability of the anarchist movement, rooted in the social life of this world, to weld a movement that was firmly based in working-class culture. The anarchists' commitment to combine the personal and political led the movement to recognize, for example, such practices as infant initiation into anarchism. If the practice seems religious, a secular baptism, it is because the anarchists adopted the old forms to teach the new and to demonstrate their rejection of the old ways. The anarchists insisted on the importance of secular education, particular scientific education, to restore the sense of justice in this life rather than the next. Their belief in the ability of science to shape a more just society was shared by many of the leading scientific thinkers of their time, among them Herbert Spencer and Ernst Haeckel, whose work the anarchists regarded as contributing to their own social theory.

The periodic uprisings that appear to be spontaneous and millenarian can be better understood against the background of a social movement firmly imbedded in union organization and urban life. The anarchists knew that they could only win demands at times of good harvests, which occurred infrequently in the late nineteenth century. Good harvests meant high employment and labor shortages that gave agricultural laborers an opportunity to organize successful strikes. This sense of the conditions under which strikes could best succeed was a fully rational strategy, and not a spontaneous explosion of rage.

The communitarian qualities achieved by the Andalusian anarchists, the solidarity expressed by the poor who attacked factories and estates in support of strikers, even when they themselves were not employed in these enterprises, has been used as evidence that the anarchists were irrational. The general strike as practiced by Andalusian anarchists was, however, a rational tactic designed to pit the weight of the masses, whatever their occupations, against the power of the government and the ruling class. The degree of organization, not the religiosity of workers and the community, accounts for mass mobilizations carried on by the Andalusian anarchists at the end of the nineteenth century.

Bibliography

This essay attempts to familiarize readers with general issues raised by the book. Aside from the archival material, printed manuscripts, and periodical literature listed below in the section on primary sources, the bibliography deals with secondary material organized topically. Since Andalusian anarchism was a peasant-labor movement, similar in many respects to organizations that grew among rural and urban craftsmen experiencing proletarianization in other nineteenth-century societies, an overview of such history is desirable before embarking upon a more inclusive listing.

Economic historians, geographers, and cultural anthropologists have studied networks of peasant communities. The work of Nicolás Sánchez-Albornoz on nineteenth-century agrarian and commercial developments in Cádiz Province and of Josep Fontana about general nineteenth-century trends has formed the substructure upon which this book rests. J. Sermet's *L'Espagne du sud* confirms the thesis, gleaned from anarchist records, that economic geography in Andalusia was a key to the development and growth of Andalusian anarchism. José Cutileiro's *Portuguese Rural Society*, focusing upon a district that borders on Spain's southwestern frontier, suggests that geography rather than administrative divisions might provide the units of study in peasant history. He illustrates how Portuguese workers in the Alentejo, the area south of the Tagus River, were linked to Huelva and Cádiz Provinces, where, in the late nineteenth century, they worked for the higher wages anarchists there had been able to secure for all laborers. Ronald Fraser's two Malagan village studies, *In Hiding* and *Tajos*, and Juan Martínez-Alier's *Labourers and Landowners in Southern Spain*, a contemporary account of latifundia work in Córdoba Province, support the thesis that capitalist develop-

ment and the transformation of peasant political consciousness are interrelated. William Christian Jr.'s *Divided Island*,
though not about an Iberian village, indicates how class conflict in a small community erupts as a result of international
transformations. It demonstrates that the concatenation of
economic and social changes are far more important than
cultural factors in determining political developments.

There is a burgeoning subfield dealing with European
peasant movements, although few of these works focus upon
anarchism as such. A situation similar to that which has been
described for Cádiz Province can be found in Anton Blok's
The Mafia of a Sicilian Village, 1869–1960. Unlike the Andalusian *caciques*, who were often parliamentary figures, the
Sicilian Mafia, composed of rural gentry and their retinue,
formed its own series of decentralized states. Because of the
Mafia's greater local control, it was more effective than the
caciques in preventing peasant insurrection. Unlikely but
useful comparisons between Eastern European peasant
movements and Andalusian anarchism can be found in Philip
Gabriel Eidelberg's *The Great Rumanian Peasant Revolt of
1907* and Peter Archinov's 1923 *History of the Makhnovist
Movement (1918–1921)*. They identify specific social con-
figurations under which relatively prosperous peasants allied
with rural artisans.

The Andalusian peasants (who are defined as people hav-
ing access to land through rental, sharecropping, or ownership of small plots), and the rural proletarians who worked
in agriculture, generally lived in cities rather than villages.
They shared the experience of local urban workers. Albert
Soboul's *The Parisian Sans-Culottes and the French Revolution, 1793–94*, E. P. Thompson's *The Making of the English
Working Class*, and David Montgomery's "Trade Union
Practice and the Origins of Syndicalist Theory in the United
States" have demonstrated that relatively skilled workers or
artisans, experiencing diminishing workers' control of production because of capitalist development, have formed the
vanguard of late eighteenth- and nineteenth-century radical

and socialist politics. Harvey J. Smith's "Village Revolution: Agricultural Workers of Cruzy (Herault) 1850–1910" (unpublished doctoral dissertation) shows trends in nineteenth-century Languedoc remarkably similar to those experienced by Jerez' vineyard workers. These same tendencies can be found among Joan Scott's *Glass Workers of Carmaux*, whose decline resembled that of Jerez' coopers. Such people have favored decentralized political structures and cooperative economic organizations. They built militant trade unions, a pattern that holds for Cádiz Province as well.

Although I have taken issue with Eric J. Hobsbawm's emphasis upon anarchist millenarianism, I owe a great deal to his insights about how workers associate, establish rituals to preserve their associations, and draw upon the larger working-class community to establish new kinds of workers' solidarity. In this respect, his *Labouring Men*, which does not deal with anarchism, has influenced my own interpretation more than *Primitive Rebels* or his more recent *Revolutionaries*.

Of the general works devoted to anarchism, the three most important for the English-reading public are James Joll's *The Anarchists*, George Woodcock's *Anarchism: A History of Libertarian Ideas and Movements*, and Paul Avrich's *The Russian Anarchists*. Had it not been for these works, this local study of Andalusian anarchism would not have been possible. But where they are concerned with how anarchist intellectual and political traditions came to be shared by remote, illiterate peasants in the Ukraine, the Romagna, and in Andalusia, this study tries to describe how one important mass movement developed. Since the great anarchist theorists formulated their doctrine of spontaneity and popular control on the basis of somewhat distorted notions about the organization of ongoing peasant and workers' struggles, detailed analysis of one such movement demonstrates the dynamic interrelationship between theory and action.

A radically new phase of Spanish anarchism began in 1917

and culminated in the Spanish Civil War. Economic changes following World War I, the impact of the Russian Revolution, and the emergence of the Spanish Communist party make the history of twentieth-century anarchism distinctively different from the nineteenth-century developments discussed here. Those interested in twentieth-century topics must turn to Gabriel Jackson's *The Spanish Republic and the Civil War, 1931–1939*, Gerald Meaker's *The Revolutionary Left in Spain, 1914–1923*, and Edward A. Malefakis' *Agrarian Reform and Peasant Revolution in Spain: Origins of the Civil War*. Noam Chomsky's "Objectivity and Liberal Scholarship," in *American Power and the New Mandarins*, attacks the interpretation of anarchist activity offered by Jackson—and by extension, those of Malefakis and Meaker. Readers should also consider César M. Lorenzo's superb *Les anarchistes et le pouvoir* and Sam Dolgoff's *Anarchist Collectives*.

The major works on nineteenth-century Spanish anarchism of the past decade—all of which draw sustenance from the monumental studies prepared by Max Nettlau—are Josep Termes' *Anarquismo y sindicalismo en España*, the definitive work on early Catalan anarchism; Manuel Tuñón de Lara's *El movimiento obrero en la historia de España*, Joan Connelly Ullman's *La semana trágica; Estudio sobre las causas socioeconómicas del anti-clericalismo en España (1898–1912)*, and Joaquín Romero Maura's "La rosa de fuego," which place the anarchists within the broad context of Spanish trade unionism and socialism; and Clara Lida's *Anarquismo y revolución en la España del siglo XIX*. Lida casts her net broadly, providing a masterful analysis of the emergence of nineteenth-century anarchism from the European utopian socialist and radical traditions. At the same time, she gives detailed descriptions of anarchist developments in every major Spanish center. The scope and sympathies of these five books mark a sharp break with older studies done by historians such as Maximiano Garcia Venero and Eduardo Comín Colomer, who supported the regime of Francisco Franco and its interpretations of Spanish history.

One final word of caution: neither the list of general works nor the lists in other categories are definitive. The books represented here are those that contributed most to the area under discussion. Because the book itself is thematic, otherwise significant works have been omitted unless they pertained to the issues discussed here.

ARCHIVES

I. *National Archives*

   A. *Archivo histórico nacional*

     Series 290. Propiedades y desamortización, fincas, adjudicaciones, permutas e indemnizaciones. Alicante, Cádiz, Jaén, 1865–99. 7,305e.

     Boletín de ventas de bienes nacionales en libros de delegación de hacienda, 1866–73. L4595, L4646–L4687.

   B. *Archivo de Simancas*

     Series xxii. Secretaría y superintendencia de hacienda.
     487/64/794—Ronda, hoja de lata, 1726–99
     541/118/1060–61—Motines y contrabando

     Series xxiv. Dirección expedientes general de las rentas y regalía de Sevilla, Cádiz, Puerto de Santa María, Jerez, y San Lúcar, 1762.

     Inventario de expedientes de hacienda. Jerez de la Frontera. 215, 441, 663, 731, 821, 876, 877.

   C. *Foreign Office Records (Public Record Office)*

     Embassy and Consular Archives—Spain. Series FO 72. General Correspondence. Cádiz Province. 1868–1903. 1190, 1192, 1197–98, 1208, 1336–38, 1340–44, 1347, 1352, 1359–60, 1380, 1421, 1447, 1483, 1490–95, 1513, 1552, 1575, 1605, 1627, 1654, 1689, 1714, 1747, 1795, 1821, 1850, 1868, 1889, 1912, 2169, 2182.

II. *Archivo de la Diputación provincial de Cádiz,* uncatalogued

A. *Propuestas para la junta de comercio de Jerez de la Frontera,* 1834, 1837.

B. *Ministrio de comercio*
Instrucción y obras públicas. *Interrogatorio* para preparar la creación de establecimientos de crédito territorial.

> Letter, 7 noviembre, 1850. P[edro] Gordon, presidente and Francisco de Lauta, secretario, Real sociedad económica de Jerez de la Frontera.

> Letter, 23 noviembre, 1850. Juan Ramos and B. de Agencia, Junta de agricultura de la provincia de Cádiz.

> Letter, enero, 1851, Corregidor de San Roque.

> Letter, 12 febrero, 1851, Barcelio Augustín y Iriberri, Medina Sidonia.

III. *Archivo municipal de Cádiz*
Actas capitulares, 1866–73.

IV. *Archivo municipal de Jerez de la Frontera*
A. *Actas capitulares.* 1861, 1868, 1869, 1872, 1882–83.

B. *Archivo memoranda 6.* 1879
f.8–Agricultura: Campiña y término, descripción científica abreviada por el ingeniero de la ciudad D. Gumersindo Fernández.

f.22. Report, 24 setiembre, 1879. Bautismos, depedidos apuntes estadísticos

C. *Archivo memoranda 10.* 1889
Padrón de 1889. Número de habitantes de octubre de 1877.

D. *Protocolos*
Año de 1851. Estadística. Documentos de ayuntamientos.

Año de 1883–84. Relación de los contribuyentes que figuran como cultivadores de viña en el amillaramiento de 1883 a 1884.

E. *Series 8. Vigilancia y orden público*
Documentos de Alcaldía. Años 1890–92. 12,592; 12,618; 12,626.

F. *Series 112. Vigilancia. Orden público.* 1852–55

G. *Series 116. Grupo vigilancia. Sección R. Sociales*
7144 (1769); 7147 (1782)

H. *Series 175*
9741 (1857). Modelo de interrogatorio sobre la producción agrícola con aplicación a las subsistencias y a la industria.

I. *Series 199. Grupo vigilancia. Sección asociaciones. Clase obrera*
10,505. 5ª Sección. Años de 1871. Fomento sobre los interrogatorios relativos a la clase obrera.

10,506. Memoria referente a las principales causas que influyen en el malestar actual de la clase obrera de esta localidad y remedios que pueden adoptarse. Informe de la comisión central, que se publica como completa de dicha memoria. Jerez. 1886.

12,591. Orden público. Huelgas. 1881.

J. *Series 224. Calamidades públicas.* 1858–68

K. *Series 579. Antecedentes de sociedades que se enviaron al gobernador civil.* 1923

L. *Series 3302. Documentos relativos a la rebelión anarquista.* Años de 1892–94

V. *Archivo municipal de Sevilla*

Archivo general, sección 6ª. 1860. 30–31, 44, 51, 61, 68, 76, 97, 102, 112, 117.

VI. *Private Archives*

A. *Archivo del Consejo regulador del Vino.*
Jerez de la Frontera. José de Soto y Molina Collection, uncatalogued. Various items: clippings from *El guadalete*, January to March, 1908. *Revista vinícola jerezana*, *Revista vitícola y vinícola*, monthly sherry company newsletters.

B. *Biblioteca pública Arús.* Barcelona
A.I.T. Consejo federal. 2 vols.
A.I.T. Comunicaciones y circulares. 8 vols.

C. *Casa de Pilatos.* Archivo de los Duques de Medinaceli y Alcalá. Archivo Alcalá. Administración de Andalucía. Siglo XIX. 1–175.

D. *International Institute of Social History.* Amsterdam.
Max Nettlau Collection and Correspondence.
Manuel Buenacasa Papers.
Juan Montseny [pseud. Federico Urales] Collection.

PRINTED MANUSCRIPTS

I. *Accounts and Papers*

Supplement to the Parliamentary Record. House of Commons. Bills, Papers, and Reports. 1865–1908.

II. *Actas de los consejos y comisión federal de la región española (1870–1874)*

Asociación internacional de los trabajadores. Colección de documentos para el estudio de los movimientos obreros en España en la época contemporánea. Carlos Seco Serrano, ed. Publicaciones de la Cátedra de historia general de España, Barcelona, 1969. 2 vols.

III. *Cartas, comunicaciones y circulares del III consejo federal de la región española*

Setiembre-diciembre 1872. Asociación internacional de los trabajadores. Colección de documentos para el estudio de los movimientos obreros en la España contemporánea (ii). Carlos Seco Serrano, ed. Publicaciones de la Cátedra de historia general de España, Barcelona, 1972. 2 vols.

IV. *Instituto de reformas sociales*

A. *Estadística de la asociación obrera* en 1º de noviembre de 1904 formada por la sección 3.ª técnico-administrativa. Madrid, 1907.

B. *Resumen de la información acerca de los obreros agrícolas* en las provincias Andalucía y Extremadura. Madrid, 1905.

V. *Los procesos de la mano negra*

A. I. *Audiencia de Jerez de la Frontera*. Proceso seguido á Cristóbal Durán Gil y Antonio Jaime Domínguez por asesinato de Fernando Olivera. Imprenta de la revista de legislación, Madrid, 1883.

B. II. *Audiencia de Jerez de la Frontera*. Proceso contra Pedro Corbacho [et al.] por asesinato de El Blanco de Benaocaz. Imprenta de la revista de legislación, Madrid, 1883.

VI. Spain. Cortes. Congreso de los diputados. *Diario de las sesiones de la Cortes*. 1892. Extracto de las sesiones celebradas por el Congreso de los diputados. Días 15, 16, y 17 de enero de 1892

VII. *Xerez de la Frontera*. Representación dirigida al Rei en 1824 por varios propietarios y labradores de Xerez de la Frontera, reclamando su derecho a los bienes enagenados como nacionales durante el régimen constitucional, seguida de otra a S. M. La Reina gobernadora, recordando la anterior. Imprenta de José Antonio Niel, Cadiz, 1834

NEWSPAPERS

(Dates are those actually consulted.)
La acracia. Revista sociológica, Barcelona, 1886–88.
La alarma. Anarquía-federación-colectivismo, Seville, 1889–90.
La Andalucía. Seville, 1869–73.
La asociación. Madrid, 1886.
La autonomía. Eco del proletariado, Seville, 1883–84.
L'Avant-Garde. Organe de la fédération française de l'association internationale des travailleurs, Berne-Chaux-de-Fonds, 1877–78.
Bandera roja. Semanario anarquista, Madrid, 1888–89.
Bandera social. Semanario anárquico-colectivista, Madrid, 1885–87.
Boletín de la federación regional española de la AIT. Alcoy, 1873.
Bulletin de la fédération jurassienne de l'asociation internationale des travailleurs, Sonvillier, Locle, La Chaux-de-Fonds, 1872–78. 2 vols. Feltrinelli reprint, Milan, 1973.
El campesino. Órgano de la federación de trabajadores agrícolas de España, Vendrell-Barcelona, 1895–96.
El combate, Bilbao, 1891.
El combate, Madrid, 1870–72.
El condenado, Barcelona, 1886.
El condenado. Pediódico colectivista, defensor de la Internacional, Madrid, 1872–73.
La controversia, Valencia, 1893.
El corsario. Órgano de la federación coruñesa, La Coruña, 1891–96.
El corsario. Periódico sociológico, Valencia, 1902.
El cosmopolita, Valladolid, 1901.
La cuestión social, Valencia, 1892.

El defensor de Cádiz y su provincia. Diario liberal-dinástico, Cadiz, 1887.

Los desesperados, Madrid, 1874.

Diario de Cádiz y su departamento. Periódico político, científico, mercantil, industrial, literario y de anuncios, Cadiz, 1887.

La emancipación. Periódico socialista, defensor de la Internacional, Madrid, 1871–73.

La federación andaluza. Diario democrático, republicano, federal, Cadiz, 1873–74.

La federación española. Revista republicana federal, Madrid, 1870–71.

La filoxera, Madrid, 1878–81.

El guadalete. Periódico político y literario, Jerez de la Frontera, 1867–68, 1872–74, 1881–83.

El heraldo de Cádiz, Cadiz, 1891.

Huelga general. Periódico libertario, Barcelona, 1901–1904.

La huelga general. Semanario anárquico, Madrid, 1906.

La igualdad. Diario democrático republicano, Madrid, 1869.

La ilustración española y americana, Madrid, 1883.

El imparcial, Madrid, 1868–1902.

El jornalero. Semanario defensor de los intereses del obrero, Alcoy, 1889–90.

La justicia humana. Quincenal comunista anárquica, Barcelona, 1886.

La legalidad. Diario político de Cádiz, Cadiz, 1872–73.

El obrero, Barcelona, 1880–87.

El obrero. Defensor de los trabajadores, Barcelona, 1887–91.

El obrero. Periódico quincenal defensor de la clase obrera, Ferrol, 1890–92.

El obrero. Publicación quincenal de sociología, ciencias, y artes. Eco de la sociedad germinal obrera, Badajoz, 1900–1902.

El obrero de Río Tinto. Órgano de "los Manumitidos," Río Tinto, 1900.

El oprimido. Periódico anarquista, anarcho-comunista, Algeciras, 1903.

El pacto federal. Diario republicano, Cadiz, 1869.

El porvenir. Diario político de Sevilla, Seville, 1868–73, 1882–83.

El productor. Barcelona, 1901–1902.

El productor. Diario, periódoco socialista, Barcelona, 1887–93.

La redención obrera. Periódico órgano de los obreros corchotaponeros, Palamos, 1900.

La revancha. Periódico comunista-anárquico, Reus, 1893.

La revista blanca. Publicación quincenal de sociología, ciencia y arte, Madrid-Barcelona, 1ᵉ serie, Madrid, 1898–1905; 2ᵉ serie, Barcelona, 1924–36.

La revista social. Órgano de la unión de los obreros manufactureros de España, Manresa, Barcelona, 1872–80.

Revista social. Eco del proletariado, Madrid, 1881–85.

La revista social, Barcelona, 1903–1908.

La revista social. Órgano de la federación tres clases de vapor de España, Barcelona, 1892.

La revista socialista, Madrid, 1903–1906.

La Révolte. Organe communiste-anarchiste, Paris, 1887–94.

Le Révolté. Organe socialiste, Geneva, 1879–87. After September 16, 1887, this journal moved to Paris and changed its name to *La révolte.*

A revolução social. Orgão communista-anarchista, Porto, 1887.

La revolución. Diario democrático jerezano, Jerez, 1868.

La revolución social. Eco de la asociación internacional de los trabajadores, Barcelona, 1884–85.

La revolución social. Órgano comunista-anárquico, Barcelona, 1889–90.

Revue des deux mondes, Paris-Brussels, 1878–81.

El socialismo, Cadiz, 1886–91.

La solidaridad, Madrid, 1870–71.

La solidaridad. Anarquía-federación-colectivismo, Seville, 1888–89.

Solidaridad ferroviaria. Órgano de la federación de obreros de los ferrocarriles de España, Madrid, 1901.

Tierra y libertad, Barcelona, 1906–13.

Tierra y libertad. Diario anti-político, Madrid, 1902–1904.

Tierra y libertad. Quincenario anárquico-comunista, Barcelona, 1888–89.

El trabajo. Eco de la clase trabajadora de Málaga, Malaga, 1882.

El trabajo. Publicación mensual obrero, Cadiz, 1899–1900.

La tribuna libre. Periódico quincenal comunista-anárquico, Seville, 1891–92.

La unión gaditana, Cadiz, 1887.

La víctima del trabajo, Valencia, 1889–90.

La voz del campesino. Órgano de la federación de obreros agricultores y sus similares en España, Barcelona-Cadiz, 1914.

SECONDARY SOURCES

I. *General Works*

Albornoz, Álvaro de. *El partido republicano. Las doctrinas republicanas en España y sus hombres. La Revolución del 68 y la República del 73. Los Republicanos después de la Restauración. La Crisis del republicanismo.* Biblioteca nueva, Madrid, 1918.

Ardant, Gabriel. *Théórie sociologique de l'impôt.* 2 vols. S.E.V.P.E.N., Paris, 1965.

Artola, Miguel. *La burguesía revolucionaria (1808–1869).* Alianza editorial, Madrid, 1973.

Barbadillo Delgado, Pedro. *Historia de la ciudad de Sanlúcar de Barrameda.* Cerón, Cadiz, 1942.

Bayo, Eliseo. *Trabajos duros de la mujer.* Plaza & Janés, Barcelona, 1970.

Bertemati y Troncoso, Manuel. *Discurso sobre la historia*

y los historiadores de Xerez de la Frontera, dirigido á la Real sociedad económica xerezana en noviembre de 1863. T. Bueno, Xerez, 1883.

Bozal Fernández, Valeriano. *Juntas revolucionarias, manifiestos y proclamas de 1868.* Cuadernos para el diálogo, Madrid, 1968.

Brenan, Gerald. *The Spanish Labyrinth: An Account of the Social and Political Background of the Civil War.* 4th ed. Cambridge University Press, Cambridge, 1962.

Bruguera, F. G. *Histoire contemporaine d'Espagne, 1789–1950.* Editions Ophrys, Paris, 1953.

Butler, Augusto. *Jerez en la canción popular andaluza.* Edit. Jerez industrial, Jerez de la Frontera, 1962.

Carr, Raymond. *Spain, 1808–1939.* Clarendon Press, Oxford, 1966.

de Castro y Rossi, Adolfo. *Historia de la muy noble, muy leal, y muy ilustre ciudad de Xeres de la Frontera.* La Sociedad de la revista médica, Cadiz, 1845.

Conard, Pierre, and Albert Lovett, "Problèmes de l'évaluation du coût de la vie en Espagne," *Mélanges de la Casa de Velázquez*, 5 (1969), pp. 411–444.

Eiras Roel, Antonio. *El partido demócrata español (1849–1868).* Ediciones Rialp, Madrid, 1961.

Elorza, Antonio. *Socialismo utópico español.* Alianza editorial, Madrid, 1970.

Ensayos sobre la economía española a mediados del siglo XIX. Edited by Pedro Schwartz Girón. Servicio de estudios del Banco de España, Madrid, 1970.

Estudio agrobiológico de la provincia de Cádiz. Publicaciones del patronato de reactivación provincial, Cadiz, n.d.

Fontana, Josep. *Cambio económico y actitudes políticas en la España del siglo XIX.* Editorial Ariel, Esplugues de Llobregat, Barcelona, 1973.

———. *La quiebra de la monarquía absoluta, 1814–1820: La crisis del antiguo régimen en España.* Ediciones Ariel, Esplugues de Llobregat, Barcelona, 1971.

García-Baquero González, Antonio. *Comercio colonial y guerras revolucionarias. La decadencia económica de Cádiz.* Publicaciones de la Escuela de estudios hispano-americanos de Sevilla, Seville, 1972.

Garrido, Fernando. *Historia del reinado del último Borbón de España.* 3 vols. Librería Plaza del Teatro, Barcelona, 1869.

Góngora, A. de. *El periodismo jerezano; apuntes para su historia.* El Guadalete, Jerez, 1900.

Gramsci, Antonio. *Selections from the Prison Notebooks.* Edited and translated by Quintin Hoare and Geoffrey Nowell Smith. International Publishers, New York, 1971.

Guerrero, Esteve. *El casco urbano de Jerez de la Frontera.* Centro de estudios históricos de Jerez de la Frontera, núm. 18. Jerez de la Frontera, 1962.

Guillamas y Galiano, Fernando. *Historia de San Lúcar de Barrameda.* Imprenta del Colegio de sordos-mudos y de ciegos, Madrid, 1851.

Gutiérrez, Bartolomé. *Historia del estado presente y antiguo de la mui noble y mui leal ciudad de Xerez de la Frontera.* 4 vols. in 2. Tipografía Ruíz, Xerez, 1886–1887.

Gutkind, E. A. *Urban Development in Southern Europe: Spain and Portugal.* International History of City Development, Vol. 3. Free Press, New York, 1967.

Kiernan, V. G. *The Revolution of 1854 in Spanish History.* Clarendon Press, Oxford, 1966.

Lida, Clara E., and Iris M. Zavala, eds. *La revolución de 1868: Historia, pensamiento, literatura.* Las Américas Publishing Company, New York, 1970.

Martínez Cuadrado, Miguel. *Elecciones y partidos políticos de España (1868–1931).* 2 vols. Taurus, Madrid, 1969.

Marx, Karl. *The 18th Brumaire of Louis Bonaparte.* International Publishers, New York, 1963.

Mayer, Arno J. *Dynamics of Counterrevolution in*

Europe, 1870–1956: An Analytic Framework. Harper and Row, New York, 1971.

Miliband, Ralph. "Marx and the State," *The Socialist Register* (1965), 278–296.

Moore, Barrington, Jr. *Social Origins of Dictatorship and Democracy: Lord and Peasant in the Making of the Modern World.* Beacon Press, Boston, 1966.

Muchado, D. Juan Pedro. *La hacienda de España y modo de reorganizarla.* Imprenta del diccionario geográfico, Madrid, 1847.

Muñoz y Gómez, Augustín. *Noticia histórica de las calles y plazas de Xerez de la Frontera; sus nombres y orígenes.* Tipografía de El Guadalete, Jerez, 1903.

Nadal, Jordi. "The Failure of the Industrial Revolution in Spain 1830–1914," in *The Emergence of Industrial Societies-2*, edited by Carlo M. Cipolla, pp. 532–626. The Fontana Economic History of Europe, No. 4. Collins/Fontana Books, London, 1973.

Nadal, Jorge. *La población española (siglos XVI a XX).* Ariel, Esplugues de Llobregat, Barcelona, 1966.

Paúl y Angulo, José. *Verdades revolucionarias en dos conferencias político-sociales dedicadas a las clases trabajadoras.* Madrid, 1872.

Pavía y Rodríguez de Alburquerque, D. Manuel. *La pacificación de Andalucía y expediente de la cruz de quinta clase de San Fernando.* Establecimiento tipográfico de M. Minuesa de los Ríos, Madrid, 1878.

La Question de la "bourgeoisie" dans le monde hispanique au XIXe siècle: Colloque international organisé par l'Institut d'Études Ibériques et Ibéro-américaines de l'Université de Bordeaux III, en février 1970. Éditions Bière, Bordeaux, 1973.

Quijano, Francisco G. "El nivel de precios en España," *Moneda y crédito*, 65 (1958), pp. 35–57.

Ramos-Oliveira, Antonio. *Historia de España.* 3 vols. Compañiá general de ediciones, S.A., Mexico, n.d.

Rodríguez-Solís, Enrique. *Historia del partido republicano.* 2 vols. Madrid, 1892.

Ruiz Lagos, Manuel. *Tareas de la Sociedad económica de amigos del país de Jerez de la Frontera (1833-1860).* Jerez de la Frontera, 1974.

Sales de Bohigas, Núria. "Some Opinions on Exemption from Military Service in Nineteenth-Century Europe," *Comparative Studies in Society and History*, 10 (1967-1968), 261-289.

Sánchez-Albornoz, Nicolás. "Cádiz, capital revolucionaria, en la encrucijada económica," in *La revolución de 1868: Historia, pensamiento, literatura,* edited by Clara E. Lida and Iris Zavala, Las Américas Publishing Co., New York, 1970, pp. 80-108.

———. "Los informes comerciales de los cónsules británicos en España, 1854-1914," *Cuadernos de historia de España*, 48-49 (1967), 243-260.

Sancho de Sopranis, Hipólito. *Xerez: sinopsis histórica.* Jerez, 1961.

Santillán, R. *Memoria histórica de las reformas hechas en el sistema general de impuestos de España.* Madrid, 1888.

Schröder, Karl Heinz. "Weinbau und Siedlung in Württemberg," *Forschungen zur deutschen Landeskunde*, 73 (1953).

Silbert, Albert. *Le Portugal méditerranéen à la fin de l'Ancien Régime, XVIIIe—début du XIXe siècle; contribution à l'histoire agraire comparée,* 24. S.E.V.P.E.N., Paris, 1966.

Solís, Ramón. *El Cádiz de las cortes; la vida en la ciudad en los años de 1810 a 1813.* Instituto de estudios políticos, Madrid, 1958.

Stein, Stanley, and Barbara Stein. *The Colonial Heritage of Latin America. Essays on Economic Dependence in Perspective.* Oxford University Press, New York, 1970.

Tamames, Ramon. *Introducción a la economía española.* Alianza editorial, Madrid, 1968.

"Tareas de la Sociedad económica de amigos del país de

Jerez de la Frontera en el año de 1836," *Folletos varios*, Vol. 84, no. 5. Imprenta de Bueno, Jerez de la Frontera, 1837.

"Tareas de la Sociedad económica de amigos del país de Jerez de la Frontera en el año de 1837," *Folletos varios*, Vol. 85, no. 5. Imprenta de Bueno, Jerez de la Frontera, 1838.

Tortella Casares, Gabriel. *Los orígenes del capitalismo en España*. Editorial Tecnos, Madrid, 1973.

Tuñón de Lara, Manuel. *Variaciones del nivel de vida en España*. Colección ibérica, 5. Ediciones Península, Madrid, 1965.

Turbino, F. M. *La historia de un cautiverio*. Madrid, 1875.

Vicens Vives, Jaime. With the collaboration of Jorge Nadal Oller. *An Economic History of Spain*. Tr. Frances López Morillas. Princeton University Press, Princeton, 1969.

Wais San Martín, Francisco. *Historia general de los ferrocarriles españoles (1830–1941)*. Editora nacional, Madrid, 1967.

Warner, Charles K. *The Winegrowers of France and the Government since 1875*. Columbia University Press, New York, 1960.

White, George Whitman. *The Heart and Songs of the Spanish Sierra*. T. Fisher Unwin, London, 1894.

Wiener, Jonathan M. "The Barrington Moore Thesis and Its Critics," *Theory and Society*, 2 (1975), 301–330.

Zavala, Iris M. *Ideología y política en la novela española del siglo XIX*. Ediciones Anaya, S.A., Salamanca, 1971.

———. *Masones, comuneros y carbonarios*. Siglo veintiuno de España, Madrid, 1971.

Zugasti, Julián. *El bandolerismo andaluz*. Espasa-Calpe, S.A., Madrid, 1934.

II. *Spanish Land, Agriculture, and Sherry*

Aller, Domingo Enrique. *Las grandes propiedades rústicas en España efectos que producen y problemas jurídicos, económicos que plantean.* Memoria que obtuvo el "Premio del Conde de Toreno" concedido por la Real academia de ciencias morales y políticas en el sexto concurso extraordinario (bienio de 1909 a 1911). Establecimiento tipográfico de Jaime Ratés, Madrid, 1912.

Anes Álvarez, Gonzalo. "La agricultura española desde comienzos del siglo XIX hasta 1868: Algunos problemas," in *Ensayos sobre la economía española a mediados del siglo XIX,* edited by Pedro Schwartz Girón. Raycar, Madrid, 1970, 235–263.

Braudel, Fernand. *The Mediterranean and the Mediterranean World in the Age of Philip II.* 2 vols. Harper and Row, New York, 1973.

Caballero, Fermín. *Fomento de la población rural de España.* 3rd ed. Imprenta nacional, Madrid, 1864.

del Castillo, Rafael. *Gran diccionario geográfico, estadístico y histórico de España y sus provincias.* 4 vols. Henrich, Barcelona, 1889–1892.

Chayanov, A. V. *The Theory of Peasant Economy.* Edited by Daniel Thorner, Basile Kerblay, and R.E.F. Smith. Published for the American Economic Association by R. D. Irwin, Homewood, Ill., 1966.

Costa, Joaquín. *Oligarquía y caciquismo, colectivismo agrario y otros escritos (Antología).* Edited by Rafael Pérez de la Dehesa. Alianza editorial, Madrid, 1967.

Croft-Cooke, Rupert. *Sherry.* Putnam, London, 1955.

de las Cuevas, José. "The Vineyards of Jerez," *Harpers* (June, 1958), pp. 125–135.

Defourneaux, Marcelin. "Le Problème de la terre en Andalousie au XVIIIᵉ siècle et les projets de réforme agraire," *Revue historique,* no. 217–218 (1957), pp. 42–57.

Delgado y Orellana, José Antonio. *La casa de Domecq d'Usquain: ensayo genealógico-nobiliario.* Impresos en gráfica sevillanas, Seville, 1966.

Diccionario geográfico de España. 17 vols. Prensa gráfica, Madrid, 1956–1961.

González Gordon, Manuel María. *Jerez-Xerez-Sheris: Noticias sobre el origen de esta ciudad, su historia y su vino.* Edición especial, Jerez de la Frontera, 1948.

Harrison, R. J. "The Spanish Famine of 1904–1906," *Agricultural History*, 47, no. 4 (1973), 300–307.

Herr, Richard. "El significado de la desamortización en España," *Moneda y crédito*, 131 (1974), 55–94.

El impuesto de consumos y los extractores de vinos de Jerez de la Frontera: De como 35 individuos comerciantes, que no destinan las existencias de sus establecimientos al consumo inmediato, han pagado el cupo de una población de más de 25,000 habitantes. Imprenta El Cronista, Jerez, 1885.

Janke, Peter. *Mendizábal y la instauración de la monarquía constitucional en España (1790–1853).* Siglo veintiuno de España, Madrid, 1974.

Jones, E. L. "The Agricultural Origins of Industry," *Past and Present*, no. 40 (1968), pp. 58–71.

Lazo Díaz, Alfonso. *La desamortización de las tierras de la iglesia en la provincia de Sevilla (1835–1845).* Publicaciones de la excma. Diputación provincial de Sevilla y del Instituto de estudios sevillanos con la colaboración de la Facultad de filosofía y letras, Seville, 1970.

Madoz, Pascual. *Diccionario geográfico-estadístico histórico de España.* 16 vols. Est. tip. de P. Madoz y L. Sagasti, Madrid, 1845–1850.

Marvaud, Angel. *L'Espagne au XXe siècle. Étude politique et économique.* 2nd ed. Librairie Armand Colin, Paris, 1915.

Muñoz Pérez, José, and Juan Benito Arranz. *Guía bibliográfica para una geografía agraria de España.* Instituto "Juan Sebastián Elcano," de geografía. Consejo superior de investigaciones científicas, Madrid, 1961.

Niemeier, Georg. *Siedlungsgeographische Untersuchungen in Niederandalusien.* Abhandlungen aus dem Gebiet der Auslandskunde, 42. Hamburg Universität, Hamburg, 1935.

"Old Sherry": The Story of the First Hundred Years of Gonzalez Byass & Co., Ltd., 1835–1935. Sir Joseph Causton & Sons, London, 1935.

Parada y Barreto, Diego. *Noticias sobre la historia y estado actual del cultivo de la vid y del comercio vinatero de Jerez de la Frontera.* El Guadalete, Jerez, 1868.

Ponsot, Pierre. "Révolution dans les campagnes espagnoles au XIX⁰ siècle: les désamortissements. Revue des études récentes," *Études rurales*, 45 (1972), 104–123.

Porres Martín-Cleto, Julio. *La desamortización del siglo XIX en Toledo.* Patronato "José María Quadrado" del Consejo superior de investigaciones científicas. Diputación provincial, Toledo, 1965.

Portillo, Joaquín. *Noches jerezanas, o sea la historia y descripción de la M.N. y M.L. ciudad de Jerez de la Frontera, y de su término, por D.J.P.* Imprenta de J. Mallen, Jerez, 1839.

Quirós, Francisco. "El comercio de los vinos de Jerez," *Estudios geográficos*, Vol. 23, no. 86 (1962), 29–44.

Sánchez-Albornoz, Nicolás. *Las crisis de subsistencia de España en el siglo XIX.* Instituto de investigaciones históricas, Rosario, Argentina, 1963.

———. "Determining Economic Regions from Time Series Data: A Factor Analysis of the 19th Century Spanish Wheat Prices," *NYU Occasional Papers*, no. 1, 1973.

———. *España hace un siglo: Una economía dual.* Colección ibérica, 24. Ediciones Península, Barcelona, 1968.

Sereni, Emilio. *Il capitalismo nelle campagne (1860–1900).* Einaudi, Turin, 1968.

Sermet, Jean. *L'Espagne du sud.* B. Arthaud, Paris, 1953.

A Short Account of Port and Sherry. The Vintaging and Treatment of the Wines. Printed at the Chiswick Press, London, 1884.

Simón Segura, F. *La desamortización española del siglo XIX.* Instituto de Estudios Fiscales, Madrid, 1973.

Vizetelly, Henry. *Facts about Sherry Gleaned in the*

Vineyards and Bodegas of the Jerez, Seville, Moguer, and Montilla Districts during the Autumn of 1875. Ward, Lock, and Tyler, London, 1876.

III. *Cultural Anthropology and Rural History*

VILLAGE STUDIES

Christian, William A., Jr. *Divided Island: Faction and Unity on Saint Pierre.* Harvard University Press, Cambridge, 1969.

Cornelisen, Ann. *Torregreca: Life, Death, Miracles.* Delta Books, Dell Publishing Co., New York, 1970.

Cutileiro, José. *A Portuguese Rural Society.* Clarendon Press, Oxford, 1971.

Fraser, Ronald. *In Hiding: The Life of Manuel Cortes.* New American Library, New York, 1972.

———. *Tajos: The Story of a Village on the Costa del Sol.* Pantheon, New York, 1973.

Le Roy Ladurie. *Les Paysans de Languedoc.* Centre de recherches historiques (École pratique des hautes études, VIᵉ). S.E.V.P.E.N., Paris, 1966.

Martinez-Alier, Juan. *Labourers and Landowners in Southern Spain.* St. Antony's Publications, no. 4. George Allen and Unwin, London, 1971.

Pitt-Rivers, J. A. *The People of the Sierra.* 2nd ed. Phoenix Books, University of Chicago Press, Chicago, 1961.

Stanislawski, Dan. *Portugal's Other Kingdom: The Algarve.* University of Texas Press, Austin, 1963.

Wolf, Eric R. *Sons of the Shaking Earth.* Phoenix Books, University of Chicago Press, Chicago, 1964.

PEASANT MOVEMENTS

Alavi, Hamza. "Peasants and Revolution," *Socialist Register* (1965), pp. 241–277.

Arshinov, Peter. *History of the Makhnovist Movement (1918–1921).* 2nd ed. Red and Black, Detroit, 1974.

Augé-Laribé, Michel. *Le Problème agraire du socialisme: la viticulture industrielle du Midi de la France*. V. Giard & E. Brière, Paris, 1907.

Aya, Roderick. *The Missed Revolution: The Fate of Rural Rebels in Sicily and Southern Spain 1840–1950*. Papers on European and Mediterranean Societies. Antropologisch-sociologisch centrum-Universiteit van Amsterdam, 1975.

Blok, Anton. "Mafia and Peasant Rebellion as Contrasting Factors in Sicilian Latifundism," *Archives européennes de sociologie*, 10 (1969), 95–116.

————. *The Mafia of a Sicilian Village, 1860–1969: A Study of Violent Peasant Entrepreneurs*. Basil Blackwell, Oxford, 1974.

Eidelberg, Philip Gabriel. *The Great Rumanian Peasant Revolt of 1907: Origins of a Modern Jacquerie*. E. J. Brill, Leiden, 1974.

Gratton, Philippe. *La Luttes de classes dans les campagnes*. Anthropos, Paris, 1971.

Loubere, Leo A. "The Emergence of the Extreme Left in Lower Languedoc, 1848–1851: Social and Economic Factors in Politics," *American Historical Review*, 73 (1968), 1019–1051.

————. *Radicalism in Mediterranean France. Its Rise and Decline, 1848–1914*. State University of New York Press, Albany, 1974.

IV. *European and American Labor History*

Anarchism and Anarcho-Syndicalism. Selected Writings by Marx, Engels, Lenin. International Publishers, New York, 1972.

Brecher, Jeremy. *Strike!* 3rd ed. Fawcett Publications, Greenwich, Conn., 1974.

del Carria, Renzo. *Proletari senza rivoluzione: Storia delle clase subalterne italiane dal 1860 al 1954*. 2 vols. Oriente, Milan.

Gilding, Dan. *The Journeymen Coopers of East London: Workers' Control in an Old London Trade.* History Workshop Pamphlets, no. 4. Oxford, 1971.

Hobsbawm, E. J. *Labouring Men: Studies in the History of Labour.* 3rd ed. Weidenfeld and Nicolson, London, 1968.

————. *Primitive Rebels: Studies in Archaic Forms of Social Movements in the 19th and 20th Centuries.* Manchester, 1959. 2nd ed. W. W. Norton and Co., New York, 1965.

————. *Revolutionaries: Contemporary Essays.* Pantheon Books, New York, 1973.

Lenin, V. I. *Alliance of the Working Class and the Peasantry.* Moscow, 1959.

Montgomery, David. "The 'New Unionism' and the Transformation of Workers' Consciousness in America, 1909–22," *Journal of Social History*, 7, no. 4 (1974), 509–529.

————. "Trade Union Practice and the Origins of Syndicalist Theory in the United States." Mimeographed, 1974.

Scott, Joan Wallach. *The Glassworkers of Carmaux: French Craftsmen and Political Action in a Nineteenth-Century City.* Harvard University Press, Cambridge, 1974.

Smith, Harvey J. "Village Revolution: Agricultural Workers of Cruzy (Herault) 1850–1910." Ph.D. Dissertation, University of Wisconsin, 1972.

Soboul, Albert. *The Parisian Sans-Culottes and the French Revolution, 1793–94.* Clarendon Press, Oxford, 1964.

Thompson, E. P. *The Making of the English Working Class.* 2nd ed. Vintage Books, New York, 1966.

Tilly, Charles, and Edward Shorter. *Strikes in France, 1830–1968.* Cambridge University Press, Cambridge, 1974.

Tilly, Louise. "I Fatti di Maggio: The Working Class of Milan and the Rebellion of 1898," in *Modern European*

Social History, edited by Robert J. Bezucha. D. C. Heath, Lexington, Mass., 1972, pp. 124–160.

V. *Anarchism*

GENERAL

Anarchism Today. Edited by David E. Apter and James Joll. Macmillan, London, 1971.

Ansart, Pierre. *Naissance de l'anarchisme; esquisse d'une explication sociologique du proudhonisme*. Presses universitaires de France, Paris, 1970.

Avrich, Paul. *The Russian Anarchists*. Princeton University Press, Princeton, 1967.

Coletti, A. *Anarchici e questori*. Marsilio editori, Padua, 1971.

Fonseca, Carlos da. *A origem da 1º internacional em Lisboa*. Ed. Estampa, Lisbon, 1973.

Joll, James. *The Anarchists*. Eyre and Spottiswoode, London, 1964.

Maitron, Jean. *Histoire du mouvement anarchiste en France (1880–1914)*. 2nd ed. Société universitaire d'éditions et de librairie, Paris, 1955.

Pernicone, Nunzio. "The Italian Anarchist Movement: The Years of Crisis, Decline, and Transformation (1879-1894)." Ph.D. Dissertation, University of Rochester, 1971.

Stafford, David. *From Anarchism to Reformism: A Study of the Political Activities of Paul Brousse within the First International and the French Socialist Movement, 1870–1890*. University of Toronto Press, Toronto, Canada, 1971.

Vianna, J. M. Gonçalves. *A evolucão anarchista em Portugal*. 2 vols. Grupo anarchista "Revolução social," Porto, 1894-1895.

Vizetelly, Ernest Alfred. *The Anarchists, Their Faith and Their Record, Including Sidelights on the Royal and Other Personages Who Have Been Assassinated*. John Lane, London, 1911.

Woodcock, George. *Anarchism: A History of Libertarian Ideas and Movements.* Meridian Books, Cleveland, 1962.

SPANISH ANARCHISM, TWENTIETH CENTURY

Balcells, Albert. *El sindicalisme a Barcelona (1916–1923).* Editorial Nova Terra, Barcelona, 1965.

Calero Amor, Antonio María. *Historia del movimiento obrero en Granada (1909–1923).* Editorial Tecnos, Madrid, 1973.

Chomsky, Noam. "Objectivity and Liberal Scholarship, II," *American Power and the New Mandarins.* Pantheon, New York, 1967, pp. 72–158.

Dolgoff, Sam, ed. *The Anarchist Collectives: Workers' Self-Management in the Spanish Revolution, 1936–1939.* Free Life Editions, New York, 1974.

Jackson, Gabriel. *The Spanish Republic and the Civil War, 1931–1939.* Princeton University Press, Princeton, 1965.

Kaplan, Temma. "Spanish Anarchism and Women's Liberation," *Journal of Contemporary History*, 6, no. 2 (1971), 101–110.

———. "Women and Spanish Anarchism," in *Becoming Visible: Women in European History.* Edited by Claudia Koonz and Renate Bridenthal. Houghton Mifflin, Boston, 1977.

Lorenzo, César. *Les Anarchistes espagnols et le pouvoir (1868–1969).* Collections esprit "la cité prochaine." Editions du Seuil, Paris, 1969.

Malefakis, Edward E. *Agrarian Reform and Peasant Revolution in Spain: Origins of the Civil War.* Yale University Press, New Haven, 1970.

Martí, Casimiro. *Orígenes del anarquismo en Barcelona.* Centro de estudios históricos internacional, Barcelona, 1959.

Meaker, Gerald H. *The Revolutionary Left in Spain, 1914–1923.* Stanford University Press, Stanford, 1974.

Payne, Stanley G. *The Spanish Revolution: A Study of the Social and Political Tensions that Culminated in the Civil War in Spain.* W. W. Norton and Co., New York, 1970.

Prat, José. *La burguesía y el proletariado. Apuntes sobre la lucha sindical.* (Valencia, 1910), Prefacio de Anselmo Lorenzo. Ediciones "Tierra y Libertad," Barcelona, 1937.

Romero Maura, Joaquín. "Terrorism in Barcelona and its Impact on Spanish Politics, 1904–1909," *Past and Present*, 41 (1968), 130–183.

Sender, Ramón José. *Casas Viejas.* Editorial Cenit, Madrid, 1933.

Ullman, Joan Connelly. *The Tragic Week: A Study of Anticlericalism in Spain, 1875–1912.* Harvard University Press, Cambridge, 1968.

―――. *La semana trágica; estudio sobre las causas socioeconómicas del anticlericalismo en España (1898–1912).* Ariel, Esplugues de Llobregat, Barcelona, 1972.

SPANISH ANARCHISM, NINETEENTH CENTURY

Abad de Santillán, Diego [pseud. Sinesio García Delgado]. *Contribución a la historia del movimiento obrero español: Desde sus orígenes hasta 1905.* Editorial Cajica, Mexico, D.F., 1962.

Álvarez Junco, José. *La comuna en España.* Siglo veintiuno de España, Madrid, 1971.

Bécarud, Jean, and Gilles Lapouge. *Anarchistes d'Espagne.* André Balland, Paris, 1970.

Buenacasa, Manuel. *El movimiento obrero español: Historia y crítica, 1886–1926: Figuras ejemplares que conocí.* (Barcelona, 1928), Familia y amigos del autor, Paris, 1966.

Carr, E. H. *Michael Bakunin.* Vintage Books, New York, 1961.

Cascales y Muñoz, José. *El apostolado moderno: estudio*

histórico-crítico del socialismo y el anarquismo hasta terminar el siglo XIX. F. Granada y Cía, editores, Madrid, n.d.

La clase obrera española a finales del siglo XIX. Serie P-núm. 18. Zero-Zyx, Algorta-Madrid, 1970.

Comín Colomer, Eduardo. *Historia del anarquismo español.* 2nd ed. 3 vols. Editorial AHR, Barcelona, 1956.

Correspondence between the British and Spanish Governments Respecting the International Society: 1872. Harrison and Sons, London, 1872. Included in *Accounts and Papers,* 70 (1872), pp. 715–720.

Elorza, Antonio, and María del Carmen Iglesias, *Burgueses y proletarios: Clase obrera y reforma social en la restauración.* Editorial Laia, Barcelona, 1973.

Engels, Frederick. "The Bakuninists at Work: Notes on the Spanish Uprising in the Summer of 1873," in *Revolution in Spain,* by Karl Marx and Frederick Engels. International Press, New York, 1939, pp. 208–236.

García Venero, Maximiano. *Historia de las Internacionales en España.* Vol. I. Ediciones del Movimiento, Madrid, 1956.

———. *Historia de los movimientos sindicalistas españoles. 1840–1933.* Ediciones del Movimiento, Madrid, 1961.

Garrido, Fernando. *Historia de las clases trabajadoras.* (Madrid, 1870.) 2nd ed. 4 vols. Biblioteca promoción del pueblo, Serie P-núm. 28. Zero-Zyx, Algorta-Madrid, 1970.

Gómez Casas, Juan. *Historia del anarco-sindicalismo español.* Biblioteca promoción del pueblo, núm. 30. Zero-Zyx, Algorta-Madrid, 1968.

Guillaume, James. *L'Internationale. Documents et souvenir (1864–1878).* 4 vols. in 2. Société nouvelle de librairie et d'édition, Paris, 1905–1910.

Hennessy, C.A.M. *The Federal Republic in Spain: Pi y Margall and the Federal Republican Movement, 1868–1874.* Clarendon Press, Oxford, 1962.

Jackson, Gabriel. "The Origins of Spanish Anarchism," *The Southwestern Social Science Quarterly*, 36 (1955), 135–147.

Jutglar Bernaus, Antonio. *Federalismo y revolución: Las ideas sociales de Pi y Margall*. Publicaciones de la Cátedra de historia general de España, Barcelona, 1966.

Lehning, Arthur. *Michel Bakounine et les conflits dans l'Internationale, 1872*. Archives Bakounine II. Brill, Leiden, 1965.

Lida, Clara E. *Anarquismo y revolución en la España del XIX*. Siglo veintiuno de España, Madrid, 1972.

———. *Antecedentes y desarrollo del movimiento obrero español (1835–1888): Textos y documentos*. Siglo veintiuno de España, Madrid, 1973.

———. "Educación anarquista en la España del ochocientos," *Revista de occidente*, 97 (1971), 33–47.

Lorenzo, Anselmo. *El proletariado militante. Memorias de un internacional*. 2 vols. Editorial del Movimiento libertario español C.N.T. en Francia, Toulouse, 1946–1947.

———. *El proletariado militante*. Edited by José Álvarez Junco. Alianza editorial, Madrid, 1974.

Maestre Alfonso, Juan. *Hechos y documentos del anarcosindicalismo español*. 2nd ed. Básica 15, Madrid, 1974.

Martí, Casimiro. *Orígenes del anarquismo en Barcelona*. Editorial Teide, Barcelona, 1959.

Martínez Shaw, Carlos. *El Cantón sevillano*. Imprenta de la Diputación Provincial, Seville, 1972.

Mella, R[icardo]. "La cooperación libre y los sistemas de comunidad," *La revista blanca*, 5 (1903), no. 119, 724–730.

Mora, Francisco. *Historia del socialismo obrero español: Desde sus primeras manifestaciones hasta nuestros días*. Imprenta de I. Calleja, Madrid, 1902.

Morato, J[uan] J[osé]. *Historia de la sección española de la Internacional (1868–1874)*. Gráfica Socialista, Madrid, 1930.

Nettlau, Max. *La anarquía a través de los tiempos.* "Colección Vertice," Mexico, n.d.

————. *Documentos inéditos sobre la Internacional y la alianza en España.* Buenos Aires, 1930.

————. "Impresiones sobre el desarrollo del socialismo en España," *La revista blanca,* 2ª época. 7–8 (1928–1929), 161–682.

————. *Impresiones sobre el desarrollo del socialismo en España.* Zero-Zyx, Algorta-Madrid, 1971.

————. *Miguel Bakunin: La Internacional y la alianza en España (1868–1873).* Edited by Clara E. Lida (Buenos Aires, 1925), Iberama Publishing Co., New York, 1971.

————. *La Première Internationale en Espagne, 1868–1888.* Edited by Renée Lamberet. D. Reidel, Dordrecht, Holland, 1969. 2 vols.

————. "Zur Geschichte der Spanischen Internationale und Landsföderations 1868 zu 1889," *Archiv für die Geschichte des Sozialismus und der Arbeiterbewegung,* 19 (1929), 1–66.

Núñez de Arenas, Manuel. *Historia del movimiento obrero español.* Annotated by Manuel Tuñón de Lara. Editorial Nova Terra, Barcelona, 1970.

La Première Internationale. L'Institution. L'Implantation. Le Rayonnement. Colloques internationaux du Centre national de la recherche scientifique. Sciences humaines. Éditions du Centre national de la recherche scientifique, Paris, 1968.

The Revolutionary Internationals, 1864–1943. Edited by Milorad M. Drachkovitch. Stanford University Press, Stanford, 1966.

Romero Maura, Joaquín. *"La rosa de fuego." Republicanos y anarquistas: la política de los obreros barceloneses entre el desastre colonial y la semana trágica, 1899–1909.* Ediciones Grijalbo, Barcelona, 1975.

Termes, Josep. *Anarquismo y sindicalismo en España: La primera Internacional (1864–1881).* Ediciones Ariel, Esplugues de Llobregat, Barcelona, 1972.

Termes Ardévol, José. *El movimiento obrero en España: La primera Internacional (1864–1881)*. Publicaciones de la Cátedra de historia general de España, Barcelona, 1965.

Trujillo, Gumersindo. *Introducción al federalismo español: Ideología y fórmulas constitucionales*. Editorial cuadernos para el diálogo, Madrid, 1967.

Tuñón de Lara, Manuel. *El movimiento obrero en la historia de España*. Taurus, Madrid, 1972.

Urales, Federico [pseud. of Juan Montseny]. *La evolución de la filosofía en España*. Edited and abridged by Rafael Pérez de la Dehesa. (Barcelona, 1934, 2 vols.), Ediciones de cultura popular, Barcelona, 1968.

Vergés Mundó, Oriol. *La I Internacional en las cortes de 1871*. Publicaciones de la Cátedra de historia general de España, Barcelona, 1964.

SPANISH ANARCHISM: ANDALUSIA

Bernal, Antonio-Miguel. "Bourgeoisie rurale et prolétariat agricole en Andalousie pendant la crise de 1868," *Mélanges de la Casa de Velázquez*, 7 (1971), pp. 327–346.

———. "Formación y desarrollo de la burguesía agraria sevillana: caso concreto de Morón de la Frontera," *La Question de la "bourgeoisie" dans le monde hispanique au XIXe siècle*. Éditions Bière, Bordeaux, 1973, pp. 47–70.

———. *La propiedad de la tierra y las luchas agrarias andaluzas*. Editorial Ariel, Esplugues de Llobregat, Barcelona, 1974.

Bernaldo de Quirós, Constancio. "Bandolerismo y delincuencia subversiva en la baja Andalucía," *Junta para la ampliación de estudios científicos. Anales*, 9 (1913), 33–55.

———. *El espartaquismo agrario andaluz*. Ed. with introduction by Luis Jiménez Asúa. Ediciones Torner, Madrid, 1974.

Bernaldo de Quirós, Constancio. "El espartaquismo agrario andaluz," *Revista general de legislación y jurisprudencia*, 18 (1919), 7–48.

Blasco Ibañez, V. *La bodega*. Sempere, Valencia, 1905.

Brey, Gérard, and Jacques Maurice. "Casas-Viejas: Réformisme et anarchisme en Andalousie (1870–1933)," *Le mouvement social*, no. 83 (1973), pp. 95–134.

Díaz del Moral, Juan. *Historia de las agitaciones campesinas andaluzas-Córdoba. (Antecedentes para una reforma agraria.)* Madrid, 1929. 2nd and 4th eds. Alianza editorial, Madrid, 1967, 1973.

de Góngora, A. *Materiales para l'historia de la M.N. y M.L. ciudad de Jerez de la Frontera*. Bibloteca "El Guadalete," Jerez, 1901.

Guichot y Parody, Joaquín. *Historia general de Andalucía, desde los tiempos más remotos hasta 1870.* 8 vols. E. Perié, Seville, 1869–1871.

Kaplan, Temma. "The Social Base of Nineteenth-Century Andalusian Anarchism in Jerez de la Frontera," *Journal of Interdisciplinary History*, 6 (1975), 47–70.

Lida, Clara E. "Agrarian Anarchism in Andalusia: Documents on the Mano Negra," *International Review of Social History*, 14 (1969), 315–352.

———. *La Mano negra: Anarquismo agrario en Andalucía*. Colección: "Lee y Discute" Serie V-núm. 29. Zero-Zyx, Algorta-Madrid, 1972.

———. "Republicanismo federal y crisis agraria en el primer año de la revolución," in *La revolución de 1868: Historia, pensamiento, literatura*. Edited by Clara E. Lida and Iris M. Zavala. Las Américas Publishing Company, New York, 1970, pp. 182–195.

Maurice, Jacques. "À propos d'une réédition récente: Remarques sur l'anarchisme andalou," *Bulletin hispanique*, 71, nos. 1–2 (1969), 318–334.

———. "Le thème des 'nuevos ricos' en Andalousie de la restauration à la IIe république," *La Question de la* *"bourgeosie" dans le monde hispanique au XIXe siècle.* Éditions Bière, Bordeaux, 1973, pp. 71–86.

Mejías y Escassy, Luis. *Las barricadas de Cádiz; Crónica detallada de los acontecimientos ocurridos en dicha ciudad, desde el día 5 de diciembre de 1868.* Edición económica. Imprenta de Arjona, Cadiz, 1869.

Mistral, Emilio. *Vida revolucionaria de Fermín Salvochea.* Valencia, 1937.

Molnár, Miklós, and Juan Pakmez. "Rural Anarchism in Spain and the 1873 Cantonalist Revolution," in *Rural Protest: Peasant Movements and Social Change.* Edited by Henry A. Landsberger. Barnes and Noble, New York, 1973, pp. 158–193.

Pérez del Álamo, Rafael. *Apuntes sobre dos revoluciones andaluzas.* (Seville, 1872), Biblioteca "Promoción del pueblo." Serie P-núm. 37. Zero-Zyx, Algorta-Madrid, 1971.

Reclus, Elie. "Impresiones de un viaje por España en días de revolución (1868–1869)," *La revista blanca* (1932–1933).

Rocker, R[udolph]. *Fermín Salvochea: Precursores de la libertad.* Tierra y libertad, Toulouse, 1945.

Sánchez Jiménez, José. *El movimiento obrero y sus orígenes en Andalucía.* 2nd ed. Zero-Zyx, Algorta-Madrid, 1969.

Sánchez Rosa, José. *Diálogo. El obrero sindicalista y su patrono.* 1ª ed. Seville, 1911.

———. *Las dos fuerzas. Reacción y progreso. Diálogo s.l., juventudes libertarias del ramo de alimentación.* 3ª ed. Tipografía de la Revista de tribunales, Seville, 1910. Reprint of 1904 article.

———. *En el campo. Dialogo.* "Revista de tribunales," Seville, 1916.

———. *La idea anarquista.* Biblioteca de "El despertar del terruño," La Linea, 1903.

Los sucesos de Jerez. Tipografía Calle San Rafael, Barcelona, 1893.

Vallina, Pedro. *Crónica de un revolucionario. Con trazos de la vida de Fermín Salvochea.* Ediciones Solidaridad Obrera, Paris, 1958.

Waggoner, Glen A. "The Black Hand Mystery: Rural Unrest and Social Violence in Southern Spain, 1881–1883," in *Modern European Social History*. Edited by Robert J. Bezucha. D. C. Heath and Co., Lexington, Mass., 1972, pp. 161–191.

Index

"Abnegation" society, 35
Abreu, Joaquín, 52
Agis, Juan, 182
agricultural workers: in Arcos, 5, 7; and the Black Hand trials, 133, 170; and the demand for labor, 27–29; in Jerez, 24–25; in the Jerez Insurrection of 1892, 173, 175; in May Day demonstrations, 169; organized, 12, 77–78, 103, 138, 143–145, 148, 156, 162, 194, 196–199, 202, 204; organized female, 159–160; paid by piece rates, 32; and the persistence of local anarchism, 123; repression of, 155; residing in cities, 214; in the Sanlúcar Cantonal Uprising, 105; strike of, 202; unrest of, 121
Agricultural Workers of the Spanish Region (Organización de agricultores de la región española; OARE), xvi, 170–172, 175, 182, 183
Agricultural Works Union, 144
Alas, Leopoldo, 23
Alba, dukes of, 13
albariza vineyards, 14–16, 20, 188; attacked by phylloxera, 189; economic decline of, 22–23, 34, 186; purchased by shippers and blenders, 32, 47
Albarracín, Severino, 111
Alcalá de los Gazules, 125, 146, 160, 196, 198
Alcalá del Valle, 126, 147, 160,

171, 177, 198; general strike in, 168, 202, 204
Alcalá Zamora, Gregorio, 67
Alcornocalejo, 90, 129–30, 132, 134
Alcoy, 107, 111
Alentejo, 151, 213
Alerini, Carlos, 99, 112
Alfonso XII (king of Spain), 122, 186
Algar, 125; organizations in, 146, 159, 160, 194, 196, 197, 198
Algarve, 151
Algeciras, 88
Alianza de los hermanos internacionales (International Brothers' Alliance), 72
Alliance, *see* International Alliance of Social Democracy; Secret Alliance
Alliance, Spanish, 96–98
Amadeo of Savoy (king of Spain), 96, 101, 104, 105
amigo del pueblo, El, 70
anarchism: and agricultural workers' organizations, 204; Andalusian, 11, 76–84; clandestine structure of 114–126 early, 61, 72–75; links with Republicanism, 70; and local economy, 12; structure and nature of, in Spain, 79; theorists of, 13n, 207–212, 215; twentieth-century, 216; "village," 204–205; and working-class culture, 61–62, 76; FTRE definition of, 165

imported by, 10, 188; vines
from, introduced to Europe,
185, 189
universal male suffrage, 59, 63
UTC (Unión de trabajadores
del campo), *see* Union of
Field Workers

Valencia, 87, 95, 201
Valle, del, vineyards, 44
Valverde, Mayor, of Jerez, 172
Vázquez, Antonio, 128
Vázquez, Pedro, 77
Vázquez, Roque, 130, 132
Vázquez Escalante, José, 175
Veracruz monastery, 44
"village anarchism," 204–205
Villamartín: anarchist and labor
organizations in, 125, 145, 146,
159, 160, 196, 198; hard times
in, 190–191; latifundist power
around, 163; population of,
125
vinetenders: economic decline
of, 23; and liberal politics, 54;
living conditions of, 19–20; in
organizations, 36, 76, 77, 84,
143, 144, 148, 156, 162, 195;
and the persistence of local
anarchism, 123; pruners dis-
placed by, 16; in the Sanlúcar
Cantonal Uprising, 105;
strike of, 145; work of, 10, 25
Vineyard Workers Center, 195
vineyards: area devoted to, 21;
description of work in, 17,
19; diseases of, 16, 20, 185–
190; expansion of, 22, 34, 37,
47–48; labor requirements
of, 15–17; locations of,
4, 10, 14
violence, 191; anarchist, 184–
185; as a tactic, 142, 148,
163; at times of high unem-

ployment, 28. *See also* crime;
incendiarism
Vizetelly, Henry, 17–19, 30–31
Volunteers for Liberty, 71

wages: average daily, 26; of
coopers and blenders, 32;
daily, demanded, 151, 201;
increases in, sought, 27, 118;
low in hill towns, 148; of
males and females, 25n, 159;
of plowmen, 19, 24; strikes
against reductions in, 124;
strikes for better, 154, 157–158,
182, 199; of treaders and
pressers, 19. *See also* piece
work and piece rates
Waggoner, Glen A., 133–134
wagon and coach makers, 29–30
War Committees (Revolutionary Action Groups), 116,
119
wheat, *see* grain
wine: blenders, 29, 32, 54;
demand for cheaper, 20, 22,
34, 186, 188; foreign trade in,
9, 10, 20, 38, 46, 126, 186–
188; making of, 17–19, 30–32;
shippers of, 23, 46–47. *See
also* sherry
winecellars and winecellarmen,
10, 30, 31, 34, 47, 65, 76, 192
women, 44, 68, 87, 109; and
anarchism, 135, 138, 140, 141;
associations of, in labor
organizations, 76, 85, 136,
159–161, 166–167, 171, 207;
earnings of, compared to
men's, 25n, 159; economic
activities of, 7–8; emancipation of, advocated, 85; equal
property rights of, advocated,
87; infant initiation apparently
started by, 86–87; in omnibus

Library of Congress Cataloging in Publication Data

Kaplan, Temma, 1942–
    Anarchists of Andalusia, 1868–1903.

    Bibliography: p.
    Includes index.
    1. Anarchism and anarchists—Spain—Andalusia—History.
I. Title.
HX928.A35K27   335′.83′09468   76–3262
ISBN 0–691–05236–0